Bravo, Bobbie and Millie!

"The book really lives up to its title."
Tulsa Tribune

"A valuable, practical tool for helping patients modify their diets without sacrificing taste. For weight maintenance programs it's a must. The recipes are clear, fast, and delicious."
Marta Smith, Registered Dietician
Nutritional Weight Management Center
York Hospital, York, PA

"Thank you for your fabulous cookbook. The recipes provide great tasting food with a reasonable calorie content. My wife and I use it all the time."
Theodore M. Brennan, Owner
Brennan's Restaurant, New Orleans

Recipes shown on cover are:	
Shrimp Scampi	page 150
Apricot-Glazed Carrots	page 235
Caesar Salad	page 32
Multi-Grain Apple Muffins	page 285
Strawberry-Topped Cheese Pie	page 398

Quantity discounts are available from Prima Publishing & Communications, Post Office Box 1260LL, Rocklin, CA 95677; Telephone: (916) 624-5718. On your letterhead, include information concerning the intended use of the books and the number of books you wish to purchase.

U.S. Bookstores and Libraries: Please submit all orders to St. Martin's Press, 175 Fifth Avenue, New York, NY 10010; Telephone: (212) 674-5151.

For information on how to arrange an appearance by the authors for your hospital or organization, write on your organization's letterhead to Prima Publishing (see address above).

LEAN ^A_N_D LUSCIOUS

Over 400 easy-to-prepare, delicious recipes for today's low-fat lifestyle. Each recipe includes at-a-glance nutritional breakdown.

BOBBIE HINMAN & MILLIE SNYDER

Illustrator: Vonnie Crist

PRIMA PUBLISHING & COMMUNICATIONS
P.O. Box 1260LL
Rocklin, CA 95677
Tel: (916) 624-5718

Distributed to the trade by St. Martin's Press (except in Canada)

Library of Congress Number 84-91380
ISBN 0-914629-20-4 Paperback
ISBN 0-914629-22-0 Hardcover

10 9 8 7 6 5 4 3 2

Printed in the United States of America

To Harry, Traci, and Mike

For your patience, encouragement, and willingness to taste and retaste, and for the love and support you gave through the long days of work that ran into the wee small hours of the night. I love you.

To Harvey, Jennifer, and Craig

For your support and encouragement, and for always continuing to reach out, and for being very special.

Important

This book is not intended as a promotion or recommendation for any specific diet, nor as a substitute for your physician's advice. Its purpose is to show you how you can follow a balanced diet and enjoy tasty, nutritious meals.

Table of Contents

About the Authors vi
Foreword by Harold Selinger, M.D. vii
Introduction: About Our Book ix
    Our Use of Sweeteners x
    Food Families xi
    How to Use the Nutritional Information
    Found in This Book xiv
Soups 1
Salads and Salad Dressings 17
Milk Dishes 52
Eggs and Cheese 77
Fish and Seafood 131
Poultry 160
Veal 187
Liver 197
Beef, Pork and Lamb 209
Vegetables 225
Starchy Vegetables 254
Breads and Grains 268
Legumes and Tofu 302
Peanut Butter 331
Fruit 348
Cakes, Pies, Cookies and Candies 377
Sauces and Toppings 427
Spice Chart 437
Index 439

ABOUT THE AUTHORS

Bobbie Hinman

Passionate about cooking, Bobbie Hinman always knew that she was destined to write a cookbook. She became a pioneer of low-fat, low-cholesterol cooking after discovering that her children were susceptible to high cholesterol levels. Her unique contribution to healthful and tasty cooking comes from her successful experiments in converting high-fat gourmet cooking into successful low-fat, low-cholesterol, low-sodium, low-sugar meals — while actually enhancing flavor. As Bobbie puts it, "I found that the flavor is *not* in the fat!" Today, Bobbie is a much-sought-after instructor and seminar leader for hospitals, schools, and individuals. In *Lean and Luscious* you are invited to taste and enjoy the results of Bobbie's creativity.

Bobbie and her husband, Harry, live in Maryland with their four children.

Millie Snyder

Together with her husband, Harvey, Millie Snyder is well known in West Virginia and surrounding states for her dedicated work in the field of weight maintenance services. She is the creator and distributor of low calorie foods, which she markets through her wholesale/retail business. In addition, at one time a victim of obesity, Millie is an outstanding motivator and speaker on the subjects of self-image and weight control. This quintessential contemporary American woman is a mother of two and is listed in *Who's Who of American Women* and *Who's Who of Finance and Industry*.

Bobbie and Millie's high school friendship was rekindled after many years. *Lean and Luscious* is the wonderful fruit of their considerable combined talents.

FOREWORD

As a cardiologist, I have been concerned that my patients keep their weight down and lower their cholesterol level. In the past, I recommended various diets that followed the general guidelines of low calories and low cholesterol and/or sodium. Unfortunately, I have been disappointed in my patients' ability to stick with them. The reason for this, I suspect, is that these diets fail to satisfy people's craving for tasty food.

As a result of the failure of these diets to be of practical benefit, my colleagues and I have had to resort to simply recommending a specific limit of calories to each patient, based on need. Also, if a patient has a special problem, such as diabetes, we have also advised on the amount of carbohydrates he or she can intake daily. For more specific help, we would make recommendations as to which foods to eliminate. But, still, we could not show them *how* to prepare allowed foods in a savory way.

In *Lean & Luscious,* by Millie Snyder and Bobbie Hinman, we found the solution! In addition to providing introductory tips on lowering calories, fats, and cholesterol, their recipes represent gourmet cooking. And to make matters even easier, each recipe gives the number of calories, the content of sodium and cholesterol, proteins, carbohydrates, and fats, as well as equivalents on the diet exchange lists. With this information, the recipes can be adapted successfully to any type of diet a physician recommends.

It is important to add that my interest in this book is more than clinical. I enjoy good food, *and* I have a weight problem. Naturally, this compounded my interest in a book that offers wonderful recipes and the opportunity for nutritional balance.

Today, more of us than ever have become conscious of our weight and nutrition. In addition to eating better, we exercise more regularly to become or remain lean and fit. I have no doubts that *Lean & Luscious* is the cookbook that will allow us to eat right and *enjoy* it!

Harold Selinger, M.D., Director
Heart Institute of West Virginia

Introduction:
About Our Book

"Lean and Luscious" is not a diet book. Rather, it is a collection of recipes created to allow you to enjoy your favorite foods without adding unnecessary calories. It is our wish that using these recipes will help you to create a new, low calorie, healthful way of cooking and eating. Our quick, easy-to-prepare dishes will transform ordinary meals into culinary delights, while teaching you and your family new, healthier eating habits.

Although many of these recipes are our own, we have included some traditional favorites, and also some that have been in our families for years. We have lowered the calorie and fat content of these recipes, and have converted them in a way that now makes them available to the weight-conscious people of the world.

For each recipe we have included calorie counts, as well as other nutritional information. It is our hope that you will use this information to help you choose recipes that fit into your own diet.

We suggest eating controlled, satisfying portions and we have included in our recipes serving sizes and amounts. Therefore, be sure, in dividing dishes into serving portions, that you divide them evenly.

In preparing and creating our recipes, we have tried to keep in mind the fact that foods have their own built-in flavors. We have used spices to enhance, not hide, these flavors. We have attempted to bring out the best in food by eliminating the use of excess sugar, salt and fats, and replacing them with unique, flavorful combinations of extracts and spices. So, be creative and experiment with your own combinations of spices. Let our Spice Chart on page 437 be your initial guide. When starting to experiment, go easy. You can always add more. Remember, you're not trying to cover up or change the flavor of food, but bring out its best.

OUR USE OF SWEETENERS

Throughout the recipes in this book we have offered the personal choice of which sweetener to use. The choice is your own. Over the years, there has been considerable confusion concerning the use of artificial sweeteners. Some have disappeared from the marketplace, while others are still being researched. We believe that all sweeteners, whether high in calories or artificial, should be used in moderation. When artificial sweeteners are selected the calories are lowered considerably. However, many people object to the use of artificial products. Therefore, we have left the choice up to you. Our calorie count for each recipe is based on the use of artificial sweeteners. We have also given the additional calorie count if sugar, fructose, or brown sugar were to be used in each recipe.

Please bear in mind that the sweetening power and end results of different sweeteners are not always uniform. Sweeteners generally have to be adjusted according to personal taste. For people who prefer artificial sweeteners we have found that generally, in baking cakes and muffins, the best end results were achieved by using half sugar or fructose and half artificial sweetener. Cakes made entirely with artificial sweeteners often had an unpleasant texture.

It is important to note that aspartame* should be used only in recipes that do not require cooking, or in those that have the sweetener added after the cooking time, because the sweetening power of this particular sweetener is lost during prolonged exposure to high temperatures.

We have also found, through our own personal testing of recipes, that whenever fructose is used as a sweetener in hot dishes, the same amount as sugar is needed. However, when we used fructose in preparing cold dishes, we were able to reduce the amount of sweetener called for, thereby saving calories.

In all of our recipes we have attempted to reduce the total amount of sweetener called for, so that even if you prefer sugar or fructose, the total caloric count of each dish has been lowered. Sweetening power can be heightened in other ways, such as the use of ripe, sweet varieties of fresh fruit in your recipes, or the addition of fruit juice concentrates. More extracts can also be added for increased flavor. We suggest that in adapting your own recipes, you try these calorie-saving methods and also try reducing the total

*Aspartame is manufactured under the name of NutraSweet by G. D. Searle and Company.

x

amount of sweetener called for. Get used to foods being less sweet and you will find that you will enjoy the flavors of the individual ingredients more when they are not overpowered by sugar.

Remember, too, that the amount of sweetener called for in each recipe is *our* recommendation. Be creative and alter each recipe, if necessary, to your own personal taste.

FOOD FAMILIES

In order to help you to develop healthy eating habits we have taken the basic food groups and derived from them Food Families. It is our hope that these food groupings will help you to plan variable menus and to greatly simplify your portion control.

The foods found in each Family are foods of comparable nutritional and calorie values. At the end of each recipe, in addition to the nutritional analysis, you will find the number of servings from each Food Family. (Example: 2 Protein Servings, 1 Fruit Serving, etc.) If you vary your menu, but choose foods from each Family daily, you will have all the nutrients needed for a balanced diet.

If you are currently following a weight reduction organization diet, it is our hope that these recipes will be easily adapted to your program. If you are not following a specific diet, and wish to lose weight, please consult your physician or other weight control expert regarding the number of servings from each Food Family that would be best for your particular daily diet.

There is a general trend in our country today toward trimming calories and developing healthy eating habits. Even if you are not following a diet, if you distribute your food evenly between Food Families, you will be assured of good nutrition.

Family #1 — Proteins

The Protein Family is made up of meats, poultry, seafood, eggs, cheese, legumes, and tofu. All of these foods are valuable sources of protein. Legumes and tofu are not of animal origin and, while high in protein, they contain no cholesterol.

There are also other nutrients available in the Protein Family. Zinc is found in crab, liver, turkey, and legumes. Legumes are also a good source of potassium. Liver and eggs are outstanding sources of iron. The B vitamins are also abundant in this Family.

Be sure, when choosing meats and poultry, that you choose the leanest cuts and discard all skin and visible fat before serving. When choosing cottage cheese or ricotta cheese, choose the lowfat varieties. And remember that peanut butter, while high in protein, also has a high fat content.

One serving from the Protein Family contains approximately 60 to 70 calories.

Family #2 – Breads

The Bread Family is made up of breads, crackers, cereals, grains, and starchy vegetables. We have included starchy vegetables in this Family because their carbohydrate levels are about the same as an equivalent serving of bread.

Enriched and whole grain breads and cereals are valuable sources of the B vitamins: thiamin, niacin, and riboflavin, and of iron. Starchy vegetables are good sources of vitamins A, C, and B. The Bread Family also provides other vitamins, minerals, and protein, and is a good source of fiber in the diet. One serving from the Bread Family contains approximately 75 to 85 calories.

Family #3 – Vegetables

The Vegetable Family provides valuable sources of vitamins, minerals, and fiber. Vitamin A is abundant in dark green vegetables such as spinach and broccoli, and in deep yellow vegetables such as carrots and pumpkin. Vitamin C is found in asparagus, broccoli, Brussels sprouts, cabbage, cauliflower, spinach, and tomatoes. Iron is found in spinach and mushrooms. Valuable sources of potassium are broccoli, Brussels sprouts, carrots, and celery.

We have excluded from this group the starchy vegetables, such as corn, peas, and potatoes. Because of their high levels of carbohydrates, we have chosen to place them in the Bread Family.

Vegetables may be fresh, frozen, or canned. In order to maintain the highest level of nutrients, we recommend choosing fresh vegetables whenever possible, and when cooking vegetables, to cook them until just tender-crisp.

One serving from the Vegetable Family contains approximately 25 to 30 calories.

Family #4 – Fats

The Fat Family is made up of margarine, mayonnaise, vegetable oils, and salad dressings. We recommend using fats of vegetable, rather than animal origin whenever possible. Vegetable oils such as sunflower, safflower, soybean, cottonseed, or corn oil are high in polyunsaturated fatty acids and are therefore preferable. If using the reduced-calorie margarine or mayonnaise, you can increase the amount you use without affecting the levels of fat you consume.

Margarine is a good source of vitamin A and vegetable oils are a good source of vitamin E.

One serving from the Fat Family contains approximately 40 to 45 calories.

Family #5 – Fruit

The Fruit Family consists of fruits and fruit juices. This Family provides valuable sources of vitamins, minerals and fiber. Vitamin A is found in peaches and apricots. Vitamin C is abundant in strawberries, raspberries, and of course, citrus fruits and juices. Potassium is found in bananas, apricots, oranges and peaches.

Fruits may be fresh, canned, dried, or frozen. Be sure when choosing canned or frozen fruit, that the fruit has been packed in water or in unsweetened fruit juice and that no sugar has been added.

One serving from the Fruit Family contains approximately 40 to 50 calories.

Family #6 – Milk

The Milk Family is made up of milk and milk products, such as buttermilk and yogurt. This Family is an excellent source of calcium. It also provides valuable protein, phosphorous, riboflavin, magnesium, and vitamins A and D.

In order to cut down on calories and fats, choose skim milk and other dairy products that are derived from skim milk.

One serving from the Milk Family contains approximately 80 to 90 calories.

Family #7 – Free Foods

The Free Food Family consists of foods that appear in our recipes, but provide no nutritional value. They are used to enhance the taste of each dish. Included in this Family are spices, herbs, extracts, unflavored gelatin, artificial sweeteners, vinegar, lemon juice, and sauces such as mustard, Worcestershire sauce, and soy sauce.

While we call them "Free," be sure to use your discretion and add these foods in moderate amounts.

One serving from the Free Food Family contains a negligible amount of calories.

Family #8 — Additional Calories

The Additional Calorie Family consists of foods that appear in our recipes in small amounts, and, while they do not appreciably alter the nutritional value of each dish, they do add calories. Among these foods are sugar and other sweeteners, ketchup, jams and jellies, seeds such as sunflower and sesame seeds, bacon bits, cocoa, broth mix, flour and other thickening agents, egg whites, and coconut.

In each recipe we have figured the additional calories for you. They appear at the end of each list of Food Family Servings where applicable. (Example: 1 Protein Serving, 2 Vegetable Servings, 15 Additional Calories.)

HOW TO USE THE NUTRITIONAL INFORMATION FOUND IN THIS BOOK

After each recipe you will find a box that contains the nutritional information for that particular recipe:

Each serving provides:

46 Calories*

2 Protein Servings	3 g	Protein
1 Fat Serving	5 g	Fat
0 Additional Calories*	27 g	Carbohydrate
	145 mg	Sodium
	0 mg	Cholesterol

*Add 20 calories if sugar or fructose is used as sweetener.

If you are not on any particular diet, and are simply enjoying the high nutritional value and good taste of our recipes, you won't need to use the information found in the box. Simply enjoy the recipe.

If you are following a weight reduction organization diet or are interested in choosing foods wisely from our Food Families, you can tell at a glance how many servings from the Food Families each portion contains. For instance, in this example each serving contains 2 servings from the Protein Family, 1 serving from the Fat Family, and no extra ingredients from the Additional Calorie Family. However, if you are using sugar or fructose in this recipe, as opposed to an artificial sweetener, you would be getting 20 additional calories.

If you are counting calories, the information in the box will tell you how many calories each serving provides. In this example one serving of this recipe contains 46 calories. However, if you are using sugar or fructose as a sweetener, add 20 calories for a total of 66 calories per serving.

If you are following any type of restrictive diet, such as diabetic, low-sodium, low-fat, or low-cholesterol, the information provided will give you a nutritional analysis of each serving that will help you to choose the best recipes for your particular diet. A zero listed before a nutrient indicates that a serving of that recipe contains a negligible amount of that particular nutrient.

If you are following a low-sodium diet, many of the ingredients in our recipes can be replaced with the new low-sodium products now available, thereby reducing the total sodium content of each serving.

It is our hope that you will use this information to help you to choose and balance your diet in a delicious and healthful way.

Enjoy!

Soups

There's nothing like hot soup to warm your bones and cheer your feelings. As a meal starter, or as the entrée itself, these soups will prove to be delicious and satisfying. We've added some cold soup recipes too, for an interesting change of pace. So, sample all of our taste treats. A world of variety awaits you.

French Onion Soup

Vive la France!

Makes 4 servings

1	tablespoon plus 1 teaspoon vegetable oil
2	cups thinly sliced onions
4	cups water
4	packets instant beef flavored broth mix
1	teaspoon Worcestershire sauce
	Salt and pepper to taste
3	tablespoons grated Parmesan cheese

In a medium nonstick saucepan, heat oil over medium heat. Add onions and sauté until golden, separating slices into rings. Add small amounts of water, if necessary, to keep onions from drying.

Add water, broth mix, Worcestershire sauce, salt and pepper. Bring soup to a boil. Reduce heat and simmer 15 minutes, stirring occasionally.

Divide soup evenly into 4 serving bowls.

Sprinkle with Parmesan cheese.

Each serving provides:

100 Calories

1/2	Vegetable Serving	4 g	Protein
1	Fat Serving	6 g	Fat
33	Additional Calories	9 g	Carbohydrate
		839 mg	Sodium
		3 mg	Cholesterol

Cabbage Soup

Makes 8 servings

2   16-ounce cans tomatoes, chopped, undrained
1/2   small cabbage, shredded (about 4 cups)
5   tablespoons lemon juice
2   tablespoons minced onion flakes
1   cup water
2   packets instant beef flavored broth mix
      Sweetener equivalent to 1 teaspoon sugar
      Salt and pepper to taste

Combine all ingredients in a large saucepan. Bring to a boil over medium heat. Reduce heat and simmer, uncovered, until cabbage is tender, about 20 minutes.

Each serving provides

38 Calories*

2 Vegetable Servings   2   g   Protein
3 Additional Calories*   1   g   Fat
                             8   g   Carbohydrate
                     342   mg   Sodium
                        0   mg   Cholesterol

*Add 2 calories if sugar or fructose is used as sweetener.

Manhattan Clam Chowder

An exquisite blend of flavors!

Makes 6 servings

2	tablespoons vegetable oil
1	cup sliced onions
1	cup diced carrots
1	cup diced celery
1	tablespoon dried parsley flakes
1	16-ounce can tomatoes, drained (Reserve liquid)
9	ounces cooked potatoes, diced
1	teaspoon salt
4	whole black peppercorns
1	bay leaf
1-1/2	teaspoons dried thyme
1/4	teaspoon dried basil
12	ounces canned clams, drained (Reserve liquid)

Heat oil in a medium saucepan over medium heat. Add onions and cook until tender, about 5 minutes.

Add carrots, celery and parsley. Cook, stirring frequently, 5 minutes.

Add tomatoes, potatoes, salt, pepper, and remaining spices.

In a 1-quart bowl or jar, combine reserved tomato liquid and clam liquid. Add water to make 1 quart. Pour liquid over vegetables and bring to a boil. Cover, reduce heat and simmer 45 minutes.

Add clams. Simmer 15 minutes, covered.

Remove and discard bay leaf before serving.

Each serving provides:

137 Calories

2	Protein Servings	7	g	Protein
1/2	Bread Serving	5	g	Fat
1-1/2	Vegetable Servings	17	g	Carbohydrate
1	Fat Serving	810	mg	Sodium
		18	mg	Cholesterol

Cream of Chicken Soup

Makes 4 servings

1-1/3 cups lowfat cottage cheese
1   cup skim milk
1   cup sliced mushrooms
3   packets instant chicken flavored broth mix
3   cups water
2   tablespoons dried chives
1   teaspoon paprika
1/8   teaspoon pepper
1/8   teaspoon ground nutmeg
8   ounces cooked chicken, cut into small cubes, discarding skin

In a blender container, combine cottage cheese and milk. Blend until smooth. Pour into a medium saucepan.

Add mushrooms, broth mix, water, chives, paprika, pepper and nutmeg. Heat, stirring, over low heat, until mixture comes to a boil.

Add chicken. Heat through.

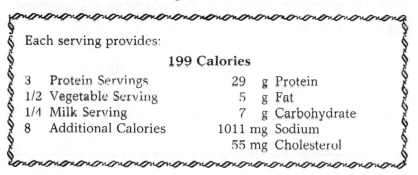

Each serving provides:

199 Calories

3	Protein Servings	29	g	Protein
1/2	Vegetable Serving	5	g	Fat
1/4	Milk Serving	7	g	Carbohydrate
8	Additional Calories	1011	mg	Sodium
		55	mg	Cholesterol

Chicken Rice Soup

Makes 4 servings

4　　cups water
4　　packets instant chicken flavored broth mix
1/2　cup diced celery
1/4　cup diced carrots
1/4　cup diced onions
1/2　teaspoon poultry seasoning
1/4　teaspoon dill weed
　　　Salt and pepper to taste
4　　ounces cooked chicken, cubed, skin discarded
1　　cup cooked rice

In a medium saucepan, combine water, broth mix, celery, carrots, onions and seasonings. Cover and cook over medium-low heat until vegetables are tender, about 20 minutes.
Add chicken and rice. Heat through.

Each serving provides:

131 Calories

1　Protein Serving　　　　11　g Protein
1/2　Bread Serving　　　　2　g Fat
1/2　Vegetable Serving　　16　g Carbohydrate
10　Additional Calories　881 mg Sodium
　　　　　　　　　　　　25 mg Cholesterol

Creole Seafood Chowder

A colorful and tasty dish . . .

Makes 4 servings

1	tablespoon plus 1 teaspoon margarine
1/4	cup chopped onions
1/4	cup chopped green pepper
1/4	cup chopped celery
2/3	cup lowfat cottage cheese
1	1-pound can tomatoes, undrained
1/2	cup water
1	packet instant chicken flavored broth mix
1/8	teaspoon dried thyme
1/2	teaspoon dried oregano
1/4	teaspoon dried basil
1/2	teaspoon dried parsley flakes
	Salt and pepper to taste
4	ounces cooked, diced shrimp, crabmeat or fish (or any combination of cooked seafood)

Melt margarine in a medium skillet over medium-high heat. Add onions, green pepper, and celery. Cook, stirring frequently, until vegetables are tender, about 10 minutes.

In a blender container, combine remaining ingredients, *except* seafood. Blend until smooth.

In a medium saucepan, combine onion mixture and cottage cheese mixture. Bring to a simmer over low heat, stirring frequently. Stir in seafood. Heat through. (Do not boil.)

Divide chowder evenly into 4 serving bowls.

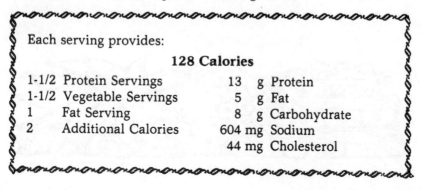

Each serving provides:

128 Calories

1-1/2	Protein Servings	13	g Protein
1-1/2	Vegetable Servings	5	g Fat
1	Fat Serving	8	g Carbohydrate
2	Additional Calories	604	mg Sodium
		44	mg Cholesterol

Fruit Soup

They won't believe this one!

Makes 4 servings

2   cups fresh strawberries (or frozen, unsweetened)
1-1/3 cups nonfat dry milk
1/2   cup cold water
1   teaspoon vanilla extract
      Sweetener equivalent to 6 teaspoons sugar
1/4   cup cold orange juice, unsweetened
4   mint sprigs to garnish

In a blender container, combine strawberries, dry milk, water, vanilla and sweetener. Blend until smooth.

Pour into a bowl and chill.

At serving time, add orange juice and beat mixture with a wire whisk until smooth.

Pour into soup bowls. Garnish each with a sprig of mint.

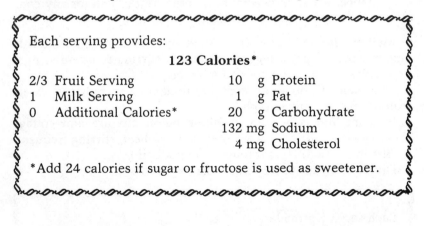

Each serving provides:

123 Calories*

2/3	Fruit Serving	10 g	Protein
1	Milk Serving	1 g	Fat
0	Additional Calories*	20 g	Carbohydrate
		132 mg	Sodium
		4 mg	Cholesterol

*Add 24 calories if sugar or fructose is used as sweetener.

Cream of Broccoli Soup

An unusual and tasty starter for any meal.

Makes 4 servings

1/2 cup chopped onions
2   cups fresh broccoli, chopped
     (or 1 10-ounce package frozen broccoli, thawed and
     chopped)
3   teaspoons instant chicken bouillon granules
1/2 teaspoon Worcestershire sauce
1/8 teaspoon seasoned salt
1/8 teaspoon celery salt
1/8 teaspoon garlic powder
     Dash nutmeg
4   cups water
2   teaspoons cornstarch
2/3 cup nonfat dry milk
2   tablespoons margarine

In a medium saucepan, combine onions, broccoli, bouillon, Worcestershire sauce, seasoned salt, celery salt, garlic powder and nutmeg. Add 3 cups of the water. Bring to a boil. Simmer over medium heat until vegetables are tender, about 20 minutes.

Stir a little of the liquid into the cornstarch, stirring until smooth; then stir into soup.

Combine dry milk and remaining water, stirring until smooth. Stir into soup.

Heat, stirring, until soup is hot. Do not boil.

Remove from heat. Stir in margarine.

Each serving provides:

155 Calories

1-1/4	Vegetable Servings	9	g Protein
1-1/2	Fat Servings	7	g Fat
1/2	Milk Serving	16	g Carbohydrate
10	Additional Calories	1128	mg Sodium
		3	mg Cholesterol

Cream of Carrot Soup

Our version of a French favorite!

Makes 6 servings

2   tablespoons margarine
3   cups diced carrots
1/2   cup chopped onions
3-1/2   cups water
5   teaspoons instant chicken bouillon granules
1   bay leaf
        Salt and pepper to taste
1-1/2   cups evaporated skim milk

In a medium saucepan, melt margarine over medium heat. Add carrots and onions. Cook 5 minutes, stirring frequently.

Add water, bouillon, bay leaf, salt and pepper. Cover, reduce heat to low, and simmer 30 minutes, until carrots are soft. Remove and discard bay leaf.

Place soup in a blender container, reserving about 1/4 cup of the carrots and onions. Blend until smooth. Return to saucepan and add reserved vegetables.

Stir in milk. Heat soup through, but do not boil.

Each serving provides:

129 Calories

1	Vegetable Serving	7 g	Protein
1	Fat Serving	5 g	Fat
1/2	Milk Serving	15 g	Carbohydrate
10	Additional Calories	1136 mg	Sodium
		3 mg	Cholesterol

Mushroom Soup

Makes 6 servings

2   tablespoons margarine
1/2   cup chopped onions
1   pound fresh mushrooms, sliced
6   cups water
5   teaspoons instant beef bouillon granules
2   cups carrots, sliced 1/4-inch thick
1/4   teaspoon dried thyme
1   teaspoon salt
1/8   teaspoon pepper
1-1/2   teaspoons sherry extract

Melt margarine in a large saucepan over medium heat. Add onions and mushrooms. Cook, stirring, until onions are tender, 5 to 10 minutes.

Reduce heat to low.

Add remaining ingredients, *except* sherry extract. Cover and simmer 1 hour. Remove from heat and stir in extract.

Each serving provides:

90 Calories

2 Vegetable Servings   3 g Protein
1 Fat Serving   4 g Fat
10 Additional Calories   9 g Carbohydrate
                                 978 mg Sodium
                                   1 mg Cholesterol

Garlic and Bean Soup

Savor the rich flavor.

Makes 4 servings

16   ounces cooked white kidney beans
1   packet instant chicken flavored broth mix
1-1/2 cups water
1   tablespoon dried parsley flakes
1   large clove garlic
2   teaspoons grated Parmesan cheese
      Salt and pepper to taste

In a blender container, combine all ingredients. Blend until smooth.

Pour mixture into a medium saucepan. Heat and serve.

Each serving provides:

143 Calories

2 Protein Servings
7 Additional Calories

10 g Protein
1   g Fat
25 g Carbohydrate
229 mg Sodium
1   mg Cholesterol

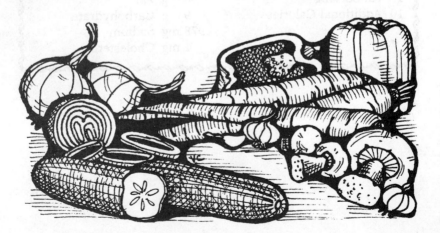

Barley-Mushroom Soup

The flavor is hearty, yet delicate.

Makes 6 servings

2   tablespoons margarine
1/2   cup chopped onions
1/2   cup chopped celery
1/2   cup chopped carrots
4   cups sliced mushrooms
4   cups water
1-1/2   cups cooked barley
4   packets instant beef flavored broth mix
1   teaspoon dried parsley flakes
1/8   teaspoon pepper

In a medium saucepan, melt margarine over medium heat. Add onions, celery and carrots. Cook 10 minutes, stirring frequently.
Add remaining ingredients.
Cover, reduce heat to low, and simmer 1 hour, or until vegetables are tender.

Each serving provides:

108 Calories

1/2	Bread Serving	4	g Protein
1-3/4	Vegetable Servings	4	g Fat
1	Fat Serving	15	g Carbohydrate
10	Additional Calories	560	mg Sodium
		0	mg Cholesterol

Potato Soup

*A delight on a chilly day, or serve
it cold for a real taste treat.*

Makes 4 servings

2   cups evaporated skim milk
12   ounces cooked potatoes, diced
2   tablespoons minced onion flakes
2   packets instant chicken flavored broth mix
1/4   teaspoon celery salt
     Dash pepper
1   tablespoon plus 1 teaspoon reduced-calorie margarine
1   teaspoon dried chives

In a medium saucepan, combine milk, potatoes, onion flakes, broth mix, celery salt and pepper. Cover and cook on low heat until heated through, about 10 minutes. Do not boil.

Remove soup from heat and stir in margarine.

Divide soup evenly into 4 serving bowls. Sprinkle dried chives on each bowl as a garnish.

Each serving provides:

182 Calories

1	Bread Serving	12 g	Protein
1/2	Fat Serving	2 g	Fat
1	Milk Serving	29 g	Carbohydrate
5	Additional Calories	703 mg	Sodium
		5 mg	Cholesterol

Tomato Squash Soup

An exciting combination of flavors!

Makes 6 servings

1   tablespoon vegetable oil
1/4   cup chopped onions
1   clove garlic, chopped
9   ounces butternut squash, peeled, cut into 1-inch cubes
1   1-pound can tomatoes, chopped, undrained
2-1/2 cups water
2   tablespoons imitation bacon bits
2   tablespoons dried parsley flakes
1   packet instant beef flavored broth mix
1   bay leaf
1/4   teaspoon dried basil
1/8   teaspoon dried thyme
1-1/2 teaspoons sherry extract

Heat oil in a medium saucepan, over medium heat. Add onions and garlic; cook until tender, about 5 minutes.

Add remaining ingredients, except sherry extract. Bring mixture to a boil, reduce heat, cover and simmer 20 minutes, or until squash is tender. Remove from heat and stir in extract.

Remove and discard bay leaf before serving.

Each serving provides:

79 Calories

1/2 Bread Serving   2 g Protein
3/4 Vegetable Serving   3 g Fat
1/2 Fat Serving   11 g Carbohydrate
6   Additional Calories   321 mg Sodium
                           0 mg Cholesterol

Vegetable Soup for a Crowd

There will be plenty left to freeze.

Makes about 24 servings

1   large head cabbage, shredded
1   bunch celery, cut into 2-inch pieces
3   1-pound cans tomatoes, undrained
4   10-ounce packages frozen cut green beans
     (or 2 pounds fresh beans)
1   pound carrots, peeled, cut into 1-inch chunks
2   8-ounce cans mushroom pieces, drained
8   packets instant chicken or beef flavored broth mix
     Salt and pepper to taste

In an 8-quart soup pot, combine all ingredients. Cover with water. Bring to a boil over medium-high heat.

Reduce heat to medium, cover, and cook 2 hours, or until vegetables are tender.

Variation: Place a measured amount of tuna or cooked chicken or fish in each serving bowl before pouring in hot soup, and be sure to count the protein as part of your meal.

Each serving provides:

49 Calories

2 Vegetable Servings
3 Additional Calories

3   g Protein
1   g Fat
10 g Carbohydrate
487 mg Sodium
0 mg Cholesterol

Salads and Salad Dressings

A salad is an appetizer.
A salad is a dessert.
A salad is a side dish.
A salad is a snack.
A salad is a main course.

So, say good-bye to the traditional lettuce and tomato salad, and say hello to the unusual. Our recipes were created to please the most discriminating tastes and add splendor, color, and excitement to every meal.

And, if you like our salads, you'll love our salad dressings. We've combined herbs and spices to show you that a dressing can make the difference between an ordinary salad and one that is spectacular.

Our Waldorf Salad

Makes 4 servings

1	cup plain lowfat yogurt
1/4	cup reduced-calorie mayonnaise
2	teaspoons lemon juice
	Sweetener equivalent to 4 teaspoons sugar
4	small, sweet apples, diced, unpeeled
1	cup chopped celery
1	tablespoon sunflower seeds

Place yogurt in a medium bowl. Stir in mayonnaise, lemon juice and sweetener.

Add remaining ingredients and mix well.

Chill to blend flavors.

Each serving provides:

158 Calories*

1/2	Vegetable Serving	5	g	Protein
1-1/2	Fat Servings	6	g	Fat
1	Fruit Serving	23	g	Carbohydrate
1/2	Milk Serving	189	mg	Sodium
15	Additional Calories*	8	mg	Cholesterol

*Add 16 calories if sugar or fructose is used as sweetener.

Tropical Ambrosia Salad

They'll think a European Chef lives in your house!

Makes 4 servings

1   cup canned pineapple chunks (unsweetened), drained
1   cup canned mandarin orange slices (unsweetened), drained
1   cup plain lowfat yogurt
1/4 teaspoon coconut extract
2   teaspoons shredded coconut (unsweetened)
1   teaspoon vanilla extract
     Sweetener equivalent to 5 teaspoons sugar

Combine all ingredients and toss to mix well.
Chill to blend flavors.

Each serving provides:

107 Calories*

1   Fruit Serving   4   g Protein
1/2 Milk Serving   1   g Fat
5   Additional Calories*   20 g Carbohydrate
                                43 mg Sodium
                                 3 mg Cholesterol

*Add 20 calories if sugar or fructose is used as sweetener.

Carrot and Raisin Salad

A truly tempting salad . . .

Makes 4 servings

2   cups grated carrots
1   cup canned crushed pineapple (unsweetened), drained
1   tablespoon lemon juice
1/4   teaspoon coconut extract
1/4   cup raisins
2   tablespoons plus 2 teaspoons reduced-calorie mayonnaise
     Sweetener equivalent to 2 teaspoons sugar

In a medium bowl, combine all ingredients. Mix well.
Chill.

Each serving provides:

117 Calories*

1 Vegetable Serving   2   g   Protein
1 Fat Serving   3   g   Fat
1 Fruit Serving   23   g   Carbohydrate
0 Additional Calories*   104 mg   Sodium
                          3 mg   Cholesterol

*Add 8 calories if sugar or fructose is used as sweetener.

South Sea Salad

Makes 1 serving

2/3 cup lowfat cottage cheese
1/2 cup sliced strawberries
1/4 cup canned crushed pineapple (unsweetened)
    Lettuce leaves to equal about 1 cup
1 teaspoon shredded coconut (unsweetened)

Combine cottage cheese, strawberries and crushed pineapple. Pile mixture on lettuce. Sprinkle with coconut.

Each serving provides:

184 Calories

2	Protein Servings	20	g	Protein
2	Vegetable Servings	3	g	Fat
1	Fruit Serving	21	g	Carbohydrate
10	Additional Calories	616	mg	Sodium
		6	mg	Cholesterol

Cranberry Salad Mold

A cool accompaniment to any dinner . . .

Makes 4 servings

2	cups fresh cranberries
1	small, sweet apple, diced, unpeeled
1/2	cup canned crushed pineapple (unsweetened) with 2 tablespoons juice
2	envelopes unflavored gelatin
1	cup water
1	cup ice cubes
1/2	cup diced celery
1	teaspoon lemon extract
1	teaspoon orange extract
	Sweetener equivalent to 16 teaspoons sugar

In a blender container or food processor, place cranberries, apples and pineapple with juice. Turn blender on and off a few times to chop fruits.

In a small saucepan, sprinkle gelatin over water and let soften a few minutes. Heat, stirring frequently, over low heat, until gelatin is completely dissolved. Remove from heat.

Stir ice into gelatin mixture. Stir until gelatin just begins to thicken. Remove and discard remaining ice.

Stir chopped fruit into gelatin. Add celery, extracts and sweetener. Mix well. Pour mixture into a 3-cup mold.

Chill until firm.

Unmold to serve.

Each serving provides:

96 Calories*

1/4	Vegetable Serving	6	g	Protein
1	Fruit Serving	0	g	Fat
0	Additional Calories*	17	g	Carbohydrate
		23	mg	Sodium
		0	gm	Cholesterol

*Add 64 calories if sugar or fructose is used as sweetener.

Tangy Tomato Aspic

We serve this dish with cottage cheese for a great lunch.

Makes 4 servings

2	tablespoons cold water
1	tablespoon lemon juice
1	envelope unflavored gelatin
2	cups tomato juice
2	tablespoons minced onion flakes
1	bay leaf
2	whole cloves
3	whole peppercorns
2	whole allspice
1/4	teaspoon dried basil
1/2	teaspoon seasoned salt
	Sweetener equivalent to 1 tablespoon firmly-packed brown sugar

In a small bowl, combine water and lemon juice. Sprinkle gelatin over this mixture and set it aside to soften.

In a medium saucepan, combine remaining ingredients. Bring to a boil over medium heat. Reduce heat to low and simmer 15 minutes. Remove from heat, strain, and discard spices.

Add gelatin mixture to tomato juice. Stir until gelatin is completely dissolved.

Pour mixture into a small mold.

Chill until firm. Unmold to serve.

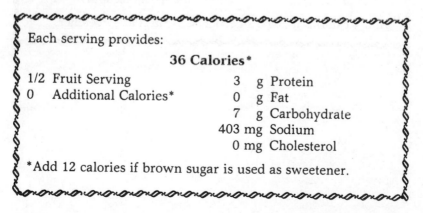

Each serving provides:

36 Calories*

1/2	Fruit Serving	3	g Protein
0	Additional Calories*	0	g Fat
		7	g Carbohydrate
		403 mg	Sodium
		0 mg	Cholesterol

*Add 12 calories if brown sugar is used as sweetener.

Marinated Artichoke Hearts

Very impressive . . .

Makes 4 servings

1   cup canned artichoke hearts, drained
1/8 teaspoon garlic powder
1   tablespoon plus 1 teaspoon vegetable oil
2   tablespoons red wine vinegar
1/4 teaspoon salt
1/4 teaspoon dried oregano
1/4 teaspoon dry mustard
     Sweetener equivalent to 1 teaspoon sugar
     Pepper to taste

Combine all ingredients in a medium bowl.
Cover and refrigerate several hours or overnight, stirring occasionally.
Serve cold.

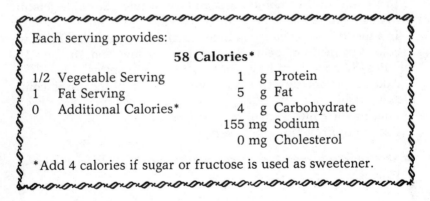

Each serving provides:

58 Calories*

1/2	Vegetable Serving	1	g	Protein
1	Fat Serving	5	g	Fat
0	Additional Calories*	4	g	Carbohydrate
		155	mg	Sodium
		0	mg	Cholesterol

*Add 4 calories if sugar or fructose is used as sweetener.

Marinated Green and Gold Salad

Makes 5 servings

1   cup zucchini, unpeeled, sliced thin
1   cup yellow squash, unpeeled, sliced thin
1/4   cup green pepper, minced
1/4   cup onions, minced
1   packet instant beef flavored broth mix
1   cup water
2   tablespoons tarragon vinegar
1   tablespoon plus 2 teaspoons vegetable oil
1   teaspoon dried parsley flakes
1/4   teaspoon salt
1   teaspoon Dijon mustard
       Pepper to taste
       Sweetener equivalent to 1 teaspoon sugar

Combine all ingredients in a medium bowl.
Cover and refrigerate several hours or overnite, stirring occasionally.
Serve cold.

Each serving provides:

59 Calories*

1 Vegetable Serving
1 Fat Serving
2 Additional Calories*

1   g Protein
5   g Fat
4   g Carbohydrate
289 mg Sodium
0 mg Cholesterol

*Add 3 calories if sugar or fructose is used as sweetener.

Italian Green Bean Salad

Makes 4 servings

2   cups green beans, cooked and drained
1   4-ounce can mushroom pieces, drained
1/2   cup tomato sauce
2   tablespoons reduced-calorie Italian dressing (6 calories per
         tablespoon)
1/4   teaspoon dried oregano
1/4   teaspoon dried basil
1/8   teaspoon garlic powder

Combine all ingredients in a bowl. Cover and chill several hours or overnight.

Serve cold or heat and serve hot.

Each serving provides:

36 Calories

1-3/4 Vegetable Servings   2   g Protein
3   Additional Calories   1   g Fat
                              7   g Carbohydrate
                      373 mg Sodium
                        0 mg Cholesterol

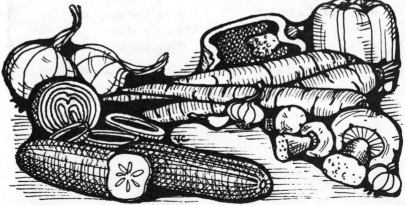

Gourmet Zucchini Salad

The name says it all.

Makes 5 servings

1-1/2 cups zucchini, unpeeled, sliced thin
1/2   cup celery, sliced thin
1/4   cup onions, sliced thin
1/4   cup green pepper, sliced thin
1/4   cup vinegar
3   tablespoons plus 1 teaspoon vegetable oil
1   tablespoon wine vinegar
1/4   teaspoon salt
1/8   teaspoon pepper
1/2   teaspoon dried basil
2   tablespoons water
          Sweetener equivalent to 6 teaspoons sugar

Layer vegetables in a shallow bowl. Combine remaining ingredients and pour over vegetables.
Refrigerate several hours or overnight, mixing occasionally.
Serve cold.

Each serving provides:

98 Calories*

1 Vegetable Serving
2 Fat Servings
0 Additional Calories*

1   g Protein
9   g Fat
4   g Carbohydrate
125 mg Sodium
0 mg Cholesterol

*Add 19 calories if sugar or fructose is used as sweetener.

Herbed Potato Salad

Makes 6 servings

18   ounces potatoes, peeled, cooked and diced†
1/2   cup plain lowfat yogurt
2   tablespoons vegetable oil
1/2   cup finely chopped onions
1   tablespoon dried parsley flakes
2   teaspoons vinegar
1/2   teaspoon dried oregano
1/4   teaspoon salt
1/8   teaspoon pepper
      Dash paprika

Place cooked potatoes in a large bowl.
Combine remaining ingredients and pour over potatoes. Toss to combine.
Chill. Serve cold.
†Note: To cook potatoes, peel, cut into quarters, place in sauce-pan and cover with water. Bring to a boil, cover, and cook about 30 minutes, or until tender. Drain.

Each serving provides:

114 Calories

1   Bread Serving   3   g Protein
1/6 Vegetable Serving   5   g Fat
1   Fat Serving   15   g Carbohydrates
17   Additional Calories   107 mg Sodium
                              1 mg Cholesterol

Best Cole Slaw

And we mean it!

Makes 8 servings

1   medium cabbage, shredded (about 4 cups)
1   large carrot, grated
     Sweetener equivalent to 10 teaspoons sugar
1   teaspoon salt
1   teaspoon celery seed
2   tablespoons vinegar
1/2 cup plus 2 tablespoons plus 2 teaspoons reduced-calorie
     mayonnaise

Place cabbage and carrots in a large bowl. Sprinkle sweetener, salt and celery seed on top. Let stand for 5 minutes.

Mix vinegar and mayonnaise together. Spoon over cabbage. Toss to blend.

Chill for several hours, tossing occasionally.

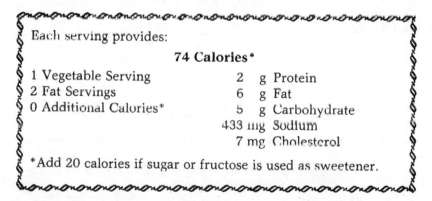

Each serving provides:

74 Calories*

1 Vegetable Serving	2 g Protein
2 Fat Servings	6 g Fat
0 Additional Calories*	5 g Carbohydrate
	433 mg Sodium
	7 mg Cholesterol

*Add 20 calories if sugar or fructose is used as sweetener.

Cucumber and Onion Salad

An excellent side dish for light summer meals . . .

Makes 8 servings

1-1/2 cups cucumber, sliced paper-thin
1/2   cup onions, sliced paper-thin
1/3   cup vinegar
5   tablespoons water
1/4   teaspoon salt
       Dash pepper
       Sweetener equivalent to 15 teaspoons sugar

Layer onions and cucumber in a jar or bowl. Combine remaining ingredients and pour over vegetables.

Refrigerate overnight, stirring or inverting jar several times.

Each serving provides:

12 Calories*

1/2 Vegetable Serving	1 g Protein
0 Additional Calories*	0 g Fat
	2 g Carbohydrate
	69 mg Sodium
	0 mg Cholesterol

*Add 30 calories if sugar or fructose is used as sweetener.

Brown Rice and Vegetable Salad

You'll love the hearty, nutty flavor of the brown rice.

Makes 4 servings

2	cups cooked brown rice
1/2	cup shredded carrots
1/2	cup shredded, unpeeled zucchini
2	tablespoons finely chopped onions
2	tablespoons lemon juice
1	tablespoon plus 1 teaspoon vegetable oil
1/2	teaspoon dried thyme
1/4	teaspoon salt
1	tablespoon dried parsley flakes
	Pepper to taste

In a medium bowl, combine rice, carrots, zucchini and onions. Toss.

In a small bowl, combine remaining ingredients. Pour over rice mixture. Toss to blend ingredients.

Chill. Serve cold.

Each serving provides:

168 Calories

1	Bread Serving	3	g	Protein
1/2	Vegetable Serving	5	g	Fat
1	Fat Serving	27	g	Carbohydrate
		145	mg	Sodium
		0	mg	Cholesterol

Caesar Salad

(Shown on cover)

We've left out the egg, but the flavor's great!

Makes 4 servings

2	slices white or whole wheat bread, cubed
1	medium head romaine lettuce, chilled, torn into bite-size pieces (about 4 cups)
1/2	teaspoon salt
1/4	teaspoon dry mustard
	Freshly ground black pepper to taste
1/4	teaspoon garlic powder
2	tablespoons lemon juice
1/2	teaspoon Worcestershire sauce
2	tablespoons plus 2 teaspoons vegetable oil
1/4	cup plus 2 tablespoons wine vinegar
3	tablespoons grated Parmesan cheese

Toast bread cubes in a 300° oven until dry and brown.

Place lettuce in a large bowl.

In a small bowl, combine seasonings, lemon juice, Worcestershire sauce, oil and vinegar. Mix well. Pour over greens. Toss.

Sprinkle with Parmesan cheese and croutons. Toss and serve.

Each serving provides:

145 Calories

1/2	Bread Serving	3	g Protein
2	Vegetable Servings	11	g Fat
2	Fat Servings	9	g Carbohydrate
22	Additional Calories	408	mg Sodium
		3	mg Cholesterol

Tangy Cucumber Salad

Makes 2 servings

1   tablespoon Dijon mustard
1/4   cup plain lowfat yogurt
1   cup cucumber, very thinly sliced

Stir mustard into yogurt in a small bowl. Gently stir in cucumbers.
Refrigerate several hours.

Each serving provides:

35 Calories

1	Vegetable Serving			
1/4	Milk Serving	2	g	Protein
		1	g	Fat
		5	g	Carbohydrate
		247	mg	Sodium
		2	mg	Cholesterol

Quick Mushroom Salad

Dresses any meal, and so easy to do . . .

Makes 4 servings

2   cups fresh mushrooms, sliced
3   tablespoons Italian dressing
1   tablespoon grated Parmesan cheese

Combine all ingredients. Mix and serve, or refrigerate for later servings.

Each serving provides:

67 Calories

1	Vegetable Serving			
1-1/2	Fat Servings	2	g	Protein
7	Additional Calories	6	g	Fat
		3	g	Carbohydrate
		115	mg	Sodium
		1	mg	Cholesterol

Marinated Vegetable Salad

Makes a colorful and tasty addition to any meal . . .

Makes 6 servings

2	cups cauliflower, cut into flowerets
1	cup carrots, cut into 1/2-inch slices
1	cup celery, cut into 2-inch sticks
1	green pepper, cut into 1/2-inch strips
1/2	cup chopped red onion
1	cup small mushrooms
12	stuffed green olives, cut in half
1/4	cup vegetable oil
1/4	cup vinegar
1/2	cup water
1-1/2	teaspoons salt
1-1/2	teaspoons dried oregano
1/2	teaspoon pepper
	Dash garlic powder
	Sweetener equivalent to 8 teaspoons sugar

In a large skillet, combine all ingredients.† Bring to a boil over medium heat, stirring occasionally.

Reduce heat to low, cover, and simmer 5 minutes.

Place mixture in a bowl and refrigerate at least 24 hours. Serve cold.

†Note: If using aspartame as sweetener, add it *after* cooking.

Each serving provides:

124 Calories*

2	Vegetable Servings	2	g	Protein
2	Fat Servings	10	g	Fat
10	Additional Calories*	8	g	Carbohydrate
		768	mg	Sodium
		0	mg	Cholesterol

*Add 26 calories if sugar or fructose is used as sweetener.

Hot German Potato Salad

Who said salads have to be cold?

Makes 4 servings

12   ounces potatoes, cooked, peeled, diced
2   teaspoons imitation bacon bits
1/4   teaspoon salt
      Pepper to taste
      Dash celery seed
1   teaspoon dry mustard
1   tablespoon dried chives
1   tablespoon minced onion flakes, reconstituted in a small
      amount of water
1/4   cup vinegar
2   tablespoons water
      Sweetener equivalent to 1 teaspoon sugar

Place potatoes in a large bowl. Sprinkle with bacon bits, salt, pepper, celery seed, mustard, chives and onion. Mix well.

In a small saucepan, heat vinegar and water until hot. (Do not boil.) Remove from heat and stir in sweetener. Pour over potatoes. Toss and serve hot.

Each serving provides:

66 Calories*

1 Bread Serving   2   g Protein
5 Additional Calories*   1   g Fat
                              14   g Carbohydrate
                             184 mg Sodium
                               0 mg Cholesterol

*Add 4 calories if sugar or fructose is used as sweetener.

Carrot Slaw

Slaw doesn't have *to mean cabbage.*

Makes 4 servings

2   cups shredded carrots
1/2   cup green pepper, minced
1/4   cup onions, minced
1   small, sweet apple, unpeeled, shredded
1/4   cup plus 2 tablespoons raisins
2   tablespoons vegetable oil
2-1/2   tablespoons vinegar
1/4   teaspoon celery seed
1/4   teaspoon salt
1/4   teaspoon dry mustard
        Sweetener equivalent to 4 teaspoons sugar

In a medium bowl, combine carrots, green pepper, onions, apple and raisins. Toss.

In a small saucepan, combine remaining ingredients. Bring to a boil over medium-high heat. Remove from heat. Pour over salad. Toss to blend.

Chill. Serve cold.

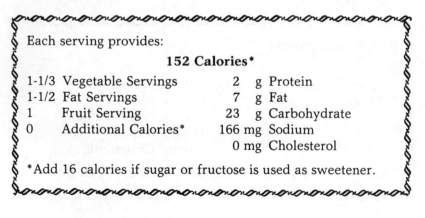

Each serving provides:

152 Calories*

1-1/3 Vegetable Servings   2 g Protein
1-1/2 Fat Servings   7 g Fat
1   Fruit Serving   23 g Carbohydrate
0   Additional Calories*   166 mg Sodium
                                0 mg Cholesterol

*Add 16 calories if sugar or fructose is used as sweetener.

Red Cabbage Salad

A bit of the old country . . .

Makes 4 servings

4   cups shredded red cabbage
1/2 cup water
1/4 cup vinegar
1   small apple, peeled, shredded
1/2 teaspoon salt
    Sweetener equivalent to 3 teaspoons sugar

Combine all ingredients in a medium saucepan. Cover and bring to a boil over medium-high heat.

Reduce heat to low. Cook, stirring occasionally, until cabbage is just tender-crisp, about 15 minutes.

Serve hot or cold.

Each serving provides:

38 Calories*

2   Vegetable Servings   1   g Protein
1/4 Fruit Serving   0   g Fat
0   Additional Calories*   9   g Carbohydrate
                          281 mg Sodium
                            0 mg Cholesterol

*Add 12 calories if sugar or fructose is used as sweetener.

Middle East Eggplant Salad

Makes 6 servings

2   tablespoons vegetable oil
3   cups eggplant, pared and cubed
1/2   cup chopped onions
1/2   cup chopped green pepper
1   clove garlic, crushed
1/2   cup chopped fresh tomato
2   tablespoons wine vinegar
1   tablespoon parsley flakes
      Salt and pepper to taste

Heat oil in a large nonstick skillet over medium-high heat. Add eggplant, onions, green pepper and garlic. Cook until eggplant is brown, stirring frequently.

Place mixture in a bowl. Add remaining ingredients. Toss. Chill. Serve cold.

Each serving provides:

66 Calories

1-1/2 Vegetable Servings
1   Fat Serving

1 g Protein
5 g Fat
6 g Carbohydrate
7 mg Sodium
0 mg Cholesterol

Italian Cauliflower Salad

Simple and delicious as a salad or an appetizer . . .

Makes 6 servings

3	cups fresh cauliflower, cut into flowerets
2	tablespoons chopped green pepper
1-1/2	teaspoons minced onion flakes
1/8	teaspoon garlic powder
3	tablespoons reduced-calorie Italian dressing (6 calories per tablespoon)
1/8	teaspoon dried basil
1/8	teaspoon dried oregano
1/4	cup water
1/2	teaspoon salt

Combine all ingredients in a medium saucepan. Cook, covered, over medium heat until cauliflower is tender, about 15 minutes. Chill.
Serve cold.

Each serving provides:

18 Calories

1 Vegetable Serving
3 Additional Calories

1 g Protein
1 g Fat
3 g Carbohydrate
297 mg Sodium
0 mg Cholesterol

Asparagus Vinaigrette

A delicious, tangy addition to any meal . . .

Makes 4 servings

1	10-ounce package frozen asparagus spears
1-1/2	teaspoons Dijon mustard
3	tablespoons red wine vinegar
2	tablespoons plus 2 teaspoons vegetable oil
3	tablespoons water
1/2	teaspoon parsley flakes
	Salt and pepper to taste

Cook asparagus according to package directions. Drain and place in a shallow bowl.

Blend mustard and vinegar in a small bowl. Add oil, water, parsley, salt and pepper. Mix well. Pour over asparagus.

Chill several hours, turning occasionally.

Serve cold.

Each serving provides:

100 Calories

1 Vegetable Serving	2	g	Protein
2 Fat Servings	9	g	Fat
	3	g	Carbohydrate
	60	mg	Sodium
	0	mg	Cholesterol

Dilly Beans

Makes 4 servings

1   pound fresh green beans
1/2 cup onions, sliced thin, broken into rings
1/2 cup vinegar
2   tablespoons plus 2 teaspoons vegetable oil
1   clove garlic, slivered
1   teaspoon dill weed
1/2 teaspoon dry mustard
1/4 teaspoon salt
1/8 teaspoon pepper
    Sweetener equivalent to 1 teaspoon sugar

Snap off the ends of the beans. Cook beans, covered, in 1 inch of boiling water until just tender-crisp, about 15 minutes. Drain, reserving liquid.

Place beans in a shallow bowl.

Add water to reserved liquid to make 1 cup. Combine liquid with remaining ingredients in a small bowl. Pour over beans.

Cover and refrigerate overnight.

Serve cold.

Each serving provides:

127 Calories*

1-1/4	Vegetable Servings	3	g Protein
2	Fat Servings	9	g Fat
0	Additional Calories*	11	g Carbohydrate
		144	mg Sodium
		0	mg Cholesterol

*Add 4 calories if sugar or fructose is used as sweetener.

Pineapple Slaw

A refreshing change . . .

Makes 4 servings

2	cups shredded cabbage
1/4	cup green pepper, diced
1/2	cup canned crushed pineapple (unsweetened), drained
2	tablespoons vinegar
1/4	cup reduced-calorie mayonnaise
2	teaspoons minced onion flakes
1/4	teaspoon curry powder
1/4	teaspoon celery seed

Combine cabbage, green pepper and pineapple in a large bowl. Toss to combine.

Stir vinegar into mayonnaise in a small bowl. Stir in seasonings. Pour over cabbage mixture. Toss to blend well.

Chill.

Toss before serving.

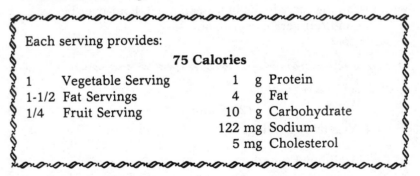

Each serving provides:

75 Calories

1	Vegetable Serving	1	g	Protein
1-1/2	Fat Servings	4	g	Fat
1/4	Fruit Serving	10	g	Carbohydrate
		122	mg	Sodium
		5	mg	Cholesterol

Herbed Yogurt Dressing

Makes 8 servings
(2-1/2 tablespoons each serving)

1	tablespoon plus 1 teaspoon vegetable oil
1	cup plain lowfat yogurt
2	tablespoons wine vinegar
1/2	teaspoon dried oregano
1/2	teaspoon dill weed
1/8	teaspoon garlic powder
1	tablespoon minced onion flakes
	Salt and pepper to taste

Stir oil into yogurt. Add remaining ingredients. Mix well.
Chill to blend flavors.
Stir before serving.

Each serving provides:

40 Calories

1/2 Fat Serving
1/4 Milk Serving

2 g Protein
3 g Fat
2 g Carbohydrate
21 mg Sodium
2 mg Cholesterol

Cucumber-Dill Dressing

*Also doubles as a dip for fresh vegetables or
as a sauce for cold fish . . .*

*Makes 8 servings
(3 tablespoons each serving)*

1	medium cucumber, peeled, seeded, shredded
1	cup plain lowfat yogurt
1/8	teaspoon salt
1/8	teaspoon garlic powder
1/2	teaspoon dill weed
2	teaspoons Dijon mustard
	Pepper to taste

Drain cucumber well on layers of paper towels.
Combine all ingredients, stirring to mix well.
Chill several hours to blend flavors.

Each serving provides:

22 Calories

1/4 Vegetable Serving
1/4 Milk Serving

2 g Protein
1 g Fat
3 g Carbohydrate
93 mg Sodium
2 mg Cholesterol

Dijon Dressing

Try this one on broccoli or asparagus.

*Makes 2 servings
(1-1/2 tablespoons each serving)*

1   tablespoon plus 1 teaspoon vegetable oil
1   tablespoon plus 1 teaspoon wine vinegar
1/8   teaspoon garlic powder
2   teaspoons Dijon mustard

Combine all ingredients in a small jar and shake to blend.

Each serving provides:

88 Calories

2 Fat Servings

    0   g Protein
    9   g Fat
    1   g Carbohydrate
151 mg Sodium
    0 mg Cholesterol

Cheesy Herb Dressing

This one is great!

Makes 5 servings
(2 tablespoons each serving)

1/4 cup plus 2 tablespoons plus 2 teaspoons reduced-calorie mayonnaise
1 tablespoon dried parsley flakes
1 tablespoon grated Parmesan cheese
1-1/2 teaspoons lemon juice
1/16 teaspoon garlic powder
1/4 teaspoon dried basil

Combine all ingredients and mix well.
Chill several hours to blend flavors.

Each serving provides:

60 Calories

2 Fat Servings
6 Additional Calories

1 g Protein
6 g Fat
2 g Carbohydrate
170 mg Sodium
7 mg Cholesterol

Creamy Italian Dressing

Makes 6 servings
(1-1/2 tablespoons each serving)

1/2   cup reduced-calorie mayonnaise
1   tablespoon skim milk
1   tablespoon wine vinegar
1/16   teaspoon garlic powder
1/4   teaspoon dried oregano
1/4   teaspoon dried basil
1/4   teaspoon sugar
       Salt and pepper to taste

Combine all ingredients. Mix well.
Chill several hours to blend flavors.

Each serving provides:

56 Calories

2 Fat Servings   0   g Protein
2 Additional Calories   5   g Fat
                               2   g Carbohydrate
                             150 mg Sodium
                               7 mg Cholesterol

French Tomato Dressing

Tart and tangy!

Makes 6 servings
(2-1/2 tablespoons each serving)

1/2 cup tomato juice
1/4 cup vegetable oil
2 tablespoons red wine vinegar
1/2 teaspoon salt
1/4 teaspoon pepper
1 teaspoon Dijon mustard
1/2 teaspoon Worcestershire sauce
1/2 teaspoon dried oregano
1/4 teaspoon dried basil
Sweetener equivalent to 1 teaspoon sugar

Combine all ingredients in a small jar and shake well.
Chill to blend flavors.

Each serving provides:

87 Calories*

2 Fat Servings
4 Additional Calories*

0 g Protein
9 g Fat
1 g Carbohydrate
247 mg Sodium
0 mg Cholesterol

*Add 3 calories if sugar or fructose is used as sweetener.

Cheesy Thousand Island Dressing

Makes 6 servings
(1/4 cup each serving)

1	cup lowfat cottage cheese
1/4	cup ketchup
1	tablespoon vegetable oil
1/2	teaspoon salt
1	teaspoon paprika
1	tablespoon pickle relish
2	tablespoons finely minced celery
2	tablespoons finely minced green pepper
1	teaspoon minced onion flakes

In a blender container, combine cottage cheese, ketchup, oil, salt and paprika. Blend until smooth.
Stir in remaining ingredients.
Chill to blend flavors.

Each serving provides:

65 Calories

1/2	Protein Serving	5 g	Protein
1/8	Vegetable Serving	3 g	Fat
1/2	Fat Serving	5 g	Carbohydrate
15	Additional Calories	471 mg	Sodium
		1 mg	Cholesterol

Bleu Cheese Dressing

Makes 4 servings
(1/4   cup each serving)

2/3   cup lowfat cottage cheese
2   ounces Bleu cheese, crumbled
1   teaspoon dry mustard
2   teaspoons wine vinegar
2   teaspoons vegetable oil
1   teaspoon minced onion flakes
      Salt and pepper to taste

Combine all ingredients in a blender container. Blend until smooth.
Chill to blend flavors.

Each serving provides:

100 Calories

1 Protein Serving	8 g Protein
1/2 Fat Serving	7 g Fat
	2 g Carbohydrate
	351 mg Sodium
	12 mg Cholesterol

Creamy Orange Dressing

Serve on fresh fruit salad for a delicious difference.

Makes 8 servings
(2-1/2 tablespoons each serving)

1   cup plain lowfat yogurt
1/4   cup frozen orange juice concentrate (unsweetened), thawed

Combine ingredients.
Serve with fresh fruit salad.

Each serving provides:

32 Calories

1/4 Fruit Serving	2 g Protein
1/4 Milk Serving	0 g Fat
	5 g Carbohydrate
	20 mg Sodium
	2 mg Cholesterol

Milk Dishes

Milk is an essential food that can be dressed up in many ways. In this section we've created for you milk recipes that are truly fine gourmet creations. Only you will know how easy they were to prepare. You'll find fluffs, puddings and dips, plus some unusual yogurt recipes. Now you can give your family healthy foods that will make them feel as important as company.

Strawberry Ice Cream in a Flash

You'll give this a 10-star rating!

Makes 2 servings

1/3	cup nonfat dry milk
	Sweetener equivalent to 5 teaspoons sugar
1/2	cup ice water
1/2	teaspoon vanilla extract
2	cups frozen strawberries (unsweetened), still frozen

In a blender container, combine dry milk, sweetener, water, vanilla and 1 cup of strawberries. Blend just until berries are chopped into small pieces.

Add remaining berries. Blend until smooth.

Spoon into 2 serving bowls.

Serve immediately.

Each serving provides:

105 Calories*

1	Fruit Serving	6	g	Protein
1/2	Milk Serving	0	g	Fat
0	Additional Calories*	20	g	Carbohydrate
		68	mg	Sodium
		2	mg	Cholesterol

*Add 40 calories is sugar or fructose is used as sweetener.

Persian Cream Pudding

Melts in your mouth!

Makes 2 servings

2/3	cup nonfat dry milk
1-1/2	cups water
2	eggs, separated
1	envelope unflavored gelatin
2	teaspoons vanilla butternut flavor
1/2	teaspoon coconut extract (*or* almond extract)
	Sweetener equivalent to 6 teaspoons sugar

In a small saucepan, combine dry milk and water. Add egg yolks and beat with a wire whisk until blended.

Sprinkle gelatin over egg yolk mixture, and let it soften a few minutes. Heat, over medium heat, stirring with a whisk until gelatin is completely dissolved and mixture starts to boil. Remove from heat.

Stir extracts and sweetener into pudding. Refrigerate 20 minutes, or until pudding is thoroughly cooled and thickened.

Beat egg whites on high speed of an electric mixer until stiff. Fold whites into chilled pudding. Beat pudding on high speed a few seconds, just until mixture is blended.

Chill.

Each serving provides:

198 Calories*

1 Protein Serving	19	g	Protein
1 Milk Serving	6	g	Fat
0 Additional Calories*	13	g	Carbohydrate
	205	mg	Sodium
	278	mg	Cholesterol

*Add 48 calories if sugar or fructose is used as sweetener.

Elegant Floating Islands

Appealing to the eye and the palate . . .

Makes 4 servings

1   cup water
1   envelope unflavored gelatin
1   cup plain lowfat yogurt
    Sweetener equivalent to 12 teaspoons sugar
1   teaspoon vanilla extract
1   teaspoon vanilla butternut flavor
1/2 teaspoon almond extract
2   cups frozen blueberries (unsweetened)

Place water in a small saucepan. Sprinkle gelatin over water and let soften a few minutes. Heat, stirring frequently, over low heat, until gelatin is completely dissolved. Remove from heat.

In a blender container, combine yogurt, sweetener, and extracts. Add gelatin mixture and blend until smooth.

Pour mixture into 4 custard cups. Chill until firm, about 1 hour. While custard is chilling, thaw blueberries.

To serve, place 1/2 cup blueberries (undrained) in each of 4 serving bowls. Unmold a custard into the center of each. Spoon a few blueberries over the top of the pudding.

Note: To unmold, dip each cup in a bowl of hot water for 10 seconds, carefully run a knife around the edge, and invert.

Each serving provides:

97 Calories*

1   Fruit Serving   6 g Protein
1/2 Milk Serving   1 g Fat
0   Additional Calories*   14 g Carbohydrate
                           45 mg Sodium
                           3 mg Cholesterol

*Add 48 calories if sugar or fructose is used as sweetener.

Whipped Topping

We like this better than the kind you can buy!

Makes 4 servings

1/2	teaspoon unflavored gelatin
1/4	cup water
2/3	cup nonfat dry milk
	Sweetener equivalent to 4 teaspoons sugar
3/4	teaspoon vanilla extract
1/4	cup ice water

Chill a medium bowl and the beaters from an electric mixer in the freezer for 30 minutes.

Sprinkle gelatin over 1/4 cup water in a small saucepan. Heat on low heat until gelatin is completely dissolved.

Remove bowl from freezer and place it in a large bowl of ice cubes. In the chilled bowl, place dry milk, sweetener, vanilla and ice water. Beat on low speed of electric mixer, gradually adding gelatin mixture.

Beat on high speed until soft peaks form.

Chill in a covered container 10 to 15 minutes before serving.

Note: Topping keeps well in the refrigerator for 2 days.

Each serving provides:

49 Calories*

1/2	Milk Serving	5 g	Protein
0	Additional Calories*	0 g	Fat
		6 g	Carbohydrate
		66 mg	Sodium
		2 mg	Cholesterol

*Add 16 calories if sugar or fructose is used as sweetener.

Tortoni

So delicious, you'll think it's fattening!

Makes 4 servings

1/3   cup ice water
1/3   cup nonfat dry milk
      Sweetener equivalent to 6 teaspoons sugar
1/2   teaspoon almond extract
1/2   teaspoon vanilla butternut flavor
1/4   ounce graham cracker crumbs
      (1 – 2-1/2-inch square, crushed)

Place ice water and dry milk in a deep bowl. Beat on medium speed of an electric mixer for 2 minutes. Increase speed to high and continue to beat for 2 more minutes.

Add sweetener. Beat 2 minutes on high speed, or until mixture is thick and forms soft peaks.

Add extracts, beating until blended.

Divide mixture evenly into 4 custard cups. Sprinkle with crumbs.

Place in freezer until set, about 1 hour. To serve, let Tortoni sit at room temperature for about 3 minutes.

Each serving provides:

35 Calories*

1/4 Milk Serving	3	g Protein
12 Additional Calories*	0	g Fat
	4	g Carbohydrate
	44 mg	Sodium
	1 mg	Cholesterol

*Add 24 calories if sugar or fructose is used as sweetener.

Piña Colada Fluff

Makes 4 servings

3/4	cup water
1	envelope unflavored gelatin
2/3	cup nonfat dry milk
	Sweetener equivalent to 4 teaspoons sugar
1	teaspoon vanilla extract
1/2	teaspoon coconut extract
1/4	teaspoon rum extract
1	cup canned crushed pineapple (unsweetened), drained
7	ice cubes

Place water in a small saucepan. Sprinkle gelatin over water and let soften a few minutes. Heat, stirring frequently, over low heat, until gelatin is completely dissolved. Remove from heat.

In a blender container, combine dry milk, sweetener, extracts and pineapple. Add gelatin mixture.

Turn on blender. Add ice cubes, 1 at a time, while blending. Blend 1 minute, or until ice is gone.

Mixture may be divided into 4 servings and eaten right away, or, if a firmer texture is desired, chilled for at least 15 minutes.

Each serving provides:

94 Calories*

1/2	Fruit Serving	6	g Protein
1/2	Milk Serving	0	g Fat
0	Additional Calories*	16	g Carbohydrate
		68	mg Sodium
		2	mg Cholesterol

*Add 16 calories if sugar or fructose is used as sweetener.

Chocolate Fluff

Light as a feather!

Makes 4 servings

3/4   cup water
1   envelope unflavored gelatin
2/3   cup nonfat dry milk
       Sweetener equivalent to 8 teaspoons sugar
1   tablespoon plus 1 teaspoon cocoa, unsweetened
1-1/2 teaspoons vanilla extract
1/2   teaspoon vanilla butternut flavor
7   ice cubes

Place water in a small saucepan. Sprinkle gelatin over water and let soften a few minutes. Heat, stirring frequently, over low heat, until gelatin is completely dissolved. Remove from heat.

In a blender container, combine dry milk, sweetener, cocoa, and extracts. Add gelatin mixture.

Turn on blender. Add ice cubes, 1 at a time, while blending. Blend one minute, or until ice is gone.

Divide into 4 servings.

This may be eaten right away or, if a firmer texture is desired, chilled for at least 15 minutes.

Variation: For Mocha Fluff, add 1-1/2 teaspoons instant coffee granules with the cocoa.

Each serving provides:

66 Calories*

1/2 Milk Serving	7 g Protein
5 Additional Calories*	0 g Fat
	7 g Carbohydrate
	68 mg Sodium
	2 mg Cholesterol

*Add 32 calories if sugar or fructose is used as sweetener.

Creamy Chocolate Pudding

This will surely be a favorite.

Makes 2 servings

1   envelope unflavored gelatin
1/4   cup water
1   cup evaporated skim milk
1   teaspoon chocolate extract
1   teaspoon unsweetened cocoa
1/2   teaspoon vanilla extract
       Sweetener equivalent to 5 teaspoons sugar

In a small saucepan, sprinkle gelatin over water. Let soften a few minutes. Heat, stirring frequently, over low heat, until gelatin is completely dissolved.

In a blender container, combine remaining ingredients. Add gelatin mixture. Blend until smooth.

Pour into a bowl and chill until set, about 20 to 30 minutes.

Beat chilled pudding on high speed of an electric mixer until creamy.

Serve, or refrigerate for a later serving.

Each serving provides:

132 Calories*

1 Milk Serving	14	g Protein
3 Additional Calories*	0	g Fat
	15	g Carbohydrate
	150 mg	Sodium
	5 mg	Cholesterol

*Add 40 calories if sugar or fructose is used as sweetener.

Orange Freeze

Makes 4 servings

1/2 cup frozen orange juice concentrate (unsweetened), thawed
1 cup skim milk
1/4 cup water
1/3 cup nonfat dry milk
1 tablespoon lemon juice
Sweetener equivalent to 8 teaspoons sugar

In a large bowl, mix orange juice concentrate with skim milk. Set aside.

In a medium bowl, beat water and dry milk on medium speed of an electric mixer for 2 minutes. Beat on high speed until soft peaks form.

Add lemon juice and continue beating on high speed until stiff. Gradually beat in sweetener.

Fold fluffy mixture into orange mixture gently, but thoroughly. Pour mixture into a 6 x 11-inch pan and place in freezer for 1 hour, or until firm, but not solid.

Spoon mixture into a bowl and beat on low speed of electric mixer until smooth. Return mixture to pan.

Cover and freeze until firm.

Let stand at room temperature for 10 minutes before serving.

Each serving provides:

105 Calories*

1	Fruit Serving	6	g Protein
1/2	Milk Serving	0	g Fat
0	Additional Calories*	20	g Carbohydrate
		67	mg Sodium
		2	mg Cholesterol

*Add 32 calories if sugar or fructose is used as sweetener.

Banana Bavarian

Makes 4 servings

2   envelopes unflavored gelatin
1/2   cup water
2   cups evaporated skim milk
2   medium, ripe bananas
       Sweetener equivalent to 4 teaspoons sugar
1   teaspoon vanilla extract
1/4   teaspoon banana extract

Sprinkle gelatin over water in a small saucepan, and let soften a few minutes. Heat, stirring frequently, until gelatin is completely dissolved.

In a blender container, combine remaining ingredients. Add gelatin mixture. Blend until smooth.

Pour into 4 individual serving bowls and chill until set.

Each serving provides:

171 Calories*

1 Fruit Serving	14	g Protein
1 Milk Serving	1	g Fat
0 Additional Calories*	28	g Carbohydrate
	151	mg Sodium
	5	mg Cholesterol

*Add 16 calories if sugar or fructose is used as sweetener.

Light-as-Air Peaches

Melt-in-your-mouth goodness . . .

Makes 2 servings

2   medium, cold, very ripe peaches
1/3   cup nonfat dry milk
      Sweetener equivalent to 2 teaspoons sugar
1   egg white ·
1/4   teaspoon cream of tartar
      Ground cinnamon *or* nutmeg

Peel peaches and remove pits.

In a blender container or food processor, combine peaches, dry milk, and sweetener. Blend until smooth.

In a medium bowl, beat egg white until foamy, on low speed of an electric mixer. Add cream of tartar and beat on high speed until stiff.

Fold peach mixture into egg white, gently, but thoroughly. Divide mixture evenly into 2 serving bowls. Sprinkle with cinnamon or nutmeg.

Serve right away.

Each serving provides:

109 Calories*

1	Fruit Serving	7	g	Protein
1/2	Milk Serving	0	g	Fat
10	Additional Calories*	21	g	Carbohydrate
		90	mg	Sodium
		2	mg	Cholesterol

*Add 16 calories if sugar or fructose is used as sweetener.

Vanilla Tapioca Pudding

Makes 2 servings

2   cups skim milk
2   tablespoons quick-cooking tapioca
1/2   teaspoon vanilla extract
1   teaspoon vanilla butternut flavor
       Sweetener equivalent to 4 teaspoons sugar

Place milk in a small saucepan. Sprinkle tapioca over milk and let it soften 5 minutes.

Cook over medium heat, stirring constantly until mixture comes to a boil. Boil, stirring, 2 minutes. Remove from heat.

Stir in vanilla extract, vanilla butternut flavor and sweetener. Divide into 2 custard cups.

Chill.

Each serving provides:

136 Calories*

1   Milk Serving
30 Additional calories*

10   g Protein
0   g Fat
20   g Carbohydrate
129 mg Sodium
5   mg Cholesterol

*Add 32 calories if sugar or fructose is used as sweetener.

Creamy Rice and Raisin Pudding

A gourmet's delight!

Makes 4 servings

2   cups skim milk
1/4   teaspoon ground cinnamon
1   tablespoon cornstarch
2   cups cooked rice
       Sweetener equivalent to 6 teaspoons sugar
2   teaspoons vanilla extract
1/4   cup raisins
       Ground cinnamon
       Ground nutmeg

In a medium saucepan, combine milk and 1/4 teaspoon cinnamon. Mix a few tablespoons of the milk into the cornstarch in a small bowl, stirring to dissolve cornstarch. Add to saucepan.

Add rice. Heat over medium heat, stirring constantly, until mixture comes to a boil. Continue to cook and stir 1 minute. Remove from heat.

Stir in sweetener, vanilla and raisins. Pour mixture into a shallow bowl.

Sprinkle generously with cinnamon.
Sprinkle with a dash of nutmeg.
Chill.

Each serving provides:

203 Calories*

1	Bread Serving	7	g Protein
1/2	Fruit Serving	0	g Fat
1/2	Milk Serving	40	g Carbohydrate
8	Additional calories*	66 mg	Sodium
		2 mg	Cholesterol

*Add 24 calories if sugar or fructose is used as sweetener.

Chocolate Upside-Down Pudding

A beautiful and delicious two-tone dessert . . .

Makes 4 servings

1-1/2 cups water
1   envelope unflavored gelatin
2/3   cup nonfat dry milk
2   tablespoons cocoa (unsweetened)
1   teaspoon vanilla butternut flavor
      Sweetener equivalent to 7 teaspoons sugar

Place half of the water in a small saucepan. Sprinkle gelatin over water and let soften a few minutes. Heat, stirring frequently, over low heat, until gelatin is completely dissolved.

Place remaining ingredients in a blender container. Add gelatin mixture. Blend just until smooth, about 5 to 10 seconds.

Pour mixture into 4 custard cups. Let them sit at room temperature for 5 minutes.

Chill until firm.

To serve, dip each cup in hot water for 20 seconds and unmold onto a serving dish.

Each serving provides:

63 Calories*

1/2 Milk Serving   7 g Protein
8   Additional Calories*   1 g Fat
                              8 g Carbohydrate
                             68 mg Sodium
                              2 mg Cholesterol

*Add 28 calories if sugar or fructose is used as sweetener.

Onion Dip

Makes 4 servings
(1/4 cup each)

1   cup plain lowfat yogurt
1   tablespoon plus 1 teaspoon minced onion flakes
2   packets instant beef flavored broth mix

In a small bowl, combine all ingredients.
Chill.
Serve with vegetable dippers.

Each serving provides:

43 Calories

1/2 Milk Serving	4	g Protein
5 Additional Calories	1	g Fat
	5	g Carbohydrate
	413 mg	Sodium
	3 mg	Cholesterol

Clam Dip

A favorite recipe goes low-calorie . . .

Makes 4 servings
(1/4 cup each)

1   cup plain lowfat yogurt
4   ounces canned minced clams, drained
1   tablespoon minced onion flakes
1/2   teaspoon salt
      Dash pepper
      Dash garlic powder
1-1/2 teaspoons Worcestershire sauce

In a small bowl, combine all ingredients.
Chill.
Serve with vegetable dippers.

Each serving provides:

67 Calories

1   Protein Serving   8   g Protein
1/2 Milk Serving   2   g Fat
                             5   g Carbohydrate
                           363 mg Sodium
                            21 mg Cholesterol

Yogurt Cheese

Tastes and spreads like real cream cheese . . .

*Makes 8 servings
(2 tablespoons each)*

2   cups plain lowfat yogurt
       Dash salt

Line a colander with 4 layers of white paper towels. Place yogurt directly on towels. Cover with 3 more towels, pressing them down onto yogurt.

Place colander in a pan to catch drippings.

Refrigerate 24 hours.

Remove cheese from towels and place in a small bowl. Sprinkle with salt. Blend with a fork.

Place cheese in a covered bowl and refrigerate.

Cheese will keep for 2 weeks, refrigerated.

(This process will not work with yogurt that contains gelatin.)

Use this cheese to make spreads and cheese balls.

Each serving provides:

35 Calories

1/2 Milk Serving

3   g Protein
1   g Fat
4   g Carbohydrate
55 mg Sodium
3 mg Cholesterol

Crab and Cheese Ball

Definitely party fare . . .

Makes 8 servings

1   cup yogurt cheese†
4   ounces crabmeat
1   tablespoon lemon juice
1   tablespoon prepared horseradish
1   teaspoon minced onion flakes
1/2   teaspoon dried chives
1/8   teaspoon salt
      Dash Worcestershire sauce

Combine all ingredients in a bowl. Blend well with a fork. Refrigerate at least 1 hour.

Shape into 1 ball or 4 small balls. Chill.

To serve, spread on toast or crackers or vegetable dippers.

†Note: To make yogurt cheese, see page 69.

Each serving provides:

32 Calories

1/2 Protein Serving   4 g Protein
1/2 Milk Serving   1 g Fat
                      2 g Carbohydrate
               95 mg Sodium
               16 mg Cholesterol

Yogurt Cheese and Cheddar Log

Makes 8 servings

1 cup yogurt cheese†
4 ounces Cheddar cheese, grated
4 ounces Bleu cheese, crumbled
Few drops bottled hot pepper sauce

Combine all ingredients in a bowl. Blend with a fork until mixture is well blended.
Shape mixture into a log or ball, or into 4 small balls.
Refrigerate several hours.
To serve, spread on toast or crackers or celery stalks.

†Note: To make yogurt cheese see page 69.

Each serving provides:

125 Calories

1	Protein Serving	8 g	Protein
1/2	Milk Serving	9 g	Fat
		2 g	Carbohydrate
		313 mg	Sodium
		27 mg	Cholesterol

Quick and Creamy Applesauce Dessert

The children will love this.

Makes 1 serving

1/2   cup applesauce (unsweetened)
1/2   cup plain lowfat yogurt
1/2   teaspoon vanilla extract
1/2   teaspoon apple pie spice
       (or 1/4 teaspoon ground cinnamon, 1/4 teaspoon ground
       nutmeg, and a pinch of ground cloves)
       Sweetener equivalent to 2 teaspoons sugar

Combine all ingredients in a bowl. Mix thoroughly.
Serve right away or chill for a later serving.

Each serving provides:

141 Calories*

1 Fruit Serving   7   g   Protein
1 Milk Serving   2   g   Fat
0 Additional Calories*   23   g   Carbohydrates
                            81 mg   Sodium
                            7 mg   Cholesterol

*Add 32 calories if sugar or fructose is used as sweetener.

Peaches 'n Creme Mold

A great use for summer's fresh peaches . . .

Makes 12 servings

6   medium, fresh peaches, peeled, pits removed
     (12 halves of canned, unsweetened, peaches may be sub-
     stituted)
     Sweetener equivalent to 15 teaspoons sugar
2   cups water
2   envelopes unflavored gelatin
1-1/2 cups plain lowfat yogurt
1   teaspoon vanilla butternut flavor
1/4 teaspoon orange *or* lemon extract

Slice 2 of the peaches in very thin slices. Sprinkle with sweetener equivalent to 3 teaspoons sugar. Set aside. (If peaches are very firm and not too ripe, you may want to cook them in about a tablespoon of water for a few minutes, until tender.)

Place 1 cup of the water in a small saucepan. Sprinkle gelatin over water and let it soften a few minutes. Heat on low heat, stirring frequently, until gelatin is completely dissolved. Remove from heat.

In a blender container, combine yogurt and remaining unsliced peaches. Blend until smooth. Add gelatin mixture, remaining 1 cup of water, remaining sweetener, and extracts. Blend until smooth. Stir in sliced peaches.

Pour into a 9-cup mold and chill several hours, until firm. Unmold to serve.

Each serving provides:

54 Calories*

1/2 Fruit Serving	4	g Protein
1/4 Milk Serving	0	g Fat
0 Additional Calories*	9	g Carbohydrate
	21 mg	Sodium
	2 mg	Cholesterol

*Add 20 calories if sugar or fructose is used as sweetener.

Three-Fruit Sherbert

A refreshing dessert . . .

Makes 4 servings

1	cup plain lowfat yogurt
1/2	cup orange juice (unsweetened)
1	cup strawberries, fresh or frozen
1	cup canned crushed pineapple (unsweetened), drained
1	tablespoon plus 1 teaspoon honey
	Sweetener equivalent to 4 teaspoons sugar

In a blender container or food processor, combine all ingredients. Process until smooth.

Pour mixture into a 7 x 11-inch glass baking dish. Freeze 1 hour, until partially frozen. While mixture is chilling, place a large bowl in the refrigerator to chill.

Place partially frozen sherbert into chilled bowl. Beat with electric mixer, on low speed, 30 seconds.

Place mixture in 1-quart container. Cover tightly.

Freeze until serving time.

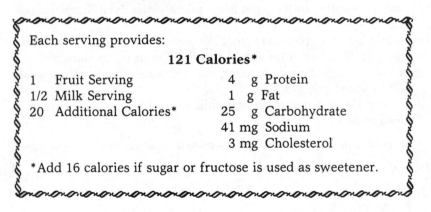

Each serving provides:

121 Calories*

1	Fruit Serving	4	g Protein
1/2	Milk Serving	1	g Fat
20	Additional Calories*	25	g Carbohydrate
		41	mg Sodium
		3	mg Cholesterol

*Add 16 calories if sugar or fructose is used as sweetener.

Fruit Yogurt

Easy to do!

Makes 1 serving

1/2 cup plain lowfat yogurt
Sweetener equivalent to 2 teaspoons sugar
1/2 teaspoon vanilla extract
Choice of any 1 of the following:
   1/4 cup canned (unsweetened) sliced pears, crushed pineapple, *or* sliced peaches, *or*
   1/4 cup frozen (unsweetened) blueberries, thawed, *or*
   1/2 cup frozen (unsweetened) strawberries, thawed

In a small bowl, combine yogurt, sweetener, and vanilla. Stir in fruit.
Enjoy!

Each serving provides:

101 Calories*

1/2	Fruit Serving	7	g Protein
1	Milk Serving	2	g Fat
0	Additional Calories*	13	g Carbohydrate
		80 mg	Sodium
		7 mg	Cholesterol

*Add 32 calories if sugar or fructose is used as sweetener.

Yogurt Fruit Mold

Makes 4 servings

3/4	cup water
1	envelope unflavored gelatin
1	cup plain lowfat yogurt
1	cup strawberries, fresh or frozen
	(If frozen berries are used, there is no need to thaw them)
1/2	cup canned crushed pineapple (unsweetened), drained
2	tablespoons juice from pineapple
	Sweetener equivalent to 12 teaspoons sugar
1	teaspoon vanilla butternut flavor
1/4	teaspoon orange extract
1/4	teaspoon lemon extract

Place water in a small saucepan. Sprinkle gelatin over water and let soften a few minutes. Heat, stirring frequently, over low heat, until gelatin is completely dissolved. Remove from heat.

In a blender container, place yogurt, strawberries, pineapple, and pineapple juice. Blend until fruit is in small pieces. Add gelatin mixture, sweetener and extracts. Blend until smooth.

Pour mixture into a 3-cup mold or a small bowl. Chill until firm. Unmold to serve.

Note: To unmold, place in a large bowl of hot water, dipping mold almost to the rim, for 10 seconds. Run a knife gently around edge of mold. Invert onto a serving plate.

Each serving provides:

84 Calories*

1/2	Fruit Serving	6 g	Protein
1/2	Milk Serving	1 g	Fat
0	Additional Calories*	11 g	Carbohydrate
		41 mg	Sodium
		3 mg	Cholesterol

*Add 48 calories if sugar or fructose is used as sweetener.

Eggs and Cheese

Which came first, the chicken or the egg?

With the almost endless recipes available for eggs, we're convinced that the egg had to get here first. Eggs are versatile, tasty, inexpensive, and are often called "one of Mother Nature's most perfect foods."

From fluffy omelets and soufflés to hearty salads, you'll find eggs just right for any meal. Browse through our other sections, too, and you'll find eggs uniquely combined with many other ingredients, and as a mainstay in many of our cakes and pies.

And . . .

Cheese is a perfect match-mate for so many foods. In this section we've created combinations of cheese, with fruits as desserts, with vegetables as main courses, and with gelatin and milk for that hungry in-between time.

In addition . . .

We've brought eggs together with cheese to create a match-up of high-protein, low calorie, scrumptious taste delights. By combining eggs and cheese with vegetables, fruits, herbs and spices, we offer you one palate-pleasing discovery after another.

Spinach Pancakes

Makes 2 servings

4   eggs, beaten
1   10-ounce package frozen chopped spinach, thawed and
     drained well
1   tablespoon minced onion flakes
1   tablespoon imitation bacon bits
     Salt and pepper to taste

Combine all ingredients in a bowl. Mix well. Drop mixture by 1/4 cupfuls onto a preheated nonstick skillet or griddle over medium heat. Turn pancakes carefully and brown on both sides.

Each serving provides:

210 Calories

2 Protein Servings   18 g Protein
2 Vegetable Servings   12 g Fat
15 Additional Calories   8 g Carbohydrate
                           362 mg Sodium
                           548 mg Cholesterol

Bacon and Egg Salad

Extra special!

Makes 1 serving

2   hard-cooked eggs, peeled and chopped
1   tablespoon plus 1 teaspoon reduced-calorie mayonnaise
2   teaspoons imitation bacon bits
2   teaspoons dried chives
1/4   cup minced celery
1/4   cup minced cucumber
        Salt and pepper to taste

In a medium bowl, combine all ingredients.
Chill.

Each serving provides:

241 Calories

2	Protein Servings	14	g	Protein
1	Vegetable Serving	18	g	Fat
2	Fat Servings	6	g	Carbohydrate
20	Additional Calories	517	mg	Sodium
		555	mg	Cholesterol

Spanish Omelet

Makes 1 serving

2	teaspoons reduced-calorie margarine
1/4	cup diced onions
1/4	cup diced green pepper
1/4	cup diced celery
1/2	cup tomato sauce
2	eggs, beaten

Melt margarine in a small saucepan over medium-low heat. Add onions, green pepper and celery. Cook until tender, adding small amounts of water if necessary, to prevent drying.

Add tomato sauce to onion mixture. Reduce heat to low and simmer while preparing eggs.

In a small nonstick skillet, cook eggs until done to taste. Transfer to a serving plate. Pour sauce over eggs.

Each serving provides:

261 Calories

2	Protein Servings	15 g Protein
2	Vegetable Servings	16 g Fat
1	Fat Serving	16 g Carbohydrate
25	Additional Calories	864 mg Sodium
		548 mg Cholesterol

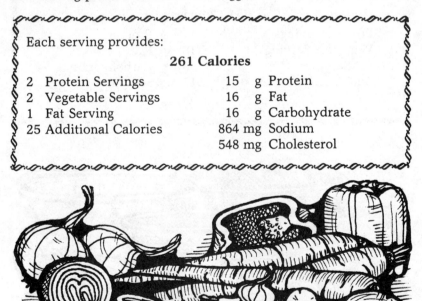

Company Egg Cups

Like miniature quiches — a real treat!

Makes 4 servings

2	tablespoons plus 2 teaspoons reduced-calorie margarine
1/2	cup chopped mushrooms
1/4	cup chopped onions
1/4	cup chopped green pepper
1	teaspoon dried oregano
1	tablespoon imitation bacon bits
	Salt and pepper to taste
8	slices thin-sliced white or whole wheat bread
8	eggs, beaten

Preheat oven to 375°.

Melt 4 teaspoons of the margarine in a small nonstick skillet over medium heat. Add mushrooms, onions, green pepper, oregano, bacon bits, salt and pepper. Cook until vegetables are tender, about 10 minutes.

Using remaining margarine, spread 1/2 teaspoon on each slice of bread. Press each slice, margarine side down, into the cup of a nonstick muffin pan, forming a crust.

Divide mushroom mixture evenly into the crusts. Divide the eggs evenly over mushroom mixture.

Bake 15 minutes, until eggs are set.

Each serving provides:

285 Calories

2	Protein Servings	16	g	Protein
1	Bread Serving	16	g	Fat
1/2	Vegetable Serving	18	g	Carbohydrate
1	Fat Serving	450	mg	Sodium
8	Additional Calories	549	mg	Cholesterol

Spinach Frittata

A hearty dish that's good for any occasion . . .

Makes 6 servings

2	tablespoons margarine
1	cup chopped onions
1	clove garlic, crushed
2	10-ounce packages frozen chopped spinach, thawed, drained well
1/4	teaspoon ground nutmeg
	Salt and pepper to taste
1/4	cup grated Parmesan cheese
12	eggs, beaten

Preheat oven to 375°.

Melt margarine in a heavy oven-proof skillet over medium heat. Add onions and garlic and cook until tender, about 5 minutes. Reduce heat to low.

Stir in spinach, nutmeg, salt, pepper, and half of the Parmesan cheese. Mix well.

Pour eggs evenly over spinach mixture. Sprinkle with remaining Parmesan cheese.

Place skillet in oven and bake 20 minutes, until eggs are set and lightly browned.

Cut into pie-shaped wedges to serve.

Each serving provides:

242 Calories

2	Protein Servings	17	g	Protein
1-1/2	Vegetable Servings	16	g	Fat
1	Fat Serving	8	g	Carbohydrate
20	Additional Calories	301	mg	Sodium
		551	mg	Cholesterol

Fruittata

A unique combination of eggs and fruit!

Makes 2 servings

4   eggs
        Sweetener equivalent to 3 teaspoons sugar
1-1/2 teaspoons vanilla butternut flavor
1/4   teaspoon orange *or* lemon extract
1/3   cup nonfat dry milk
1/3   cup water
1/8   teaspoon ground cinnamon
2   teaspoons margarine
1/3   cup frozen blueberries (unsweetened)
1/3   cup crushed pineapple (unsweetened), drained
1/3   cup canned peaches (unsweetened), cut into small chunks,
        drained
        Ground cinnamon
Topping
1/2   cup plain lowfat yogurt
1/2   teaspoon vanilla butternut flavor
        Sweetener equivalent to 2 teaspoons sugar

Preheat oven to 375°. In a blender container, combine eggs, sweetener, vanilla butternut flavor, extract, milk, water and 1/8 teaspoon cinnamon. Blend for a few seconds, until just blended. Melt margarine in a small oven-proof skillet or baking dish over medium heat. Add fruit, stirring to distribute evenly in pan. Pour egg mixture over fruit. Sprinkle with additional cinnamon. Cook 3 minutes. Do not stir. Place in oven. Bake 20 to 25 minutes, until set.

Combine yogurt, vanilla butternut and sweetener. Serve as a topping on hot fruittata. (Leftovers are delicious cold.)

Each serving provides:

337 Calories*

2 Protein Servings	20	g Protein
1 Fat Serving	16	g Fat
1 Fruit Serving	24	g Carbohydrate
1 Milk Serving	290 mg	Sodium
0 Additional Calories*	554 mg	Cholesterol

*Add 40 calories if sugar or fructose is used as sweetener.

Dutch Apple Pancake

A nice brunch dish for friends . . .

Makes 2 servings

2	teaspoons margarine
2	small, sweet apples, peeled, cut into 1/2-inch cubes
2	eggs
1/3	cup nonfat dry milk
3	tablespoons all-purpose flour
1/4	cup water
1/2	teaspoon ground cinnamon
1/4	teaspoon ground nutmeg
1	teaspoon vanilla extract
1/4	teaspoon double-acting baking powder
	Sweetener equivalent to 4 teaspoons sugar

Melt margarine in a heavy ovenproof skillet over medium-high heat. Add apples and cook until tender, about 5 minutes, stirring. Remove from heat.

Preheat oven to 500°.

Combine remaining ingredients in a blender container. Blend until smooth. Pour over apples.

Bake 20 minutes, or until brown.

Serve hot.

Each serving provides:

267 Calories*

1	Protein Serving	12	g	Protein
1/2	Bread Serving	10	g	Fat
1	Fat Serving	31	g	Carbohydrate
1	Fruit Serving	230	mg	Sodium
1/2	Milk Serving	276	mg	Cholesterol
0	Additional Calories*			

*Add 32 calories if sugar or fructose is used as sweetener.

Applesauce Pancakes

Makes 2 servings

2   eggs
1/2   cup applesauce (unsweetened)
1/2   teaspoon ground cinnamon
1/4   teaspoon ground nutmeg
2   slices white or whole wheat bread, crumbled
2   teaspoons vegetable oil
1/3   cup nonfat dry milk
1   teaspoon double-acting baking powder
1   teaspoon vanilla extract
       Sweetener equivalent to 3 teaspoons sugar

In a blender container, combine all ingredients. Blend until smooth.

Preheat a nonstick griddle or skillet over medium-high heat.

Pour mixture onto griddle, making eight 4-inch pancakes. Turn once, carefully, when edges of pancakes appear dry. Brown on both sides.

Note: To make turning pancakes easier, spray both sides of your spatula with a nonstick cooking spray.

Each serving provides:

263 Calories*

1	Protein Serving	12	g Protein
1	Bread Serving	11	g Fat
1	Fat Serving	26	g Carbohydrate
1/2	Fruit Serving	457 mg	Sodium
1/2	Milk Serving	277 mg	Cholesterol
0	Additional Calories*		

*Add 24 calories if sugar or fructose is used as sweetener.

Banana Puff

A delicious breakfast treat . . .

Makes 4 servings

2	eggs, separated
	Sweetener equivalent to 6 teaspoons sugar
1	cup plain lowfat yogurt
2	tablespoons margarine, melted
1	teaspoon vanilla extract
1/2	teaspoon vanilla butternut flavor
3/4	cup all-purpose flour
2	teaspoons double-acting baking powder
1	teaspoon baking soda
1/8	teaspoon salt
1/4	teaspoon ground cinnamon
1	medium, ripe banana, diced

Preheat oven to 400°.

Combine egg yolks, sweetener, yogurt and margarine. Beat on low speed of an electric mixer until blended. Add extracts and beat 1 minute.

Sift flour, baking powder, baking soda, salt and cinnamon. Beat into first mixture until all ingredients are moistened.

In a separate bowl, beat egg whites on high speed until stiff. Fold into batter, gently but thoroughly.

Fold in bananas.

Spread batter in a 9-inch round cake pan that has been sprayed with a nonstick cooking spray. Sprinkle with additional cinnamon.

Bake 20 minutes, until puffy. Serve warm.

Each serving provides:

247 Calories*

1/2	Protein Serving	9	g	Protein
1	Bread Serving	10	g	Fat
1-1/2	Fat Servings	30	g	Carbohydrate
1/2	Fruit Serving	472	mg	Sodium
1/2	Milk Serving	140	mg	Cholesterol
0	Additional Calories*			

*Add 24 calories if sugar or fructose is used as sweetener.

Lemon Soufflé

So elegant!

Makes 4 servings

4   eggs, separated
        Sweetener equivalent to 9 teaspoons sugar†
1/2   teaspoon vanilla extract
1   teaspoon lemon extract
1/4   teaspoon grated lemon peel
1/4   teaspoon cream of tartar

Preheat oven to 350°.

In a large bowl, beat egg yolks on medium speed of an electric mixer for 1 minute. Add a portion of the sweetener equivalent to 6 teaspoons sugar, the extracts, and lemon peel. Beat mixture on high speed for 2 minutes.

In another bowl, beat egg whites and cream of tartar on high speed until soft peaks form. Add remaining sweetener and beat until egg whites are stiff.

Fold egg whites into yolk mixture, 1/3 at a time, folding gently until the 2 mixtures are just blended.

Pour mixture into a 1-1/2 quart soufflé dish or baking dish that has been sprayed with a nonstick cooking spray. Place in a shallow pan; pour hot water in pan to a depth of 1 inch.

Bake 30 minutes. Do not open oven door during baking time. Serve immediately.

†Do not use liquid sweetener in this recipe.

Note: It is important to work quickly and get the soufflé into the oven as quickly as possible.

Each serving provides:

91 Calories*

1 Protein Serving   6   g Protein
0 Additional Calories*   6   g Fat
                                2   g Carbohydrate
                               73 mg Sodium
                              274 mg Cholesterol

*Add 36 calories is sugar or fructose is used as sweetener.

Banana Fritters

Makes 2 servings

2   eggs
1   medium, ripe banana
2   slices white or whole wheat bread, crumbled
1/3   cup nonfat dry milk
1   teaspoon vanilla extract
1   teaspoon double-acting baking powder
2   teaspoons vegetable oil
      Sweetener equivalent to 2 teaspoons sugar

In a blender container, combine all ingredients. Blend until smooth.

Preheat a nonstick griddle or skillet over medium-high heat.

Pour mixture onto griddle, making eight 4-inch fritters. Turn over carefully when edges of fritters become dry. Cook until golden brown on each side.

(To make turning pancakes easier, spray both sides of your spatula with a nonstick cooking spray.)

Each serving provides:

286 Calories*

1	Protein Serving	13	g Protein
1	Bread Serving	11	g Fat
1	Fat Serving	32	g Carbohydrate
1	Fruit Serving	456	mg Sodium
1/2	Milk Serving	277	mg Cholesterol
0	Additional Calories*		

*Add 16 calories if sugar or fructose is used as sweetener.

Baked Custard

An old-time favorite we never get tired of . . .

Makes 4 servings

2   eggs, slightly beaten
      Sweetener equivalent to 6 teaspoons sugar
2   cups skim milk
1   teaspoon vanilla
      Ground nutmeg

Preheat oven to 350°.

In a medium bowl, combine eggs and sweetener. Add milk slowly, stirring constantly. Add vanilla. Stir.

Pour mixture into 4 custard cups. Spinkle with nutmeg.

Place cups in a baking pan. Pour hot water around them to almost the height of the custard.

Bake 30 minutes, until a knife inserted near the edge of the cup comes out clean.

Cool on a rack. Chill.

(Custard will set as it cools.)

Each serving provides:

87 Calories*

1/2 Protein Serving	7	g Protein
1/2 Milk Serving	3	g Fat
0 Additional Calories*	6	g Carbohydrate
	99 mg	Sodium
	139 mg	Cholesterol

*Add 24 calories if sugar or fructose is used as sweetener.

Orange Upside-Down French Toast

Makes 4 servings

2   tablespoons plus 2 teaspoons reduced-calorie margarine
      Sweetener equivalent to 6 teaspoons sugar
1/2   teaspoon ground cinnamon
4   eggs
1/2   teaspoon orange extract
1/2   teaspoon vanilla extract
1/2   teaspoon maple extract
1/4   cup frozen orange juice concentrate (unsweetened), thawed
1/4   cup water
4   slices white or whole wheat bread

Preheat oven to 400°.

Place margarine in an 8-inch square baking pan and place in oven until margarine is melted.

Tilt pan back and forth to spread margarine evenly.

Combine sweetener and cinnamon. Sprinkle evenly over margarine.

In a shallow bowl, combine eggs, extracts, orange juice concentrate and water. Dip each slice of bread in egg mixture, soaking well. Arrange bread evenly in pan. Spoon any remaining egg mixture on bread.

Bake 25 minutes. Let stand 1 minute before serving.

To serve, turn cinnamon-side up.

Each serving provides:

210 Calories*

1	Protein Serving	9	g Protein
1	Bread Serving	10	g Fat
1	Fat Serving	19	g Carbohydrate
1/2	Fruit Serving	280	mg Sodium
0	Additional Calories*	275	mg Cholesterol

*Add 24 calories if sugar or fructose is used as sweetener.

Almond Bread Puff

A sensational variation of French toast!

Makes 2 servings

2   eggs, separated
2   tablespoons skim milk
2   teaspoons vanilla butternut flavor
1/2 teaspoon almond extract
     Sweetener equivalent to 3 teaspoons sugar
2   slices white or whole wheat bread

Preheat oven to 350° degrees.

In a 4 x 8-inch baking pan, combine egg yolks, milk, 1 teaspoon of the vanilla butternut flavor, 1/4 teaspoon of the almond extract, and *half* of the sweetener. Place bread in mixture, turning carefully until all liquid is absorbed.

In a medium bowl, beat egg whites until stiff, using high speed of an electric mixer. Beat in remaining vanilla butternut, almond extract and sweetener. Spread over bread.

Bake 10 to 15 minutes, or until browned.

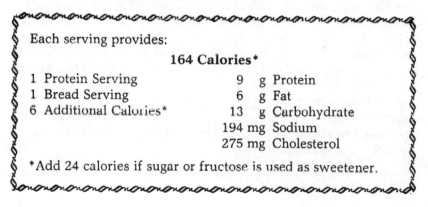

Each serving provides:

164 Calories*

1 Protein Serving   9 g Protein
1 Bread Serving   6 g Fat
6 Additional Calories*   13 g Carbohydrate
                            194 mg Sodium
                            275 mg Cholesterol

*Add 24 calories if sugar or fructose is used as sweetener.

Italian Eggplant and Cheese Casserole

They'll ask for this one again and again!

Makes 6 servings

1	large eggplant, unpeeled, cut into 1/2-inch slices
2	tablespoons vegetable oil
2	8-ounce cans tomato sauce
2	tablespoons minced onion flakes
1/4	teaspoon garlic powder
1	teaspoon dried basil
2-3/4	cups part-skim ricotta cheese
3	tablespoons water
1/2	teaspoon salt
1/4	teaspoon pepper
1	tablespoon dried parsley flakes
1	ounce grated Parmesan cheese

Arrange eggplant in a single layer on a nonstick baking sheet. Broil 4 to 5 inches from heat for a total of 20 minutes, or until brown, turning once. Preheat oven to 375°. In a medium bowl, combine oil, tomato sauce, half of the onion flakes, half of the garlic powder, and all of the basil. In another bowl, combine ricotta cheese, remaining onion flakes, remaining garlic powder, water, salt, pepper, and parsley flakes. Mix well with a fork. Spread a thin layer of the sauce in the bottom of a 9 x 13-inch baking pan that has been sprayed with a nonstick cooking spray. Arrange half of the eggplant slices over the sauce. Spread cheese mixture evenly over eggplant. Top with a thin layer of sauce, then remaining eggplant, and then remaining sauce. Sprinkle with Parmesan cheese. Bake, uncovered, 30 minutes.

Each serving provides:

278 Calories

2 Protein Servings	17	g Protein
2 Vegetable Servings	16	g Fat
1 Fat Serving	19	g Carbohydrate
8 Additional Calories	811	mg Sodium
	39	mg Cholesterol

Cheese Herbed Onions

Makes 4 servings

2   pounds baby onions, peeled
4   tablespoons reduced-calorie margarine
3   tablespoons all-purpose flour
1/2   cup skim milk
1/2   teaspoon salt
        Dash pepper
3/4   teaspoon dried marjoram
1-1/3   cups lowfat cottage cheese
3   tablespoons dry bread crumbs

Cook onions, covered, in boiling water until tender, about 20 minutes. Drain. Place in a 6 x 10-inch baking dish that has been sprayed with a nonstick cooking spray.

Preheat oven to 375°.

Melt margarine in a medium saucepan over medium heat. Add flour, stirring.

Add milk and cook, stirring constantly, for 1 minute. Remove from heat. Stir in salt, pepper, marjoram and cheese. Spread evenly over onions. Sprinkle with crumbs.

Bake, uncovered, 25 minutes.

Each serving provides:

237 Calories

1	Protein Serving	14	g Protein
1/2	Bread Serving	7	g Fat
2	Vegetable Servings	32	g Carbohydrate
1-1/2	Fat Servings	784	mg Sodium
13	Additional Calories	4	mg Cholesterol

Italian Veggie Bake

If you like Italian food, don't miss this.

Makes 4 servings

1	cup zucchini, unpeeled, cut into 1-inch cubes
1	cup mushrooms, halved
1	cup broccoli, cut into flowerets
1/2	cup yellow squash, unpeeled, cut into 1-inch cubes
1/2	cup cauliflower, cut into flowerets
1/2	cup chopped onions
1/2	green pepper, sliced
1	16-ounce can tomatoes, chopped, undrained
1/2	teaspoon dried basil
1/4	teaspoon garlic powder
1	teaspoon dried oregano
	Salt and pepper to taste
8	ounces shredded Mozzarella cheese
3	tablespoons grated Parmesan cheese

Preheat oven to 375°.

Combine vegetables and spices in a large baking pan that has been sprayed with a nonstick cooking spray. Cover.

Bake 45 minutes, stirring once after half the cooking time.

Uncover vegetables and sprinkle evenly with Mozzarella and Parmesan cheese. Bake, uncovered, 10 minutes.

Let stand for 10 minutes before serving.

Each serving provides:

245 Calories

2	Protein Servings	17	g	Protein
3-1/2	Vegetable Servings	14	g	Fat
23	Additional Calories	15	g	Carbohydrate
		449	mg	Sodium
		47	mg	Cholesterol

Zucchini Cheese Bake

Gives new taste dimensions to zucchini . . .

Makes 2 servings

3   cups zucchini, thinly sliced
2/3 cup lowfat cottage cheese
1   tablespoon plus 1 teaspoon reduced-calorie margarine
2   ounces shredded Cheddar cheese
2   slices white or whole wheat bread, crumbled
1   tablespoon minced onion flakes
1/2 teaspoon dried oregano
     Salt and pepper to taste

Steam zucchini in a covered saucepan containing 1 inch of boiling water for 5 minutes, or until just tender-crisp. Drain. Place in a shallow baking dish that has been sprayed with a nonstick cooking spray.

Preheat oven to 375°.

In a blender container, combine remaining ingredients. Blend until smooth. Pour evenly over zucchini.

Bake, uncovered, 20 minutes, until hot and lightly browned.

Each serving provides:

302 Calories

2 Protein Servings	21	g Protein
1 Bread Serving	15	g Fat
3 Vegetable Servings	22	g Carbohydrate
1 Fat Serving	693	mg Sodium
	33	mg Cholesterol

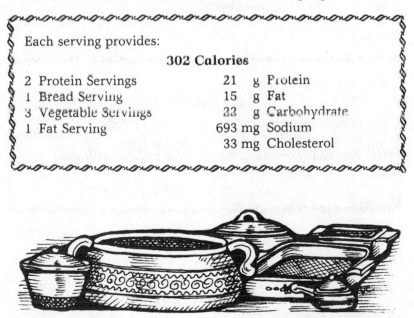

Noodles and Cheese Casserole

Serve with a leafy green salad for a colorful luncheon plate.

Makes 4 servings

2	cups cooked noodles
1-1/3	cups lowfat cottage cheese
3	ounces grated Cheddar cheese
1	cup plain lowfat yogurt
2	teaspoons minced onion flakes
1/8	teaspoon garlic powder
	Salt and pepper to taste
1/2	teaspoon Worcestershire sauce
1	8-ounce can mushroom pieces, drained
1	ounce grated Parmesan cheese

Preheat oven to 350°.

Place noodles in an 8-inch square baking pan that has been sprayed with a nonstick cooking spray.

In a blender container, combine remaining ingredients, *except* mushrooms and Parmesan cheese. Blend until smooth. Stir in mushrooms. Pour evenly over noodles. Mix together lightly.

Sprinkle with Parmesan cheese.

Bake, uncovered, 25 to 30 minutes, or until hot and lightly browned.

Each serving provides:

319 Calories

2	Protein Servings	25 g	Protein
1	Bread Serving	12 g	Fat
1/2	Vegetable Serving	27 g	Carbohydrate
1/2	Milk Serving	841 mg	Sodium
		59 mg	Cholesterol

Chili-Cheddar Cheese Ball

Makes 4 servings

8   ounces grated Cheddar cheese
2   tablespoons minced onion flakes
1   packet instant beef flavored broth mix
2   tablespoons lemon juice
2   tablespoons plus 2 teaspoons reduced-calorie margarine
1   tablespoon bottled chili sauce
1   teaspoon dry mustard

In a large bowl, combine all ingredients. Mix with a fork until well blended.

Shape mixture into 1 large ball or 4 small balls. Chill several hours.

To serve, spread on toast or crackers.

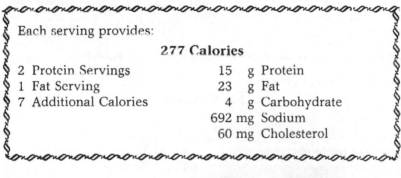

Each serving provides:

277 Calories

2 Protein Servings	15 g Protein
1 Fat Serving	23 g Fat
7 Additional Calories	4 g Carbohydrate
	692 mg Sodium
	60 mg Cholesterol

Cheese-Stuffed Pita

Makes 2 servings

1/2   cup part-skim ricotta cheese
2   ounces shredded Provolone cheese
2   teaspoons grated Parmesan cheese
1   4-ounce can mushroom pieces, drained
1   teaspoon imitation bacon bits
1   teaspoon dried parsley flakes
       Dash onion powder
       Salt and pepper to taste
2   pita breads, 1-ounce each

Preheat oven to 350°.

In a small bowl, combine all ingredients, *except* pita. Mix with a fork until well blended.

Open one end of each pita, forming a pocket. Divide cheese mixture evenly and spoon into the pockets. Wrap in foil.

Bake 20 minutes.

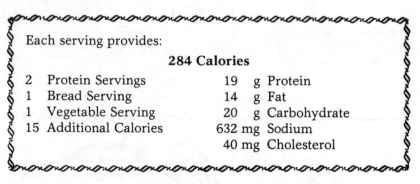

Each serving provides:

284 Calories

2 Protein Servings   19   g Protein
1 Bread Serving   14   g Fat
1 Vegetable Serving   20   g Carbohydrate
15 Additional Calories   632 mg Sodium
                              40 mg Cholesterol

Chocolate Ricotta

For the taste of chocolate cheesecake — ready in 1 minute!

Makes 1 serving

1/2   cup part-skim ricotta cheese
1   teaspoon cocoa (unsweetened)
1/2   teaspoon vanilla extract
1/2   teaspoon chocolate extract
      (1/4 teaspoon almond *or* rum extract – optional)
      Sweetener equivalent to 4 teaspoons sugar

Combine all ingredients in a bowl. Mix well with a spoon or fork.
Enjoy!

Each serving provides:

201 Calories*

2 Protein Servings	16	g	Protein
5 Additional Calories*	10	g	Fat
	7	g	Carbohydrate
	155	mg	Sodium
	38	mg	Cholesterol

*Add 64 calories if sugar or fructose is used as sweetener.

Pineapple Bavarian Cream

Makes 4 servings

1/2 cup water
1 cup canned crushed pineapple (unsweetened), drained
1/4 cup liquid from pineapple
1 envelope unflavored gelatin
1-1/3 cups lowfat cottage cheese
Sweetener equivalent to 6 teaspoons sugar
1-1/2 teaspoons vanilla butternut flavor

In a small saucepan, combine water and pineapple liquid. Sprinkle with gelatin and let soften a few minutes. Heat over low heat until gelatin is completely dissolved, stirring frequently.

In a blender container, combine gelatin mixture, cottage cheese, sweetener and flavoring. Blend until smooth. Pour into a bowl and chill until slightly set, about 10 minutes.

Add pineapple and stir until mixed well. Divide mixture into 4 dessert bowls or parfait glasses.

Chill.

Note: This may also be poured into a 3-cup mold, chilled until firm, and unmolded to serve.

Each serving provides:

142 Calories*

1	Protein Serving	12	g Protein
1/2	Fruit Serving	1	g Fat
0	Additional Calories*	21	g Carbohydrate
		305	mg Sodium
		3	mg Cholesterol

*Add 24 calories if sugar or fructose is used as sweetener.

Quick Peach Melba

A French classic you can enjoy any time . . .

Makes 1 serving

1/2   cup part-skim ricotta cheese
      Sweetener equivalent to 2 teaspoons sugar
1   teaspoon vanilla extract
1/2   cup canned, sliced peaches (unsweetened), *or* 1 medium,
      very ripe, fresh peach, peeled and sliced
2   teaspoons reduced-calorie raspberry spread (16 calories per 2
      teaspoons)

In a small bowl, combine ricotta cheese, sweetener and vanilla.
Mix well with a fork or spoon.
Spoon peaches over cheese.
Spoon raspberry spread over peaches.

Each serving provides:

238 Calories*

2   Protein Servings   16   g Protein
1   Fruit Serving   10   g Fat
16 Additional Calories*   18   g Carbohydrate
                                  159 mg Sodium
                                  38   mg Cholesterol

*Add 32 calories if sugar or fructose is used as sweetener.

Red, White and Blueberry Parfaits

Makes 4 servings

1/2 cup fresh or frozen blueberries (unsweetened)†
1 cup fresh or frozen strawberries (unsweetened)†
1 cup part-skim ricotta cheese
 Sweetener equivalent to 6 teaspoons sugar
1 teaspoon vanilla extract
1/4 teaspoon almond extract

In a small bowl, combine blueberries with 1 teaspoon of the sweetener. Toss to coat berries.

In another bowl, combine strawberries with 1 teaspoon of the sweetener. Toss.

In a third bowl, combine ricotta cheese, remaining sweetener and extracts. Mix well with spoon.

In each of 4 parfait glasses, place 2 tablespoons of the strawberries. Top with 2 tablespoons of ricotta cheese. Divide blueberries evenly over the parfaits. Divide remaining ricotta cheese evenly over blueberries. Top with remaining strawberries.

†Note: If using frozen berries, thaw and drain them slightly before using.

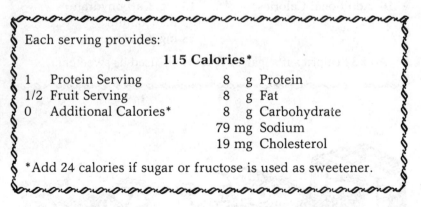

Each serving provides:

115 Calories*

1 Protein Serving   8 g Protein
1/2 Fruit Serving   8 g Fat
0 Additional Calories*   8 g Carbohydrate
                          79 mg Sodium
                          19 mg Cholesterol

*Add 24 calories if sugar or fructose is used as sweetener.

Tropical Cheese Pudding

Makes 4 servings

1   envelope unflavored gelatin
3/4   cup water
1-1/3   cups lowfat cottage cheese
         Sweetener equivalent to 6 teaspoons sugar
1   teaspoon vanilla butternut flavor
1/2   teaspoon coconut extract
1/2   medium, ripe banana
1/2   cup canned crushed pineapple (unsweetened)

Sprinkle gelatin over water in a small saucepan and let soften a few minutes. Heat over low heat until gelatin is completely dissolved, stirring frequently.

In a blender container, combine gelatin mixture with remaining ingredients, *except* pineapple. Blend until smooth. Stir in pineapple.

Pour into 1 bowl or 4 individual serving bowls.

Chill until firm.

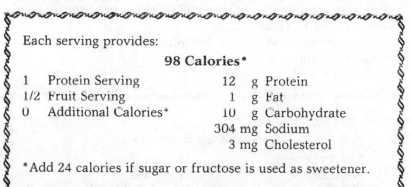

Each serving provides:

98 Calories*

1	Protein Serving	12 g	Protein
1/2	Fruit Serving	1 g	Fat
0	Additional Calories*	10 g	Carbohydrate
		304 mg	Sodium
		3 mg	Cholesterol

*Add 24 calories if sugar or fructose is used as sweetener.

Strawberry Cheese Mold

A favorite with company and family . . .

Makes 4 servings

2   envelopes unflavored gelatin
3/4   cup water
1-1/3 cups lowfat cottage cheese
2/3   cup nonfat dry milk
1   teaspoon lemon juice
1   teaspoon vanilla extract
1/4   teaspoon strawberry extract
        Sweetener equivalent to 12 teaspoons sugar
2   cups fresh or frozen strawberries (If using frozen straw-
        berries, thaw and drain before using.)

Sprinkle gelatin over water in a small saucepan. Heat over low heat until gelatin is completely dissolved, stirring frequently.

In a blender container, combine gelatin mixture with remaining ingredients, reserving half of the strawberries. Blend until smooth.

Pour mixture into a 5- or 6-cup mold that has been sprayed with a nonstick cooking spray.

Slice remaining strawberries. Stir into mold.

Chill until firm.

Unmold to serve.

Each serving provides:

142 Calories*

1	Protein Serving	18 g	Protein
1/2	Fruit Serving	1 g	Fat
1/2	Milk Serving	14 g	Carbohydrate
0	Additional Calories*	373 mg	Sodium
		5 mg	Cholesterol

*Add 48 calories if sugar or fructose is used as sweetener.

Plum Cheese Cobbler

Makes 4 servings

2   cups canned purple plums (unsweetened), drained, pitted,
     quartered
     Sweetener equivalent to 6 teaspoons sugar
1/2 teaspoon ground cinnamon
Topping
2   slices white or whole wheat bread, crumbled
1-1/4 cups part-skim ricotta cheese
     Sweetener equivalent to 4 teaspoons sugar
2   teaspoons double-acting baking powder
1   teaspoon vanilla extract
1   egg

Preheat oven to 375°.
Place plums in an 8-inch square baking pan that has been
sprayed with a nonstick cooking spray. Sprinkle evenly with 6 teaspoons sugar (or equivalent), and cinnamon.

In a blender container, combine topping ingredients. Blend until
smooth. Pour mixture evenly over plums. Sprinkle with additional
cinnamon.

Bake, uncovered, 25 minutes, until set and lightly browned.
Serve warm, or chill and serve cold.

Variation: Substitute canned peaches for the plums.

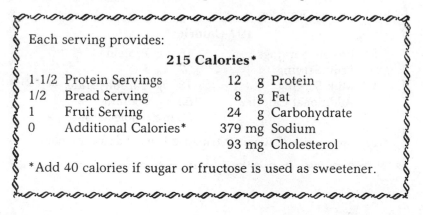

Each serving provides:

215 Calories*

1-1/2	Protein Servings	12 g	Protein
1/2	Bread Serving	8 g	Fat
1	Fruit Serving	24 g	Carbohydrate
0	Additional Calories*	379 mg	Sodium
		93 mg	Cholesterol

*Add 40 calories if sugar or fructose is used as sweetener.

Rum Raisin Pudding

So elegant, yet so easy.

Makes 4 servings

1	envelope unflavored gelatin
3/4	cup water
1-1/2	cups part-skim ricotta cheese
1/3	cup nonfat dry milk
	Sweetener equivalent to 9 teaspoons sugar
1	teaspoon vanilla extract
1/2	teaspoon vanilla butternut flavor
1	teaspoon rum extract
1/4	cup raisins
	Ground nutmeg

Sprinkle gelatin over water in a small saucepan and let soften a few minutes. Heat over low heat until gelatin is completely dissolved, stirring frequently.

In a blender container, combine gelatin mixture with remaining ingredients, *except* raisins and nutmeg. Blend until smooth.

Stir in raisins.

Pour into 1 serving bowl or individual serving bowls. Sprinkle with nutmeg.

Chill until firm.

Each serving provides:

197 Calories*

1-1/2	Protein Servings	16	g	Protein
1/2	Fruit Serving	7	g	Fat
1/4	Milk Serving	15	g	Carbohydrate
0	Additional Calories*	152	mg	Sodium
		30	mg	Cholesterol

*Add 36 calories if sugar or fructose is used as sweetener.

Blueberry Cheese Pudding

Makes 4 servings

1   envelope unflavored gelatin
3/4   cup water
1-1/3 cups lowfat cottage cheese
       Sweetener equivalent to 6 teaspoons sugar
1   teaspoon vanilla extract
1/4   teaspoon orange extract
1   cup fresh or frozen blueberries (If frozen, thaw and drain well.)

Sprinkle gelatin over water in a small saucepan and let soften a few minutes. Heat over low heat until gelatin is completely dissolved, stirring frequently.

In a blender container, combine gelatin mixture, cottage cheese, sweetener, extracts and *half* of the blueberries. Blend until smooth.
Stir in remaining blueberries.
Pour into 4 individual bowls or 1 large bowl.
Chill until firm.

Each serving provides:

88 Calories*

1	Protein Serving	12	g Protein
1/2	Fruit Serving	1	g Fat
0	Additional Calories*	7	g Carbohydrate
		306 mg	Sodium
		3 mg	Cholesterol

*Add 24 calories if sugar or fructose is used as sweetener.

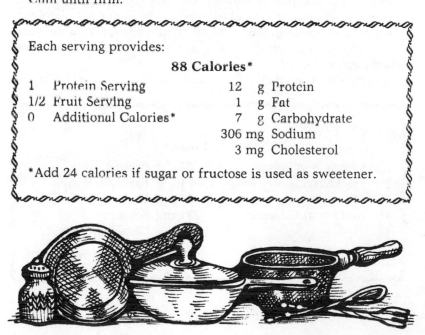

Pears Belle Helene

Chocolate-topped pears and cheese!

Makes 1 serving

1/2   cup part-skim ricotta cheese
      Sweetener equivalent to 2 teaspoons sugar
1   teaspoon vanilla extract
1/2   cup canned pears (unsweetened), sliced
Chocolate topping
1-1/2 teaspoons cocoa (unsweetened)
1   teaspoon cornstarch
1/4   cup evaporated skim milk
      Sweetener equivalent to 2 teaspoons sugar
1/4   teaspoon vanilla extract
1/8   teaspoon chocolate extract

In a serving bowl, combine ricotta cheese, sweetener equivalent to 2 teaspoons sugar, and vanilla. Mix well.

Place pears on cheese.

In a small saucepan, combine cocoa and cornstarch. Slowly stir in evaporated milk, mixing until most of the lumps are dissolved.

Cook over medium-low heat, stirring constantly, until sauce thickens. Remove from heat, stir in sweetener and extracts, and spoon over pears.

Serve right away.

Each serving provides:

306 Calories*

2	Protein Servings	22	g Protein
1	Fruit Serving	11	g Fat
1/2	Milk Serving	27	g Carbohydrate
18	Additional Calories*	231	mg Sodium
		41	mg Cholesterol

*Add 64 calories if sugar or fructose is used as sweetener.

Cottage Cheese Cinnamon Toast

Makes 1 serving

2/3   cup lowfat cottage cheese
1/2   teaspoon ground cinnamon
      Sweetener equivalent to 1 teaspoon sugar
1   teaspoon vanilla extract
2   slices thin-sliced white or whole wheat bread
      (80 calories per 2 slices), lightly toasted

In a small bowl, combine cottage cheese, cinnamon, sweetener and vanilla. Mix well with a spoon until blended.

Spread cheese on toast. Sprinkle with additional cinnamon.

Place in a shallow pan or on a baking sheet. Broil 4 inches from heat for 3 minutes, or until hot and bubbly.

Each serving provides:

205 Calories*

2 Protein Servings	21 g	Protein
1 Bread Serving	2 g	Fat
0 Additional Calories*	19 g	Carbohydrate
	753 mg	Sodium
	7 mg	Cholesterol

*Add 16 calories if sugar or fructose is used as sweetener.

Pineapple-Orange Danish Toast

Quick and easy!

Makes 1 serving

1/4   cup part-skim ricotta cheese
1/4   cup canned crushed pineapple (unsweetened)
2   tablespoons reduced-calorie orange marmalade
       (16 calories per 2 teaspoons)
1/4   teaspoon ground cinnamon
2   slices thin-sliced white or whole wheat bread
       (80 calories per 2 slices), lightly toasted

In a small bowl, combine cheese, pineapple, orange spread and cinnamon. Spread on toast.

Broil under a broiler or in a toaster-oven until hot and bubbly. Serve hot.

Each serving provides:

249 Calories

1	Protein Serving	10	g	Protein
1	Bread Serving	6	g	Fat
1/2	Fruit Serving	40	g	Carbohydrate
16	Additional Calories	222	mg	Sodium
		20	mg	Cholesterol

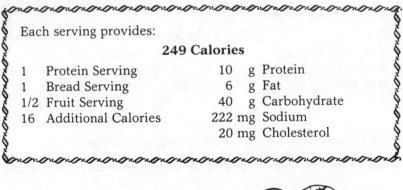

Asparagus Cheese Tart

So elegant!

Makes 4 servings

1   10-ounce package frozen asparagus spears
1-1/3 cups lowfat cottage cheese
2/3   cup nonfat dry milk
1/2   cup water
1/4   cup plus 2 tablespoons all-purpose flour
2   teaspoons double-acting baking powder
2   tablespoons plus 2 teaspoons reduced-calorie margarine
3   eggs
2   teaspoons minced onion flakes
1   packet instant chicken flavored broth mix
1   ounce grated Parmesan cheese, divided in half

Cook asparagus spears according to package directions, cooking a little less than recommended time, so that spears are tender-crisp. Drain.

Preheat oven to 350°.

Cut each asparagus spear into 3 pieces. Arrange pieces in a 9-inch pie pan that has been sprayed with a nonstick cooking spray.

In a blender container, combine remaining ingredients, using only half of the Parmesan cheese. Blend until smooth. Pour over asparagus.

Sprinkle with remaining Parmesan cheese.

Bake 30 minutes, until lightly browned.

Cool 5 minutes. Serve hot.

Each serving provides:

288 Calories

2	Protein Servings	25	g Protein
1/2	Bread Serving	11	g Fat
1	Vegetable Serving	22	g Carbohydrate
1	Fat Serving	1061	mg Sodium
1/2	Milk Serving	216	mg Cholesterol
3	Additional Calories		

Easy Cheesy

A quick and easy onion-flavored cheese casserole!

Makes 4 servings

1-1/3 cups lowfat cottage cheese
4   ounces Cheddar cheese, cubed or grated
4   eggs
1   teaspoon minced onion flakes
1   envelope instant onion flavored broth mix
       Dash garlic powder
1   tablespoon all-purpose flour
2   teaspoons vegetable oil

Preheat oven to 350°.

In a blender container, combine all ingredients. Blend until smooth.

Pour mixture into an 8-inch square baking pan that has been sprayed with a nonstick cooking spray.

Bake 30 minutes, until puffy and lightly browned.

Cut into squares and serve hot.

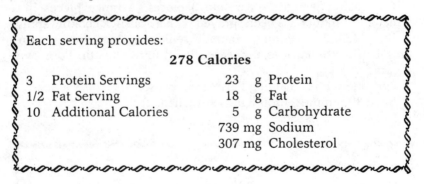

Each serving provides:

278 Calories

3   Protein Servings   23 g Protein
1/2 Fat Serving   18 g Fat
10 Additional Calories   5 g Carbohydrate
                             739 mg Sodium
                             307 mg Cholesterol

Broccoli Cheese Puff

What an effective combination!

Makes 4 servings

4	slices white or whole wheat bread
4	ounces grated Cheddar cheese
1	10-ounce package frozen chopped broccoli, cooked, drained†
4	eggs
2	cups skim milk
1/4	teaspoon salt
1/8	teaspoon pepper
1	teaspoon minced onion flakes
1/2	teaspoon dry mustard

Place 2 slices of the bread in the bottom of a 4 x 8-inch nonstick loaf pan. Sprinkle with half of the cheese.

Spread broccoli over the cheese. Top with remaining cheese, then remaining bread.

In a blender container, place eggs, milk, salt, pepper, onion flakes and mustard. Blend until smooth. Pour evenly over bread.

Refrigerate 1 hour.

Preheat oven to 350°.

Bake 40 minutes, or until golden brown.

†For best results, partially cook the broccoli, leaving it tender-crisp.

Each serving provides:

321 Calories

2	Protein Servings	22 g	Protein
1	Bread Serving	16 g	Fat
1	Vegetable Serving	23 g	Carbohydrate
1/2	Milk Serving	572 mg	Sodium
		307 mg	Cholesterol

Potato Cheese Casserole

Makes 4 servings

12   ounces cooked potatoes, thinly sliced
3   ounces shredded Cheddar cheese
2   eggs
1   cup lowfat cottage cheese
2   tablespoons minced onion flakes
1   teaspoon dried parsley flakes
      Salt and pepper to taste

Preheat oven to 350°.

Place half of the potatoes in a 1-1/2 quart baking dish that has been sprayed with a nonstick cooking spray. Top with half of the Cheddar cheese, then the remaining potatoes, and then the remaining Cheddar.

In a blender container, combine the remaining ingredients. Blend until smooth. Pour mixture evenly over potatoes.

Bake, uncovered, 30 minutes, until lightly browned.

Each serving provides:

226 Calories

2 Protein Servings   17   g Protein
1 Bread Serving   11   g Fat
                           16   g Carbohydrate
                          397 mg Sodium
                          162 mg Cholesterol

Almost a Quiche

As good as the fattening kind!

Makes 4 servings

1	small onion, very thinly sliced, separated into rings
1	tablespoon plus 1 teaspoon imitation bacon bits
4	ounces shredded Swiss cheese
4	eggs
2	cups skim milk
1/4	teaspoon salt
1/8	teaspoon pepper
1	tablespoon plus 1 teaspoon reduced-calorie margarine
2	tablespoons plus 2 teaspoons all-purpose flour
2	slices white or whole wheat bread, crumbled
1/2	teaspoon baking soda
	Dash ground nutmeg

Preheat oven to 350°.

Spread onion rings in a 9-inch pie pan that has been sprayed with a nonstick cooking spray. Sprinkle with bacon bits, and then cheese.

Combine remaining ingredients in a blender. Blend for 3 minutes. Pour evenly over onion mixture. Let stand 5 minutes.

Bake 35 to 40 minutes, until top is lightly browned.

Let stand 5 minutes before cutting.

Each serving provides:

313 Calories

2	Protein Servings	21	g Protein
1/2	Bread Serving	16	g Fat
1/4	Vegetable Serving	20	g Carbohydrate
1/2	Fat Serving	571	mg Sodium
1/2	Milk Serving	303	mg Cholesterol
30	Additional Calories		

Cauliflower-Cheese Bake

Makes 2 servings

2 cups cauliflower, cut into flowerets, or 1 10-ounce package frozen cauliflower
1/2 cup part-skim ricotta cheese
2 eggs, beaten
1 tablespoon plus 1 teaspoon grated Parmesan cheese
2 teaspoons minced onion flakes
Salt and pepper to taste

Cook cauliflower according to package directions. If using fresh cauliflower, steam in 1-inch of boiling water, covered, for 5 minutes. Drain.

Preheat oven to 350°.

Place cooked cauliflower in a small baking dish that has been sprayed with a nonstick cooking spray.

Combine remaining ingredients and mix well. Pour over cauliflower.

Bake, uncovered, 20 minutes.

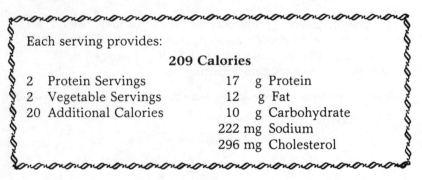

Each serving provides:

209 Calories

2	Protein Servings	17	g	Protein
2	Vegetable Servings	12	g	Fat
20	Additional Calories	10	g	Carbohydrate
		222	mg	Sodium
		296	mg	Cholesterol

Spinach 'n Herb Bake

You'll love this blend of spinach and herbs.

Makes 8 servings

2   10-ounce packages frozen chopped spinach, thawed, drained
2   cups cooked white or brown rice
8   ounces grated Cheddar cheese
2   tablespoons minced onion flakes
1/2   teaspoon dried rosemary, crushed
      Salt and pepper to taste
2   tablespoons plus 2 teaspoons reduced-calorie margarine
1-1/3 cups nonfat dry milk
2   cups water
4   eggs
1   teaspoon Worcestershire sauce

Preheat oven to 350°.

In a large bowl, combine spinach, rice, cheese, onion flakes, rosemary, salt and pepper. Toss to combine well. Place mixture in an 8-inch square baking pan that has been sprayed with a nonstick cooking spray.

In a blender container, combine margarine, milk, water, eggs and Worcestershire sauce. Blend until smooth. Pour over spinach mixture.

Bake, uncovered, 35 minutes, until set.

Each serving provides:

290 Calories

1-1/2	Protein Servings	18	g Protein
1/2	Bread Serving	15	g Fat
1	Vegetable Serving	23	g Carbohydrate
1/2	Fat Serving	371	mg Sodium
1/2	Milk Serving	169	mg Cholesterol

Quiche for One

Go ahead — treat yourself!

Makes 1 serving

1   egg
1/2   cup skim milk
1   teaspoon margarine, melted
1/8   teaspoon salt
        Pepper to taste
        Dash nutmeg
1   teaspoon imitation bacon bits
1/2   cup chopped mushrooms, fresh or canned
1   teaspoon dried chives
1   ounce grated Swiss cheese

Preheat oven to 350°.

In a small bowl, beat egg and milk. Beat in margarine, salt, pepper and nutmeg. Stir in remaining ingredients. Pour into an individual small baking pan that has been sprayed with a nonstick cooking spray.

Bake 30 minutes, until set.

Let stand for 5 minutes before serving.

Each serving provides:

283 Calories

2	Protein Servings	20	g	Protein
1	Vegetable Serving	18	g	Fat
1	Fat Serving	10	g	Carbohydrate
1/2	Milk Serving	631	mg	Sodium
10	Additional Calories	303	mg	Cholesterol

Creamy Egg Salad

Makes 2 servings

2	hard-cooked eggs, chopped
1/2	cup part-skim ricotta cheese
1/4	teaspoon dill weed
1/8	teaspoon salt
1/4	teaspoon dry mustard
1/2	cup chopped celery
2	teaspoons minced onion flakes
2	teaspoons lemon juice
	Pepper to taste

In a medium bowl, combine all ingredients *except* eggs. Mix with a fork until smooth and well-blended. Stir in eggs. Chill.

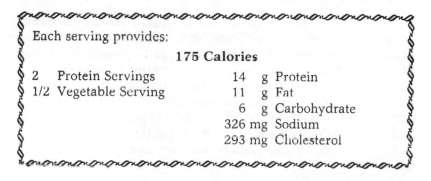

Each serving provides:

175 Calories

2	Protein Servings	14 g	Protein
1/2	Vegetable Serving	11 g	Fat
		6 g	Carbohydrate
		326 mg	Sodium
		293 mg	Cholesterol

Spinach Cheese Puffs

Make them the night before and forget about them until time to bake.
Makes 6 servings

2	tablespoons vegetable oil
1/2	cup chopped onions
1	10-ounce package frozen chopped spinach, thawed, drained well
2	eggs, slightly beaten
2	ounces grated Parmesan cheese
2	ounces shredded Cheddar cheese
1/8	teaspoon garlic powder
1/4	cup reduced-calorie Italian dressing (6 calories per tablespoon)
2	teaspoons double-acting baking powder
4-1/2	ounces corn meal

Heat oil in a large skillet over medium-high heat. Add onions and cook until golden. Remove from heat. Stir in spinach. Combine eggs, Parmesan cheese, Cheddar cheese, garlic powder and Italian dressing. Stir into spinach mixture. Stir baking powder into corn meal. Add to spinach mixture, mixing thoroughly. Place mixture in a bowl and chill several hours or overnight. When ready to prepare, preheat oven to 375°. Shape mixture into balls, about 1-1/2 inches in diameter.† Place on a nonstick baking sheet.

Bake 10 to 12 minutes, until bottoms are lightly browned. Serve hot.

†Makes 36 balls.

Each serving provides:

247 Calories

1	Protein Serving	12	g	Protein
1	Bread Serving	13	g	Fat
3/4	Vegetable Serving	21	g	Carbohydrate
1	Fat Serving	570	mg	Sodium
4	Additional Calories	109	mg	Cholesterol

Broccoli Pancakes

Makes 2 servings

1	10-ounce package frozen chopped broccoli
2	eggs
2/3	cup lowfat cottage cheese
2	slices white or whole wheat bread
1	tablespoon minced onion flakes
2	teaspoons grated Parmesan cheese
2	teaspoons vegetable oil
	Salt and pepper to taste
	Dash ground nutmeg

Cook broccoli according to package directions. Drain.

In a blender container, combine all ingredients, *except* broccoli. Blend until smooth. Pour into a bowl and stir in broccoli.

Drop mixture by 1/4 cupfuls onto a preheated nonstick skillet or griddle over medium heat. Cook, turning once, until pancakes are brown on both sides.

Makes 8 pancakes.

Each serving provides:

289 Calories

2	Protein Servings	23 g	Protein
1	Bread Serving	13 g	Fat
2	Vegetable Servings	23 g	Carbohydrate
1	Fat Serving	547 mg	Sodium
10	Additional Calories	279 mg	Cholesterol

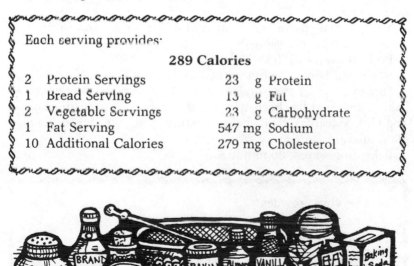

Eggplant Pastitsio

A low-cal version of a Greek favorite . . .

Makes 4 servings

2   tablespoons vegetable oil
1   large eggplant, peeled, cut into 1-inch cubes
1/2   cup chopped onions
1/2   cup tomato paste
1/2   cup dry white wine
1/2   teaspoon salt
1/4   teaspoon ground cinnamon
1/4   teaspoon ground allspice
1/2   teaspoon dried oregano
4   eggs, beaten
1-1/3 cups lowfat cottage cheese
2   tablespoons grated Parmesan cheese
2   cups cooked elbow macaroni

Heat oil over medium heat in a large nonstick skillet. Add eggplant and onions. Cook 10 minutes, stirring frequently. Reduce heat to low.

Stir in tomato paste, wine, salt and spices. Cover and simmer 15 minutes, stirring occasionally.

Preheat oven to 350°.

In a small bowl, combine eggs and cheeses.

Spread 1 cup of the eggplant in the bottom of an 8-inch square baking dish that has been sprayed with a nonstick cooking spray. Top with macaroni, then cheese mixture, and then remaining eggplant mixture.

Bake, uncovered, 30 minutes.

Each serving provides:

360 Calories

2	Protein Servings	22 g	Protein
1	Bread Serving	15 g	Fat
1-1/2	Vegetable Servings	37 g	Carbohydrate
1-1/2	Fat Servings	955 mg	Sodium
40	Additional Calories	279 mg	Cholesterol

Tomato Cheddar Bake

Colorful tomatoes in a golden custard . . .

Makes 4 servings

1	tablespoon plus 1 teaspoon margarine
1	cup chopped onions
2	16-ounce cans tomatoes, drained, chopped
1/2	teaspoon salt
1/8	teaspoon pepper
1/2	teaspoon dried oregano
1/2	teaspoon dried basil
	Dash garlic powder
4	ounces grated Cheddar cheese
4	eggs, beaten
3	tablespoons dry bread crumbs

In a medium saucepan, melt margarine over medium heat. Add onions and cook until lightly browned.

Preheat oven to 350°.

Stir tomatoes into onions. Cook 5 minutes, or until most of liquid has evaporated.

Stir in salt, pepper, oregano, basil and garlic powder. Remove from heat.

Stir in cheese and pour mixture into a 1-1/2 quart casserole that has been sprayed with a nonstick cooking spray. Pour eggs over mixture.

Sprinkle with crumbs.

Bake 45 minutes, uncovered.

Each serving provides:

311 Calories

2	Protein Servings	17 g	Protein
1/4	Bread Serving	20 g	Fat
2	Vegetable Servings	18 g	Carbohydrate
1	Fat Serving	893 mg	Sodium
		304 mg	Cholesterol

Apple-Cheddar Custard

A delicious apple and cheddar combination . . .

Makes 4 servings

4   small, sweet apples, peeled, cut in 1/4-inch slices
1   tablespoon plus 1 teaspoon all-purpose flour
4   ounces grated Cheddar cheese
4   eggs
2/3 cup nonfat dry milk
1-1/2 cups water
1/4 teaspoon ground nutmeg

Preheat oven to 350°.

In a medium bowl, toss apples with flour. Place apples in an 8-inch square baking dish that has been sprayed with a nonstick cooking spray.

Sprinkle cheese over apples.

In a blender container, combine eggs, milk, water and nutmeg. Blend 20 seconds. Pour evenly over apples and cheese.

Bake 35 to 40 minutes, until set.

Serve hot or cold.

Each serving provides:

303 Calories

2	Protein Servings	18 g	Protein
1	Fruit Serving	15 g	Fat
1/2	Milk Serving	24 g	Carbohydrate
10	Additional Calories	311 mg	Sodium
		306 mg	Cholesterol

Sweet Cheese Puff

An excellent brunch dish!

Makes 4 servings

1-1/3	cups lowfat cottage cheese
1	egg yolk
1/2	teaspoon vanilla extract
1	teaspoon vanilla butternut flavor
1/8	teaspoon ground cinnamon
	Sweetener equivalent to 9 teaspoons sugar
3	eggs plus 1 egg white
1/2	cup plain lowfat yogurt
1/3	cup nonfat dry milk
1/4	cup orange juice (unsweetened)
1/4	cup reduced-calorie margarine
1	teaspoon double-acting baking powder
1/2	cup all-purpose flour
1/2	teaspoon almond extract

Preheat oven to 350°. In a medium bowl, combine cottage cheese, egg yolk, vanilla, vanilla butternut, cinnamon, and sweetener equivalent to 3 teaspoons of the sugar. Mix well. Spread mixture evenly in the bottom of a 9-inch pie pan that has been sprayed with a nonstick cooking spray. In a blender container, combine remaining ingredients. Blend until smooth. Slowly and evenly, pour mixture over cottage cheese mixture. Bake 45 minutes, until puffed and golden brown. Let stand 5 minutes before serving.

Each serving provides:

295 Calories*

2	Protein Servings	21	g	Protein
1/2	Bread Serving	13	g	Fat
1-1/2	Fat Servings	22	g	Carbohydrate
1/2	Milk Serving	663	mg	Sodium
20	Additional Calories*	279	mg	Cholesterol

*Add 36 calories if sugar of fructose is used as sweetener.

No Noodle Fruit Kugel

It looks like noodles, but you're in for a surprise!

Makes 8 servings

1	small cabbage (about 1-1/2 pounds), shredded into 1/2-inch strips
2	small, sweet apples, peeled, coarsely shredded
1	cup canned crushed pineapple (unsweetened), drained
1/4	cup plus 2 tablespoons raisins
1/2	cup orange juice
1	teaspoon ground cinnamon
4	eggs
1-1/3	cups lowfat cottage cheese
2	teaspoons vanilla extract
2	tablespoons plus 2 teaspoons reduced-calorie margarine
	Sweetener equivalent to 9 teaspoons sugar

Place cabbage in a medium saucepan and add water to cover. Bring to a boil over medium-high heat. Reduce heat to medium, cover, and cook until cabbage is tender, about 20 minutes. Drain cabbage well in a strainer or colander, and then on paper towels.

Preheat oven to 350°.

Combine cabbage, apples, pineapple and raisins, mixing well. Place mixture in an 8-inch square baking pan that has been sprayed with a nonstick cooking spray. In a blender container, combine remaining ingredients. Blend until smooth. Pour over cabbage mixture. Bake 45 minutes, until set. Let kugel stand 5 minutes before cutting, or refrigerate and serve cold.

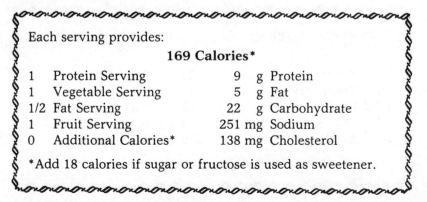

Each serving provides:

169 Calories*

1	Protein Serving	9	g Protein
1	Vegetable Serving	5	g Fat
1/2	Fat Serving	22	g Carbohydrate
1	Fruit Serving	251	mg Sodium
0	Additional Calories*	138	mg Cholesterol

*Add 18 calories if sugar or fructose is used as sweetener.

Spaghetti Squash Kugel

Makes 4 servings

4   eggs
1-1/3 cups lowfat cottage cheese
1/4   teaspoon ground cinnamon
      Sweetener equivalent to 3 teaspoons sugar
1   teaspoon vanilla butternut flavor
3   cups cooked, drained, spaghetti squash†

Preheat over to 350°.

In a large bowl, beat eggs. Add cottage cheese, cinnamon, sweetener and vanilla butternut. Beat until well blended.

Add spaghetti squash to egg mixture. Mix well. Pour into a casserole that has been sprayed with a nonstick cooking spray.

Sprinkle with additional cinnamon.

Bake 30 minutes, or until set and lightly browned.

†Note: To cook spaghetti squash, cut squash in half lengthwise. Remove seeds. Bake, cut-side down, in a baking pan containing 1 to 2 inches of water, for 45 minutes, at 350°. Drain. Pull strands free with a fork.

Each serving provides:

164 Calories*

2	Protein Servings	16	g	Protein
1-1/2	Vegetable Servings	7	g	Fat
0	Additional Calories*	9	g	Carbohydrate
		371	mg	Sodium
		277	mg	Cholesterol

*Add 12 calories if sugar or fructose is used as sweetener.

Cottage Cheese Latkes (Pancakes)

A traditional holiday favorite you can now enjoy all year long . . .

Makes 2 servings

2/3	cup lowfat cottage cheese
2	eggs
2	teaspoons vanilla extract
2	slices white or whole wheat bread, crumbled
2	teaspoons vegetable oil
	Sweetener equivalent to 3 teaspoons sugar
1/2	cup applesauce (unsweetened)
	Ground cinnamon

In a blender container, combine all ingredients, *except* applesauce and cinnamon. Blend until smooth.

Pour mixture onto a preheated nonstick skillet or griddle over medium-high heat, making eight 3-inch pancakes. Turn pancakes when edges appear dry. Brown lightly on both sides.

To serve, place pancakes on serving plates. Divide applesauce evenly among pancakes, putting 1 tablespoon of applesauce in the center of each. Sprinkle with cinnamon.

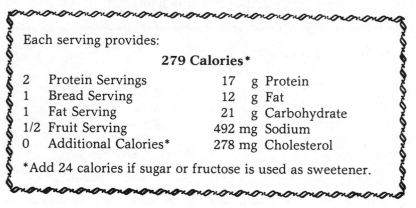

Each serving provides:

279 Calories*

2	Protein Servings	17	g Protein
1	Bread Serving	12	g Fat
1	Fat Serving	21	g Carbohydrate
1/2	Fruit Serving	492	mg Sodium
0	Additional Calories*	278	mg Cholesterol

*Add 24 calories if sugar or fructose is used as sweetener.

Cottage Apple Bake

Makes 6 servings

6   small, sweet apples, peeled and sliced very thin
1/2   cup water
1/2   teaspoon ground cinnamon
1/2   teaspoon ground nutmeg
3   eggs
1   cup lowfat cottage cheese
1/3   cup nonfat dry milk
2   teaspoons vanilla extract
    Sweetener equivalent to 8 teaspoons sugar
    Dash salt

Place apples and water in a large nonstick skillet. Sprinkle with cinnamon and nutmeg. Simmer over medium heat 10 minutes, until apples are slightly tender. Remove from heat.

Preheat oven to 350°.

In a blender container, combine eggs, cottage cheese, dry milk, vanilla, sweetener and salt. Blend until smooth.

Spread apples evenly in the bottom of an 8-inch square baking pan that has been sprayed with a nonstick cooking spray. Pour cottage cheese mixture evenly over apples. Sprinkle with additional cinnamon, if desired.

Bake, uncovered, 25 minutes, until set.

Chill.

Each serving provides:

144 Calories*

1	Protein Serving	9	g Protein
1	Fruit Serving	4	g Fat
17	Additional Calories*	18	g Carbohydrate
		229	mg Sodium
		139	mg Cholesterol

*Add 21 calories if sugar or fructose is used as sweetener.

Cinnamon Raisin Cheese Squares

Guaranteed to be a hit!

Makes 4 servings

2	tablespoons plus 2 teaspoons reduced-calorie margarine, melted
3	ounces Grape-Nuts® cereal
1/4	teaspoon ground cinnamon
1-2/3	cups lowfat cottage cheese
3	eggs
	Sweetener equivalent to 9 teaspoons sugar
1	cup applesauce (unsweetened)
2	tablespoons frozen orange juice concentrate (unsweetened), thawed
3	tablespoons all-purpose flour
1/2	teaspoon ground cinnamon
1/4	teaspoon ground nutmeg
1-1/2	teaspoons vanilla extract
1/4	cup plus 2 tablespoons raisins

Preheat oven to 325°.

In an 8-inch square baking pan, combine margarine, Grape-Nuts®, and 1/4 teaspoon cinnamon. Mix until cereal is moistened. Press firmly in bottom of pan. Bake 10 minutes.

In a blender container, combine remaining ingredients, *except* raisins. Blend until smooth. Stir in raisins. Pour mixture over crust.

Bake 40 minutes, until set.

Cool slightly; then chill.

Each serving provides:

348 Calories*

2	Protein Servings	20	g	Protein
1	Bread Serving	9	g	Fat
1	Fat Serving	47	g	Carbohydrate
1-1/2	Fruit Servings	676	mg	Sodium
23	Additional Calories*	209	mg	Cholesterol

*Add 36 calories if sugar or fructose is used as sweetener.

Fish and Seafood

Fish and seafood are so vital to a balanced diet. Low in fat and high in protein, our recipes offer you a variety of delicious, easy-to-prepare seafood dishes. Our selections will please your taste buds, delight your family and friends, and charm your waistline.

Sole and Peppers

Makes 4 servings

1	tablespoon plus 1 teaspoon vegetable oil
2	green peppers, cut into thin strips
1/2	cup chopped onions
1	packet instant onion flavored broth mix
2	8-ounce cans tomato sauce
1	bay leaf
1/4	teaspoon dried oregano
1/4	teaspoon dried thyme
1-1/2	pounds sole or flounder fillets
	Salt and pepper to taste
1/8	teaspoon garlic powder

Heat oil in a large nonstick skillet over medium heat. Add green peppers, onions and broth mix. Cook, stirring frequently, until onions and peppers are tender, about 10 minutes. Add small amounts of water if necessary, to prevent drying.

Add tomato sauce, bay leaf, oregano and thyme. Simmer 10 minutes, uncovered. Remove and discard bay leaf.

Preheat oven to 375°.

Arrange fish in a shallow baking pan. Sprinkle with salt, pepper, and garlic powder. Pour sauce evenly over fish.

Bake, uncovered, 30 minutes.

Each serving provides:

237 Calories

4	Protein Servings	31 g	Protein
2	Vegetable Servings	7 g	Fat
1	Fat Serving	13 g	Carbohydrate
28	Additional Calories	930 mg	Sodium
		85 mg	Cholesterol

Fish Parmigiana

Your family will rate this a winner.

Makes 4 servings

3/4   cup dry bread crumbs
2   teaspoons dried oregano
1/8   teaspoon garlic powder
1-1/2   pounds flounder fillets (or any non-oily fish, e.g., sole or orange roughy)
1   tablespoon plus 1 teaspoon margarine
3   tablespoons grated Parmesan cheese
Sauce
1   8-ounce can tomato sauce
2   tablespoons minced onion flakes
1/8   teaspoon garlic powder
1/8   teaspoon dried oregano
1/4   teaspoon dried basil
  Salt and pepper to taste

Preheat oven to 350°.

In a shallow bowl, combine bread crumbs, oregano, and garlic powder. Dip fish fillets first into a bowl of water, and then in crumbs.

Place fish in a shallow baking pan that has been sprayed with a nonstick cooking spray. Sprinkle any remaining crumbs over fish.

Dot with margarine.

Bake, uncovered, 20 minutes.

Combine all sauce ingredients in a small bowl. Pour evenly over baked fillets. Sprinkle with Parmesan cheese.

Bake, uncovered, 20 minutes longer.

Each serving provides:

289 Calories

4	Protein Servings	33	g Protein
1	Bread Serving	8	g Fat
1	Vegetable Serving	20	g Carbohydrate
1	Fat Serving	691	mg Sodium
23	Additional Calories	89	mg Cholesterol

Breaded Fillet of Fish

Makes 4 servings

1/4   cup plus 2 tablespoons dry bread crumbs
2/3   cup nonfat dry milk
2   tablespoons minced onion flakes
1/8   teaspoon garlic powder
2   packets instant chicken flavored broth mix
1-1/2 pounds fish fillets, e.g., flounder, turbot, haddock, bluefish
       or sole
1   tablespoon plus 1 teaspoon margarine

Preheat oven to 350°.

In a shallow bowl, combine bread crumbs, dry milk, onion flakes, garlic powder and broth mix.

Dip each fillet first in a bowl of water, and then in crumb mixture. Place fillets in a shallow baking dish that has been sprayed with a nonstick cooking spray. Sprinkle any remaining crumb mixture evenly over fish.

Dot with margarine.

Bake, uncovered, 30 minutes.

Each serving provides:

260 Calories

4	Protein Servings	37 g	Protein
1/2	Bread Serving	5 g	Fat
1	Fat Serving	15 g	Carbohydrate
1/2	Milk Serving	704 mg	Sodium
5	Additional Calories	105 mg	Cholesterol

Caribbean Fish

A unique blend of flavors!

Makes 4 servings

1-1/2 pounds flounder or sole fillets
1/4 teaspoon salt
1-1/2 tablespoons lime juice
1/2 teaspoon dried oregano
1/4 teaspoon garlic powder
1/2 teaspoon onion powder
1/4 teaspoon pepper
1 bay leaf, crumbled
1 6-ounce can tomato paste
1-1/2 teaspoons coconut extract
1/2 cup water

Preheat oven to 350°.

Place fillets in a shallow baking dish that has been sprayed with a nonstick cooking spray.

Combine remaining ingredients and pour over fish.

Bake 30 minutes, uncovered.

Each serving provides:

176 Calories

4 Protein Servings	30 g	Protein
1/3 Vegetable Serving	2 g	Fat
	9 g	Carbohydrate
	604 mg	Sodium
	85 mg	Cholesterol

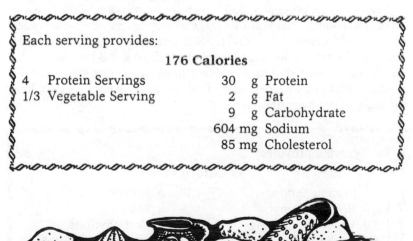

Snapper Creole

Use snapper or any firm, non-oily fish, or shrimp.

Makes 4 servings

2	tablespoons vegetable oil
1-1/2	pounds snapper fillets
1/2	cup chopped onions
1/2	cup green pepper, sliced thin
1/2	cup celery, sliced thin
2	8-ounce cans tomato sauce
1	tablespoon vinegar
	Sweetener equivalent to 1 teaspoon sugar
1/2	cup water
1/4	teaspoon salt
	Pepper to taste
1	teaspoon Worcestershire sauce
1/8	teaspoon garlic powder
1/4	teaspoon chili powder
1	small bay leaf
2	cups cooked white or brown rice

Bake fish in a preheated 350° oven for 20 minutes. Cool fish and flake into chunks. Heat oil in a large saucepan. Sauté onions, green peppers and celery until tender. Stir frequently, and add a small amount of water, if necessary, to prevent drying. Add remaining ingredients, *except* fish and rice. Heat until sauce just starts to boil. Remove and discard bay leaf. Reduce heat. Add fish and heat through. Serve over rice.

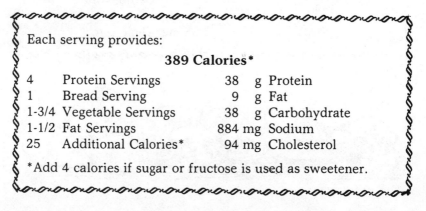

Each serving provides:

389 Calories*

4	Protein Servings	38	g Protein
1	Bread Serving	9	g Fat
1-3/4	Vegetable Servings	38	g Carbohydrate
1-1/2	Fat Servings	884	mg Sodium
25	Additional Calories*	94	mg Cholesterol

*Add 4 calories if sugar or fructose is used as sweetener.

French Fish

A rich-flavored sauce dresses up this fish.

Makes 4 servings

1-1/2 pounds flounder or sole fillets
1/4   cup sweet and spicy French dressing
2   tablespoons plus 2 teaspoons grated Parmesan cheese
2   tablespoons minced onion flakes
1   tablespoon lemon juice
1   tablespoon water

Place fish in a shallow pan.
Combine remaining ingredients and spread evenly over fish.
Marinate in the refrigerator 4 to 5 hours, or overnight, turning fish occasionally.
Bake fish, uncovered, in a preheated 350° oven for 30 minutes.
Place under the broiler for 5 minutes to brown.

Each serving provides:

219 Calories

4	Protein Servings	30	g Protein
2	Fat Servings	8	g Fat
20	Additional Calories	5	g Carbohydrate
		375	mg Sodium
		88	mg Cholesterol

Italian Baked Fish

Makes 4 servings

1-1/2 pounds flounder or sole fillets (or any other non-oily fish,
      e.g., orange roughy)
3   tablespoons reduced-calorie Italian dressing
      (6 calories per tablespoon)
3   tablespoons lemon juice
3   tablespoons Worcestershire sauce
1/8   teaspoon garlic powder
      Salt and pepper to taste

Place fish in a shallow baking pan.

Combine remaining ingredients and pour evenly over fish.

Marinate several hours in the refrigerator, turning fish occasionally.

Preheat oven to 350°.

Bake fish 30 minutes, uncovered.

Broil for 5 minutes, or until fish is crisp.

Each serving provides:

154 Calories

4 Protein Servings   29 g Protein
4 Additional Calories   2 g Fat
                           3 g Carbohydrate
                 427 mg Sodium
                  85 mg Cholesterol

Fish Cakes

A wonderful stand-in for expensive crab meat!

Makes 4 servings

12   ounces cooked fish, flaked (Any non-oily fish is good, e.g., flounder or sole.)

2   slices white or whole wheat bread, crumbled

1   egg, slightly beaten

1   teaspoon Worcestershire sauce

    Salt and pepper to taste

1   teaspoon seafood seasoning

1   tablespoon plus 1 teaspoon reduced-calorie mayonnaise

1   teaspoon double-acting baking powder

2   teaspoons vegetable oil

In a large bowl, combine fish and bread crumbs. Combine remaining ingredients, *except* oil, mixing well. Add to fish and mix with a fork until well blended.

Divide mixture evenly and shape into 8 patties.

Heat oil in a nonstick skillet or griddle over medium heat. Place fish cakes in skillet and cook until brown on both sides.

Each serving provides:

259 Calories

3	Protein Servings	28	g Protein
1/2	Bread Serving	12	g Fat
1	Fat Serving	7	g Carbohydrate
12	Additional Calories	783	mg Sodium
		147	mg Cholesterol

Springtime Broiled Fish

Makes 4 servings

1-1/2 pounds fish fillets (flounder, sole, or any non-oily fish)
1/4   cup reduced-calorie margarine
2   teaspoons lemon juice
1   teaspoon dill weed
1/2   teaspoon onion powder
1/2   teaspoon grated lemon peel
1/8   teaspoon pepper
        Salt to taste
        Dash dried oregano
        Dash paprika

Place fish in a shallow broiler pan.

Melt margarine in a small saucepan over low heat. Stir in remaining ingredients. Spread half of mixture evenly over fish.

Place fish, margarine-side-up, under a preheated broiler, or margarine-side-down, on a preheated grill.

Cook fish for 5 minutes. Then turn, baste with remaining margarine mixture, and cook 5 to 8 minutes, until fish is done.

Each serving provides:

187 Calories

4   Protein Servings   29 g Protein
1-1/2   Fat Servings   7 g Fat
                                    1 g Carbohydrate
                                  273 mg Sodium
                                   85 mg Cholesterol

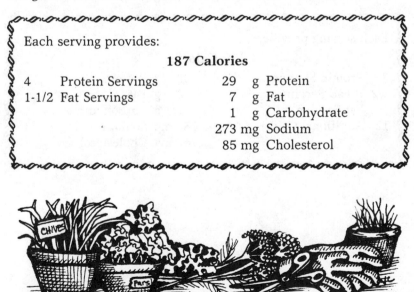

'Pretend' Salmon Salad

You'll fool the most discriminating gourmet.

Makes 4 servings

1-1/2 pounds haddock fillets
2   tablespoons lemon juice
1/2   cup plain lowfat yogurt
1/4   cup chili sauce
1/4   cup reduced-calorie mayonnaise
1/2   cup chopped celery
1   tablespoon plus 1 teaspoon minced onion flakes
1/4   teaspoon salt
1/8   teaspoon pepper
1/8   teaspoon celery salt
       Sweetener equivalent to 1 teaspoon sugar

Preheat oven to 350°.

Place fish in a shallow baking pan that has been sprayed with a nonstick cooking spray. Sprinkle with lemon juice. Bake 30 minutes. Cool.

Flake fish into a large bowl.

Add remaining ingredients and blend well with a fork.

Chill several hours.

Each serving provides:

218 Calories*

4	Protein Servings	34	g	Protein
1/4	Vegetable Serving	5	g	Fat
1-1/2	Fat Servings	9	g	Carbohydrate
1/4	Milk Serving	664	mg	Sodium
17	Additional Calories*	109	mg	Cholesterol

*Add 4 calories if sugar or fructose is used as sweetener.

Lemony Stuffed Fish

An unusual combination with delightful results . . .

Makes 4 servings

1/4 cup plus 1 tablespoon plus 1 teaspoon reduced-calorie margarine
1/2 cup finely minced onions
1/2 cup minced celery
1/2 cup plain lowfat yogurt
1 tablespoon grated lemon peel
1 teaspoon paprika
1/2 teaspoon salt
2 tablespoons lemon juice
1 teaspoon imitation butter flavor
1 teaspoon dill weed
4 slices white or whole wheat bread, cubed
1-1/2 pounds flounder fillets
Paprika

Preheat oven to 375°.

Melt margarine in a small skillet over medium heat. Add onions and celery and cook until tender, about 5 minutes. Place mixture in a large bowl.

Add yogurt, lemon peel, paprika, salt, lemon juice, butter flavor, and dill weed.

Add bread cubes. Mix well.

Place half of the fillets in a small baking dish that has been sprayed with a nonstick cooking spray.

Spread stuffing evenly over fish and top with remaining fillets. Press fish down gently onto stuffing.

Sprinkle with paprika.

Bake, uncovered, 30 minutes.

Each serving provides:

299 Calories

4	Protein Servings	33	g Protein
1	Bread Serving	10	g Fat
1/2	Vegetable Serving	17	g Carbohydrate
2	Fat Servings	741	mg Sodium
1/4	Milk Serving	87	mg Cholesterol

Potato-Fish Patties

Makes 4 servings

1	pound cod fillets
2	tablespoons minced onion flakes
1/4	cup evaporated skim milk
12	ounces cooked potatoes, mashed
1	tablespoon plus 1 teaspoon reduced-calorie margarine
1	tablespoon plus 1 teaspoon Worcestershire sauce
1/8	teaspoon garlic powder
	Salt and pepper to taste
	Paprika to garnish

Preheat oven to 350°.

Bake fish in a shallow nonstick pan for 30 minutes. Cool and flake fish.

Meanwhile, place onion flakes in milk and let stand for 5 minutes. Add onions and milk to potatoes in a large mixing bowl.

Add remaining ingredients, including fish. Mix well. Refrigerate mixture several hours or place in the freezer, covered, for 20 minutes.

Form mixture into 8 patties. Place on a nonstick baking sheet. Sprinkle with paprika.

Bake in a preheated 350° oven for 40 minutes, or until lightly browned.

Each serving provides:

183 Calories

3	Protein Servings	23	g	Protein
1	Bread Serving	2	g	Fat
1/2	Fat Serving	16	g	Carbohydrate
12	Additional Calories	203	mg	Sodium
		57	mg	Cholesterol

Lemon-Broiled Scallops

Incredible!

Makes 2 servings

12   ounces scallops
2   tablespoons reduced-calorie margarine, melted
2   tablespoons lemon juice
1/2 teaspoon salt
1/2 teaspoon Worcestershire sauce
1/4 teaspoon dried tarragon
1/4 teaspoon dried basil

Preheat broiler.
Place scallops in a shallow baking dish.
Combine remaining ingredients. Baste scallops with half of this mixture.
Broil 3 inches from heat for 5 minutes.
Turn scallops. Baste with remaining sauce and broil 5 minutes, or until done.

Each serving provides:

194 Calories

4   Protein Servings   26 g Protein
1-1/2 Fat Servings   6 g Fat
                                         7 g Carbohydrate
                                  1129 mg Sodium
                                     60 mg Cholesterol

Teriyaki Scallops

Soy sauce lends a delightful Cantonese flavor.

Makes 4 servings

1-1/2 pounds scallops
1/4 cup soy sauce
2 teaspoons sherry extract
1 tablespoon plus 1 teaspoon vegetable oil
Sweetener equivalent to 2 teaspoons sugar
1 teaspoon ground ginger
1/8 teaspoon garlic powder

Place scallops in a shallow bowl.

Add remaining ingredients and marinate in the refrigerator for several hours. Drain, reserving marinade.

Preheat broiler.

Place scallops on broiler pan. Baste with marinade. Broil 3 inches from heat for 5 minutes. Turn scallops, baste with marinade and broil 4 to 5 minutes.

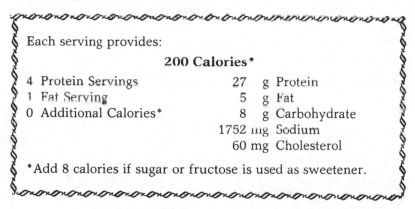

Each serving provides:

200 Calories*

4 Protein Servings	27 g Protein
1 Fat Serving	5 g Fat
0 Additional Calories*	8 g Carbohydrate
	1752 mg Sodium
	60 mg Cholesterol

*Add 8 calories if sugar or fructose is used as sweetener.

Clams Casino

Entertain with this very special item.

Makes 4 servings

16 ounces canned minced clams, drained, reserving juice
1/2 cup reserved clam juice (Add water if necessary to equal 1/2 cup.)
3/4 cup dry bread crumbs
1/4 teaspoon garlic powder
2 tablespoons minced onion flakes
2 teaspoons dried parsley flakes
1/2 teaspoon salt
1/2 teaspoon dried oregano
2 tablespoons plus 2 teaspoons vegetable oil
1 tablespoon plus 1 teaspoon grated Parmesan cheese

Preheat oven to 375°.

In a medium bowl, combine all ingredients *except* Parmesan cheese. Mix well with a fork.

Divide mixture evenly and spoon into real or ceramic clam shells.

Sprinkle with Parmesan cheese. Place shells on a cookie sheet.

Bake 25 minutes, until hot and bubbly.

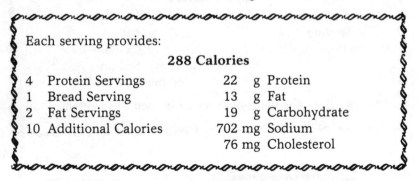

Each serving provides:

288 Calories

4	Protein Servings	22	g	Protein
1	Bread Serving	13	g	Fat
2	Fat Servings	19	g	Carbohydrate
10	Additional Calories	702	mg	Sodium
		76	mg	Cholesterol

Chesapeake Bay Crab Puffs

Our version of the deep-fried delicacy . . .

Makes 2 servings

2	eggs
1	slice white or whole wheat bread, crumbled
2	tablespoons reduced-calorie margarine
1/3	cup nonfat dry milk
1/4	cup water
1-1/2	teaspoons Worcestershire sauce
1	teaspoon lemon juice
1	teaspoon double-acting baking powder
1/2	teaspoon baking soda
1/2	teaspoon seafood seasoning
1	tablespoon plus 1 teaspoon all-purpose flour
4	ounces crabmeat

Preheat oven to 350°.

In a blender container, combine all ingredients *except* crabmeat and 1 teaspoon of the margarine. Blend until smooth.

Combine half of this mixture with crabmeat in a small bowl. Mix well.

Divide crab mixture evenly into 4 nonstick muffin cups.

Pour remaining sauce evenly over crab mixture.

Place 1/4 teaspoon of the remaining margarine on top of each muffin.

Bake 12 to 15 minutes, until brown. Cool in pan 10 minutes.

Each serving provides:

281 Calories

3	Protein Servings	22	g	Protein
1/2	Bread Serving	13	g	Fat
1-1/2	Fat Servings	18	g	Carbohydrate
1/2	Milk Serving	1108	mg	Sodium
20	Additional Calories	333	mg	Cholesterol

Crab and Cheddar Casserole

Definitely deserves rave reviews!

Makes 4 servings

2	tablespoons plus 2 teaspoons reduced-calorie margarine
1/4	cup plus 2 tablespoons all-purpose flour
2/3	cup nonfat dry milk
1	cup water
2	ounces grated Cheddar cheese
1/2	teaspoon salt
1/4	teaspoon pepper
2	teaspoons sherry extract
2	teaspoons dried parsley flakes
14	ounces crabmeat

Preheat oven to 350°.

In a small saucepan, melt margarine over medium-low heat. Stir in flour.

Dissolve dry milk in water and gradually stir into flour mixture.

Add Cheddar cheese, salt, pepper, sherry extract, and parsley flakes. Heat, stirring, until cheese is melted.

Stir in crabmeat.

Spoon mixture into a casserole that has been sprayed with a non-stick cooking spray.

Bake, uncovered, 20 minutes.

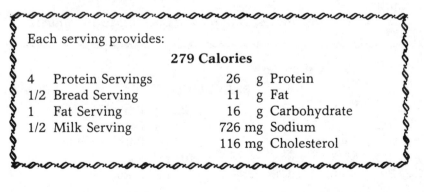

Each serving provides:

279 Calories

4	Protein Servings	26 g	Protein
1/2	Bread Serving	11 g	Fat
1	Fat Serving	16 g	Carbohydrate
1/2	Milk Serving	726 mg	Sodium
		116 mg	Cholesterol

French Herbed Shrimp

Makes 4 servings

2	tablespoons vegetable oil
1/2	cup chopped onions
3	cloves garlic, minced
2	tablespoons all-purpose flour
2-1/2	cups water
1	cup tomato purée
2	bay leaves
1	tablespoon Worcestershire sauce
4	drops bottled hot pepper sauce
1	teaspoon salt
	Sweetener equivalent to 1/2 teaspoon sugar
1/2	teaspoon dried thyme
1/4	teaspoon pepper
1	pound cooked shrimp, peeled

Heat oil in a medium saucepan over medium heat. Sauté onions and garlic in oil until tender.

Stir in flour. Cook, stirring constantly, until mixture is lightly browned. Remove from heat.

Add remaining ingredients, *except shrimp.* Simmer on low heat, uncovered, for 25 minutes. Remove and discard bay leaves.

Add shrimp and heat through.

Each serving provides:

248 Calories*

4	Protein Servings	30	g	Protein
1-1/4	Vegetable Servings	8	g	Fat
1-1/2	Fat Servings	13	g	Carbohydrate
15	Additional Calories*	988	g	Sodium
		170	mg	Cholesterol

*Add 2 calories if sugar or fructose is used as sweetener.

Shrimp Scampi

(shown on cover)

A classic!

Makes 4 servings

1-1/2 pounds cleaned raw shrimp
2   tablespoons plus 2 teaspoons vegetable oil
1/4   teaspoon pepper
2   tablespoons plus 2 teaspoons grated Parmesan cheese
1   tablespoon dried parsley flakes
1/8   teaspoon garlic powder
1/4   teaspoon salt
1   teaspoon dried oregano
3   tablespoons lemon juice
2   tablespoons Worcestershire sauce
1/4   cup dry white wine

Combine shrimp with remaining ingredients in a shallow bowl. Marinate in the refrigerator for several hours.

Remove shrimp from marinade and place in a shallow baking pan. Broil 8 inches from heat for 15 to 20 minutes, turning once. Place in serving bowl.

While shrimp is broiling, heat marinade in a small saucepan. Pour over shrimp. Toss lightly.

Each serving provides:

266 Calories

4 Protein Servings	33	g Protein
2 Fat Servings	12	g Fat
33 Additional Calories	6	g Carbohydrate
	523 mg	Sodium
	258 mg	Cholesterol

Tuna Noodle Casserole

Traci's favorite dish!

Makes 4 servings

1	cup lowfat cottage cheese
1	cup plain lowfat yogurt
1	tablespoon minced onion flakes
1/8	teaspoon garlic powder
1	tablespoon Worcestershire sauce
	Salt and pepper to taste
10	ounces canned tuna, packed in water, drained and flaked
2	cups cooked noodles
1	8-ounce can mushroom pieces, drained
3	ounces grated Cheddar cheese

Preheat oven to 350°.

In a blender container or food processor, combine cottage cheese, yogurt, onion flakes, garlic powder, Worcestershire sauce, salt and pepper.

Pour mixture into a large bowl. Stir in tuna, noodles and mushrooms.

Pour into an 8-inch square pan that has been sprayed with a nonstick cooking spray.

Sprinkle with Cheddar cheese.

Bake 30 minutes, or until hot and cheese is melted.

Each serving provides:

356 Calories

4	Protein Servings	38	g	Protein
1	Bread Serving	10	g	Fat
1/2	Vegetable Serving	27	g	Carbohydrate
1/2	Milk Serving	956	mg	Sodium
		95	mg	Cholesterol

Miracle Italian Tuna Pie

Makes 4 servings

8	ounces canned tuna, packed in water, drained and flaked
1/4	cup chopped onions
1	1-pound can tomatoes, drained, chopped
1	4-ounce can mushroom pieces, drained
1/4	cup chopped green pepper
4	eggs
2/3	cup nonfat dry milk
1-1/4	cups water
2	slices white or whole wheat bread, crumbled
1/4	teaspoon garlic powder
1/4	cup all-purpose flour
2	tablespoons plus 2 teaspoons reduced-calorie margarine
1-1/2	teaspoons dried oregano
1/2	teaspoon salt
1/2	teaspoon dried basil
1/4	teaspoon pepper

Preheat oven to 375°.

Spray an 8-inch square pan with a nonstick cooking spray.

Layer tuna, onions, tomatoes, mushrooms and green peppers in pan.

Combine remaining ingredients in a blender container. Blend 2 minutes. Pour mixture evenly over tuna.

Let stand for 5 minutes.

Bake 45 minutes, until set. Let stand 10 minutes before cutting.

Each serving provides:

317 Calories

3	Protein Servings	29	g	Protein
3/4	Bread Serving	11	g	Fat
1	Vegetable Serving	27	g	Carbohydrate
1	Fat Serving	1049	mg	Sodium
1/2	Milk Serving	311	mg	Cholesterol
8	Additional Calories			

Tuna Seashell Salad

A filling summer dinner and so easy to do . . .

Makes 2 servings

8	ounces canned tuna, packed in water, drained and flaked
1	cup cooked seashell macaroni
1/2	cup sliced celery
2	tablespoons dried parsley flakes
2	tablespoons minced onion flakes
3	tablespoons plus 1 teaspoon reduced-calorie mayonnaise
2	tablespoons lemon juice
1/2	teaspoon celery seed
1	tablespoon vinegar
1/2	teaspoon dill weed
1/4	teaspoon salt
	Pepper to taste

In a large bowl, combine macaroni with flaked tuna. Add celery.

In a small bowl combine remaining ingredients. Mix well. Pour mixture over tuna. Toss to combine.

Chill to blend flavors.

Each serving provides:

298 Calories

4	Protein Servings	33	g	Protein
1	Bread Serving	8	g	Fat
1/2	Vegetable Serving	24	g	Carbohydrate
2-1/2	Fat Servings	967	mg	Sodium
		76	mg	Cholesterol

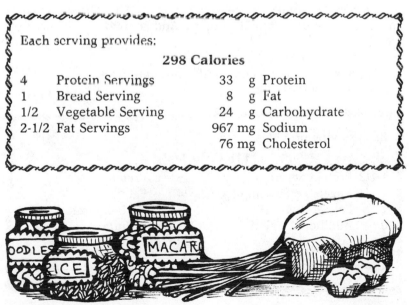

Tuna Mousse

May be varied with salmon . . .

Makes 4 servings

1   envelope unflavored gelatin
1/2   cup water
1   8-ounce can tomato sauce
4   ounces canned tuna, packed in water, drained
2/3   cup lowfat cottage cheese
2   tablespoons plus 2 teaspoons reduced-calorie mayonnaise
      Sweetener equivalent to 3 teaspoons sugar
1/8   teaspoon salt
1/4   teaspoon pepper
1/2   cup finely diced celery
2   tablespoons finely diced onions

Sprinkle gelatin over water in a small bowl and let soften a few minutes.

In a small saucepan, over medium heat, heat tomato sauce to boiling. Reduce heat to low and stir in gelatin mixture. Heat, stirring, for 1 minute.

In a blender container, combine tuna, cottage cheese, mayonnaise, sweetener, salt and pepper. Add tomato sauce mixture. Blend until smooth.

Stir in celery and onions.

Pour mixture into a 3-cup mold. Chill until firm.

Unmold to serve.

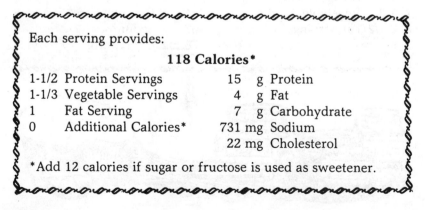

Each serving provides:

118 Calories*

1-1/2	Protein Servings	15	g	Protein
1-1/3	Vegetable Servings	4	g	Fat
1	Fat Serving	7	g	Carbohydrate
0	Additional Calories*	731	mg	Sodium
		22	mg	Cholesterol

*Add 12 calories if sugar or fructose is used as sweetener.

Salmon Paté

Makes 4 servings

8	ounces canned salmon, drained
1/2	teaspoon dried tarragon
1/8	teaspoon pepper
1	teaspoon dill weed
1/8	teaspoon garlic powder
2	teaspoons vegetable oil
1/4	teaspoon onion powder

Combine all ingredients in a blender or food processor. Blend until smooth. Pour into a bowl that has been lined with plastic wrap.

Chill 3 to 4 hours.

To serve, turn paté out onto a serving plate. Peel off plastic wrap.

Each serving provides:

108 Calories

2	Protein Servings	15 g Protein
1/2	Fat Serving	5 g Fat
		0 g Carbohydrate
		208 mg Sodium
		20 mg Cholesterol

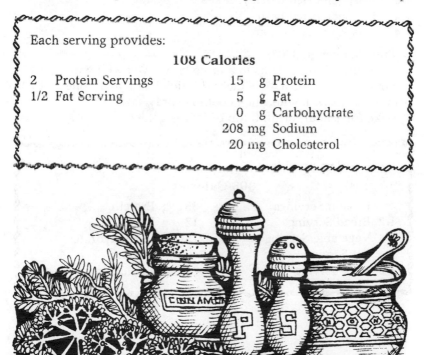

Superb Salmon Loaf

Makes 4 servings

14	ounces canned salmon, drained and flaked
2	eggs, beaten
2	slices white or whole wheat bread, crumbled
2/3	cup nonfat dry milk
3/4	cup water
1/2	cup minced green pepper
2	tablespoons minced onion flakes
1	teaspoon lemon juice
1	tablespoon plus 1 teaspoon margarine, melted
1/2	teaspoon celery salt
1/2	teaspoon grated lemon peel
1/4	teaspoon pepper
1/2	teaspoon dried parsley flakes
1/4	teaspoon dried basil
1/4	teaspoon dry mustard

Preheat oven to 350°.

Combine all ingredients in a large bowl. Mix well with a fork.

Pour mixture into a 4 x 8-inch nonstick loaf pan, or one that has been sprayed with a nonstick cooking spray.

Bake for 1 hour, or until top of loaf is golden.

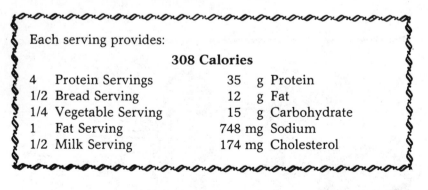

Each serving provides:

308 Calories

4	Protein Servings	35	g	Protein
1/2	Bread Serving	12	g	Fat
1/4	Vegetable Serving	15	g	Carbohydrate
1	Fat Serving	748	mg	Sodium
1/2	Milk Serving	174	mg	Cholesterol

Bengal Seafood Salad

Adds an exotic twist to seafood . . .

Makes 4 servings

12	ounces crab meat
4	ounces cooked shrimp, cut into 1-inch pieces
1/4	cup minced onion
1	cup finely sliced celery
3	ounces sliced water chestnuts
1	cup canned crushed pineapple (unsweetened)
1/4	cup raisins
2	tablespoons sunflower seeds
3	tablespoons lemon juice
5	tablespoons plus 1 teaspoon reduced-calorie mayonnaise
1	cup plain lowfat yogurt
1	teaspoon coconut extract
1	tablespoon curry powder

Combine all ingredients in a bowl. Mix well. Chill.

Each serving provides:

326 Calories

4	Protein Servings	27	g	Protein
1/4	Bread Serving	11	g	Fat
1/2	Vegetable Serving	31	g	Carbohydrate
2	Fat Servings	456	mg	Sodium
1	Fruit Serving	138	mg	Cholesterol
1/2	Milk Serving			
30	Additional Calories			

Seafood Quiche

Makes 4 servings

3/4	cup all-purpose flour
1/4	cup reduced-calorie margarine
2	tablespoons ice water
4	ounces cooked fish, shrimp or crabmeat, cut into small chunks
4	ounces shredded Swiss cheese
1	4-ounce can mushroom pieces, drained
1/2	cup thinly sliced green onions
4	eggs
1	teaspoon imitation butter flavor
2/3	cup nonfat dry milk
1-1/3	cups water
1	tablespoon grated Parmesan cheese
	Dash ground nutmeg

Preheat oven to 400°. Combine flour, margarine and ice water, mixing to form a dough. With your hands, work dough into a ball. Place between wax paper and roll into an 11-inch circle. Place in a 9-inch pie pan, fold edges under, and flute with a fork. Prick the bottom and sides of crust with a fork about 30 times. Bake 10 minutes.

Reduce oven temperature to 350°. Sprinkle seafood, Swiss cheese, mushrooms and onions evenly in crust. In a blender container, combine remaining ingredients. Blend until smooth. Pour over seafood. Bake 45 to 50 minutes, until lightly browned. Let stand 10 minutes before cutting.

Each serving provides:

413 Calories

3	Protein Servings	28	g	Protein
1	Bread Serving	20	g	Fat
3/4	Vegetable Serving	28	g	Carbohydrate
1-1/2	Fat Servings	536	mg	Sodium
1/2	Milk Serving	339	mg	Cholesterol
8	Additional Calories			

Bouillabaise

A "whole meal" soup you'll serve time and again . . .

Makes 6 servings

2-1/4 pounds fresh seafood (Use any combination of flounder, sole,
      haddock, scallops, shrimp, lobster or crab meat.)
1/4 cup vegetable oil
1/4 cup chopped carrots
1/2 cup chopped onions
2 fresh leeks, chopped
2 cups canned tomatoes, drained, chopped
4 cups water
1 clove garlic, minced
1/4 teaspoon saffron, crumbled
1 small bay leaf
1/4 teaspoon dried thyme
1-1/2 teaspoons salt
1 tablespoon dried parsley flakes
     Pepper to taste

Cut seafood into 1-inch pieces.

Heat oil in a large saucepan over medium heat. Sauté carrots, onions and leeks for 10 minutes, or until lightly browned.

Add remaining ingredients *except* seafood. Bring to a boil. Reduce heat, cover, and simmer for 30 minutes.

Add seafood. Cook 15 minutes, uncovered. Remove and discard bay leaf.

Divide seafood evenly into 6 bowls. Spoon soup over seafood.

Each serving provides:

257 Calories

4 Protein Servings	31	g Protein
1 Vegetable Serving	10	g Fat
2 Fat Servings	9	g Carbohydrate
	876	mg Sodium
	130	mg Cholesterol

Poultry

Our recipes for chicken, turkey, and Cornish hens are low in fat, high in protein, easy to prepare, and are delicious alternatives to red meat. Poultry, whether broiled, stewed, roasted, stir-fried, or diced in a salad, will add taste and variety of which you'll never tire.

Chicken Scampi

You've seen it with shrimp. Now, try this!

Makes 4 servings

1-1/4 pounds boneless chicken parts, cut into 1-inch strips, skin removed
2   tablespoons plus 2 teaspoons vegetable oil
1/4   teaspoon pepper
3   tablespoons grated Parmesan cheese
1   tablespoon dried parsley flakes
1/8   teaspoon garlic powder
1/4   teaspoon salt
1   teaspoon dried oregano
3   tablespoons lemon juice
2   tablespoons Worcestershire sauce
1/4   cup dry white wine

Combine chicken with remaining ingredients in a shallow bowl. Marinate in the refrigerator for several hours.

Preheat broiler.

Remove chicken from marinade and place in a shallow pan. Broil 8 inches from heat, turning once, until chicken is no longer pink inside, about 15 minutes.

Heat marinade in a small saucepan. Pour over the chicken. Toss and serve.

Each serving provides:

282 Calories

4 Protein Servings	32 g	Protein
2 Fat Servings	15 g	Fat
35 Additional Calories	4 g	Carbohydrate
	402 mg	Sodium
	102 mg	Cholesterol

Chicken and Peppers

Makes 4 servings

1/4   cup soy sauce
1/4   cup sherry
2   teaspoons ground ginger
1-1/4 pounds boneless chicken parts, cut into 1-inch slices, skin
      removed
2   tablespoons vegetable oil
1   cup chopped onions
2   cloves garlic, crushed
4   medium red or green peppers, sliced 1/4-inch thick
1/2   cup water

In a medium bowl, combine soy sauce, sherry, ginger and chicken. Marinate several hours.

In a large nonstick skillet, heat oil over medium heat. Add onions and garlic. Cook 3 minutes, stirring frequently.

Add peppers. Cook 3 minutes.

Add chicken and marinade. Cook, stirring frequently, until chicken loses its pink color.

Reduce heat to low. Add water, cover, and cook 15 minutes, stirring occasionally.

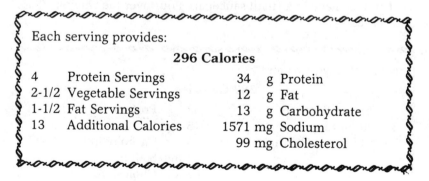

Each serving provides:

296 Calories

4   Protein Servings   34 g Protein
2-1/2 Vegetable Servings   12 g Fat
1-1/2 Fat Servings   13 g Carbohydrate
13   Additional Calories   1571 mg Sodium
                               99 mg Cholesterol

Oriental Chicken and Mushrooms

Makes 4 servings

1-1/4 pounds boneless chicken parts, skin removed
1   tablespoon minced onion flakes
1/4   cup soy sauce
2   teaspoons honey
       Dash garlic powder
1/2   cup chopped green pepper
2-1/2 cups sliced mushrooms

Preheat oven to 350°.

Place chicken in a 6 x 10-inch baking dish. Sprinkle with onion flakes.

In a small bowl, combine soy sauce, honey and garlic powder and pour mixture evenly over chicken.

Cover and bake 30 minutes.

Spread green pepper and mushrooms evenly over chicken and continue to bake, covered, 20 more minutes, until mushrooms are tender.

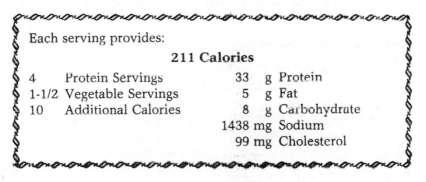

Each serving provides:

211 Calories

4	Protein Servings	33	g	Protein
1-1/2	Vegetable Servings	5	g	Fat
10	Additional Calories	8	g	Carbohydrate
		1438	mg	Sodium
		99	mg	Cholesterol

Chicken in Wine Sauce

This dish tastes best when made a day ahead and reheated!

Makes 4 servings

1-1/4 pounds boneless chicken parts, skin removed
1   cup rosé wine
1/4   cup soy sauce
2   tablespoons plus 2 teaspoons vegetable oil
2   tablespoons water
1   clove garlic, minced
1   teaspoon ground ginger
1/4   teaspoon dried oregano
       Sweetener equivalent to 1 tablespoon firmly-packed brown
       sugar

In a covered casserole or baking dish, combine all ingredients.
Marinate several hours.†
Preheat oven to 375°.
Bake chicken, covered, for 1 hour.
†Note: If chicken is to be served the following day, marinating
        is not necessary. Just bake and refrigerate. Reheat before
        serving.

Each serving provides:

263 Calories*

4   Protein Servings   34 g Protein
2   Fat Servings   11 g Fat
50 Additional Calories*   5 g Carbohydrate
                            1419 mg Sodium
                              82 mg Cholesterol

*Add 12 calories if brown sugar is used as sweetener.

Pineapple Mandarin Chicken

Makes 4 servings

1-1/4 pounds boneless chicken parts, skin removed
1/4 cup canned crushed pineapple (unsweetened)
1 small orange, peeled and sectioned
1/4 cup orange juice (unsweetened)
1 tablespoon cornstarch
1 tablespoon plus 1 teaspoon vegetable oil
1/4 cup soy sauce
1/2 teaspoon dry mustard
1 tablespoon vinegar
1 tablespoon minced onion flakes
1/4 teaspoon garlic powder

Preheat oven to 350°.

Place chicken in a baking dish that has been sprayed with a non-stick cooking spray.

Spread crushed pineapple and orange sections evenly over chicken.

In a small bowl, combine orange juice and cornstarch, stirring to dissolve cornstarch. Add remaining ingredients and pour over chicken.

Cover and bake 1 hour.

Each serving provides:

263 Calories

4	Protein Servings	32	g	Protein
1	Fat Serving	9	g	Fat
1/2	Fruit Serving	12	g	Carbohydrate
8	Additional Calories	1429	mg	Sodium
		99	mg	Cholesterol

Golden Crowned Chicken

Apples and carrots make this an outstanding flavor treat.

Makes 4 servings

1-1/4 pounds boneless chicken parts, skin removed
2   small, sweet apples, peeled, cut into 1-inch chunks
       (Stayman, Winesap, Jonathan, or McIntosh are good choices
       for this dish.)
1   16-ounce can cooked carrots, drained, cut into 1/2-inch
       chunks (about 2 cups)
1   packet instant chicken flavored broth mix
1   tablespoon plus 1 teaspoon honey
1/4   cup plus 2 tablespoons dry bread crumbs
2   tablespoons plus 2 teaspoons reduced-calorie margarine

Preheat oven to 350°.

Place chicken in a shallow baking pan that has been sprayed with a nonstick cooking spray.

In a small bowl, combine apples and carrots. Stir in broth mix and honey.

Spoon carrot mixture on top of chicken. Sprinkle with crumbs. Dot with margarine.

Cover and bake 30 minutes.

Uncover and bake 30 minutes more.

Each serving provides:

302 Calories

4	Protein Servings	35 g	Protein
1/2	Bread Serving	6 g	Fat
1	Vegetable Serving	26 g	Carbohydrate
1	Fat Serving	637 mg	Sodium
1/2	Fruit Serving	83 mg	Cholesterol
23	Additional Calories		

Orange Barbecue Chicken

A crowd-pleaser!

Makes 6 servings

1	8-ounce can tomato sauce
3	tablespoons reduced-calorie orange marmalade (16 calories per 2 teaspoons)
1	teaspoon vinegar
1/8	teaspoon garlic powder
1	tablespoon minced onion flakes
1	teaspoon Worcestershire sauce
	Salt and pepper to taste
2	pounds boneless chicken parts, skin removed

In a small bowl, combine all ingredients, *except* chicken. Let mixture stand 15 to 20 minutes.

Preheat oven to 350°.

Place chicken in a shallow baking pan that has been sprayed with a nonstick cooking spray. Spread half of the sauce over chicken.

Bake, uncovered, 1 hour, basting with sauce several times. Heat any remaining sauce and serve with chicken.

Each serving provides:

197 Calories

4	Protein Servings	31	g	Protein
1/2	Vegetable Serving	5	g	Fat
12	Additional Calories	6	g	Carbohydrate
		318	mg	Sodium
		99	mg	Cholesterol

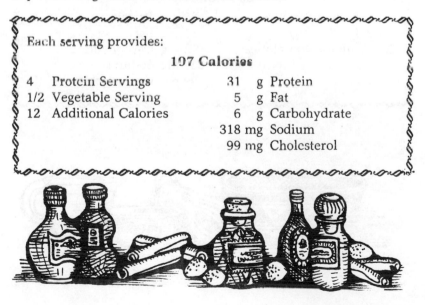

Wine Barbecued Chicken

Makes 4 servings

1-1/4	pounds boneless chicken parts, skin removed
2	tablespoons vegetable oil
1/2	cup dry white wine
1	tablespoon plus 1 teaspoon minced onion flakes
1/2	teaspoon salt
1/2	teaspoon celery salt
1/2	teaspoon pepper
1/4	teaspoon dried thyme
1/4	teaspoon dried marjoram
1/4	teaspoon dried rosemary

Place chicken in a shallow baking pan. Combine remaining ingredients and pour over chicken. Marinate several hours.

Preheat oven to 350°.

Bake chicken, uncovered, 1 hour, basting frequently.

Each serving provides:

238 Calories

4	Protein Servings	30	g	Protein
1-1/2	Fat Servings	11	g	Fat
25	Additional Calories	2	g	Carbohydrate
		559	mg	Sodium
		99	mg	Cholesterol

Spice-Glazed Chicken

This recipe has been a family favorite for years!

Makes 4 servings

1-1/4 pounds boneless chicken parts, skin removed
1/4 cup ketchup
2 tablespoons vinegar
3/4 teaspoon dry mustard
1 bay leaf
1/4 cup water
2 tablespoons plus 2 teaspoons vegetable oil
1 teaspoon Worcestershire sauce
1 cup thinly sliced onion, separated into rings after measuring
Sweetener equivalent to 8 teaspoons sugar

Preheat oven to 350°.

Place chicken in a shallow baking pan that has been sprayed with a nonstick cooking spray.

In a small saucepan, combine remaining ingredients. Bring to a boil over medium-low heat. Boil 2 minutes, stirring frequently.

Baste chicken with a little of the sauce, leaving the onions in the saucepan.

Bake chicken 1 hour, uncovered, basting frequently with sauce while baking. During the last 20 minutes of baking, arrange onion rings over chicken.

Serve any remaining sauce with the cooked chicken.

Each serving provides:

288 Calories*

4	Protein Servings	31 g	Protein
1/2	Vegetable Serving	14 g	Fat
2	Fat Servings	9 g	Carbohydrate
15	Additional Calories*	305 mg	Sodium
		99 mg	Cholesterol

*Add 32 calories if sugar or fructose is used as sweetener.

Chicken Cacciatore

Offered in many other cookbooks, but certainly best in ours!

Makes 4 servings

2	tablespoons vegetable oil
1	cup sliced onions
1	clove garlic, minced
1	1-pound can tomatoes, chopped, undrained
1	8-ounce can tomato sauce
1	teaspoon salt
1/4	teaspoon pepper
1	teaspoon dried oregano
1/2	teaspoon celery seed
1	bay leaf
1-1/4	pounds boneless chicken parts, skin removed
1/4	cup dry white wine
2	cups cooked noodles

Heat oil in a large saucepan over medium heat. Add onions and garlic and cook until tender, about 10 minutes.

Add tomatoes, tomato sauce, and spices, stirring to blend.

Add chicken. Cover, reduce heat to low, and simmer 1 hour, stirring occasionally.

Add wine. Cook, uncovered, 15 minutes.

Remove and discard bay leaf before serving.

Serve over noodles.

Each serving provides:

395 Calories

4	Protein Servings	36	g	Protein
1	Bread Serving	13	g	Fat
2-1/2	Vegetable Servings	33	g	Carbohydrate
1-1/2	Fat Servings	1100	mg	Sodium
12	Additional Calories	124	mg	Cholesterol

Peachy Spiced Chicken

Makes 4 servings

1-1/4   pounds boneless chicken parts, skin removed
3   fresh peaches, peeled and sliced, or 1-1/2 cups canned peach
        slices (unsweetened), drained
1/2   cup orange juice (unsweetened)
1   tablespoon vinegar
1/2   teaspoon ground nutmeg
1/2   teaspoon dried basil
1/8   teaspoon garlic powder
1   tablespoon plus 1 teaspoon vegetable oil
1/2   teaspoon imitation butter flavor
        Sweetener equivalent to 1 tablespoon firmly-packed brown
        sugar

Several hours before baking, place chicken in an 8-inch square
baking pan that has been sprayed with a nonstick cooking spray.

Combine peaches with remaining ingredients. Pour over
chicken. Marinate in the refrigerator for several hours. Return to
room temperature.

Preheat oven to 350°.

Cover chicken and bake 1 hour.

Each serving provides:

270 Calories

4 Protein Servings	31 g Protein
1 Fat Serving	9 g Fat
1 Fruit Serving	15 g Carbohydrate
0 Additional Calories*	115 mg Sodium
	99 mg Cholesterol

*Add 12 calories if brown sugar is used as sweetener.

Honey Crunch Chicken

Your children will choose this one time after time!

Makes 4 servings

1-1/4 pounds boneless chicken parts, skin removed
2   tablespoons plus 2 teaspoons reduced-calorie mayonnaise
1-1/2 ounces Grape-Nuts® cereal, crushed
1   tablespoon plus 1 teaspoon honey

Wash chicken and pat dry. Place in a small shallow baking pan.
Using a pastry brush, spread mayonnaise over both sides of chicken.

Sprinkle crushed cereal evenly over top side of chicken.

Drizzle evenly with honey.

Preheat oven to 375°.

Let chicken stand at room temperature for 10 minutes.

Bake, uncovered, 45 minutes.

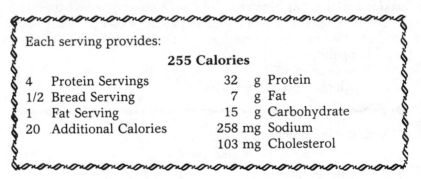

Each serving provides:

255 Calories

4	Protein Servings	32 g	Protein
1/2	Bread Serving	7 g	Fat
1	Fat Serving	15 g	Carbohydrate
20	Additional Calories	258 mg	Sodium
		103 mg	Cholesterol

Lazy Day Chicken

So quick to prepare!

Makes 4 servings

1-1/4 pounds boneless chicken parts, skin removed
1   8-ounce can tomato sauce
2   tablespoons minced onion flakes
1   packet instant beef flavored broth mix
1/2   cup water

Preheat oven to 350°.
Place chicken in a baking pan that has been sprayed with a non-stick cooking spray.
In a small bowl, combine remaining ingredients and pour over chicken.
Cover, and bake 30 minutes.
Remove cover and continue baking 30 minutes longer.

Each serving provides:

196 Calories

4 Protein Servings   31 g Protein
1 Vegetable Serving   5 g Fat
2 Additional Calories   6 g Carbohydrate
                             595 mg Sodium
                              99 mg Cholesterol

Polynesian Chicken Salad

Makes 4 servings

2	teaspoons cornstarch
2	cups canned pineapple tidbits (unsweetened), drained
1/2	cup liquid from pineapple
1/4	cup water
1/4	teaspoon dry mustard
2	tablespoons vinegar
2	tablespoons ketchup
2	teaspoons Worcestershire sauce
1/4	teaspoon salt
2	teaspoons soy sauce
1/4	teaspoon paprika
1/4	teaspoon garlic powder
12	ounces cooked chicken, cubed (*or* turkey)
1/2	cup diced green pepper

In a medium saucepan, combine cornstarch, pineapple liquid, water and mustard. Cook over medium heat, stirring constantly, until thick and bubbly. Cool 10 minutes.

Add vinegar, ketchup, Worcestershire sauce, salt, soy sauce, paprika and garlic powder. Mix well.

Stir in chicken, green pepper and pineapple.

Chill.

Each serving provides:

261 Calories

3	Protein Servings	26	g Protein
1/4	Vegetable Serving	7	g Fat
1	Fruit Serving	25	g Carbohydrate
10	Additional Calories	550	mg Sodium
		76	mg Cholesterol

Apricot-Glazed Chicken

An outstanding flavor treat . . .

Makes 4 servings

1-1/4 pounds boneless chicken parts, skin removed
1/4   cup reduced-calorie French dressing (16 calories per table-
       spoon)
2   tablespoons reduced-calorie apricot spread (16 calories per 2
       teaspoons)
1   tablespoon minced onion flakes
1   packet instant beef flavored broth mix
2   tablespoons plus 2 teaspoons vegetable oil
2   tablespoons water

Preheat oven to 350°.
Place chicken in a shallow baking pan that has been sprayed
with a nonstick cooking spray.
In a small bowl, combine remaining ingredients, mixing well.
Spread sauce over chicken.
Bake, uncovered, 1 hour.

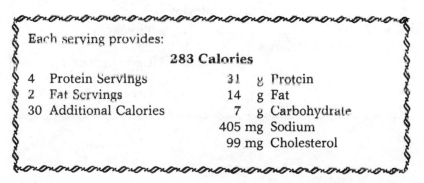

Each serving provides:

283 Calories

4 Protein Servings   31 g Protein
2 Fat Servings   14 g Fat
30 Additional Calories   7 g Carbohydrate
                             405 mg Sodium
                              99 mg Cholesterol

Chicken Delicious

This will soon become one of your family's favorites.

Makes 4 servings

1-1/4 pounds boneless chicken parts, skin removed
1/2   cup reduced-calorie sweet and spicy French dressing (16
       calories per tablespoon)
2   tablespoons minced onion flakes
2   packets instant beef flavored broth mix

Place chicken in a shallow baking pan.

In a small bowl, combine remaining ingredients and pour over
chicken. Marinate in the refrigerator 4 to 5 hours, or overnight.
Turn chicken pieces occasionally.

When ready to prepare, bring chicken to room temperature.

Preheat oven to 350°.

Cover, and bake 1 hour.

Each serving provides:

212 Calories

4   Protein Servings   31   g Protein
37 Additional Calories   5   g Fat
                                  8   g Carbohydrate
                                700 mg Sodium
                                 99 mg Cholesterol

Chicken Dijon

Spicy and delicious!

Makes 4 servings

1-1/4   pounds boneless chicken parts, skin removed
1/2   teaspoon salt
1/4   teaspoon pepper
2   tablespoons plus 2 teaspoons margarine, melted
1   tablespoon plus 2 teaspoons Dijon mustard
1/8   teaspoon garlic powder
2   teaspoons dried parsley flakes
1/2   teaspoon dried rosemary, crumbled
1/2   teaspoon paprika
1/4   teaspoon dried thyme

Preheat oven to 350°.

Place chicken in a shallow baking pan that has been sprayed with a nonstick cooking spray.

Combine remaining ingredients in a small bowl. Mix well and spread over chicken.

Cover and bake 30 minutes.

Remove cover, baste chicken and bake 30 more minutes.

Each serving provides:

247 Calories

4 Protein Servings
2 Fat Servings

31 g Protein
12 g Fat
2   g Carbohydrate
649 mg Sodium
99 mg Cholesterol

Savory Roast Chicken

Makes 6 servings

1	4-1/2 pound roasting chicken
1	small celery stalk
1	lemon wedge
1/4	cup water
2	tablespoons margarine, melted
1	tablespoon lemon juice
1	teaspoon salt
1/8	teaspoon pepper
1/2	teaspoon dried oregano

Preheat oven to 325°.

Place chicken on a rack in a shallow roasting pan.

Place celery and lemon wedge inside cavity.

In a small bowl, combine remaining ingredients. Whisk until blended. Brush chicken (including cavity) with the sauce.

Roast 1-1/2 hours, or until the internal temperature reaches 190° on a meat thermometer. (About 20 minutes per pound.)

Remove and discard skin before serving.

Weigh and serve desired amount.

Each serving provides:

198 Calories

3	Protein Servings, or as desired (weigh before serving)	25	g	Protein
		10	g	Fat
		1	g	Carbohydrate
1	Fat Serving	483	mg	Sodium
		76	mg	Cholesterol

Chicken and Broccoli Bake

Your family and friends will rave about this one!

Makes 4 servings

1   10-ounce package frozen chopped broccoli
1   tablespoon plus 1 teaspoon margarine
1   cup finely chopped onions
8   ounces cooked chicken, cubed, skin removed
4   eggs
2/3   cup nonfat dry milk
1 1/4 cups water
1/4   cup all-purpose flour
1/4   teaspoon salt
1/8   teaspoon pepper
1   teaspoon double-acting baking powder
2   teaspoons Worcestershire sauce
4   ounces Cheddar cheese, grated

Cook broccoli according to package directions, but cook only half of the recommended time. Drain. Place in an 8-inch square baking pan that has been sprayed with a nonstick cooking spray.

In a small saucepan, melt margarine over medium heat. Add onions and cook until tender, about 10 minutes. Spoon onions over broccoli.

Spread chicken evenly over broccoli and onions.

Preheat oven to 350°.

In a blender container, combine eggs, dry milk, water, flour, salt, pepper, baking powder and Worcestershire sauce. Blend until smooth. Pour over chicken.

Sprinkle evenly with Cheddar cheese.

Bake, uncovered, 30 minutes, until top is brown and mixture is set. Let stand for 5 minutes before serving.

Each serving provides:

447 Calories

4	Protein Servings	38	g Protein
1-1/2	Vegetable Servings	23	g Fat
1	Fat Serving	21	g Carbohydrate
1/2	Milk Serving	685	mg Sodium
30	Additional Calories	356	mg Cholesterol

Cranberry Stuffed Cornish Hens

Makes 4 servings

1	cup chopped cranberries
	Sweetener equivalent to 9 teaspoons sugar
1	teaspoon grated orange peel
1/2	teaspoon salt
1/8	teaspoon ground cinnamon
4	slices white or whole wheat bread, cut into cubes and toasted in a 300° oven until dry
2	tablespoons raisins
2	tablespoons plus 2 teaspoons reduced-calorie margarine
2	tablespoons water
4	1-pound Cornish hens

Preheat oven to 375°.

In a medium bowl, combine cranberries, sweetener, orange peel, salt and cinnamon. Mix well.

Add bread cubes and raisins. Toss.

Add margarine and water. Mix well.

Lightly stuff hen cavities with cranberry mixture. Fold neck skin under birds.

Place hens, breast-side up, on a rack in a shallow roasting pan. Cover loosly with aluminum foil, forming a tent.

Roast 1 hour.

Remove and discard skin before serving.

Each serving provides:

340 Calories*

4	Protein Servings, or as desired (weigh before serving)	35 g	Protein
		13 g	Fat
		19 g	Carbohydrate
1	Bread Serving	579 mg	Sodium
1	Fat Serving	102 mg	Cholesterol
1/2	Fruit Serving		
0	Additional Calories*		

*Add 36 calories if sugar or fructose is used as sweetener.

Deviled Cornish Hens

Superb! A great company dish!

Makes 4 servings

2   Cornish hens, weighing a total of 2-1/4 pounds, skin removed
2   tablespoons water
1/4 cup soy sauce
1/2 cup red wine
1   tablespoon sherry extract
1   tablespoon Dijon mustard
1/2 teaspoon bottled hot pepper sauce
2   tablespoons vegetable oil
1/2 teaspoon pepper
3   tablespoons dry bread crumbs

Split hens in half down the back. Place in a shallow pan.

In a small bowl, combine remaining ingredients, *except* bread crumbs, and pour over hens.

Marinate several hours, turning hens occasionally.

Preheat oven to 350°.

Sprinkle half the bread crumbs over hens. Bake 30 minutes.

Turn hens. Sprinkle with remaining crumbs. Bake 30 minutes more.

Each serving provides:

275 Calories

3	Protein Servings, or as desired (weigh before serving)	26	g Protein
		14	g Fat
		7	g Carbohydrate
1/4	Bread Serving	1546	mg Sodium
1-1/2	Fat Servings	76	mg Cholesterol
25	Additional Calories		

Turkey Divan

May be varied with chicken . . .

Makes 4 servings

2   10-ounce packages frozen broccoli spears
12   ounces cooked, sliced turkey, skin and bone removed
1/4   cup plus 1 tablespoon plus 1 teaspoon reduced-calorie margarine
1/4   cup plus 2 tablespoons all-purpose flour
2   cups water
2   packets instant chicken flavored broth mix
1/2   cup plain lowfat yogurt
1/2   teaspoon Worcestershire sauce
1   tablespoon plus 1 teaspoon prepared mustard
2   tablespoons minced onion flakes
2   teaspoons sherry extract
3   tablespoons grated Parmesan cheese
     Salt and pepper to taste

Cook broccoli according to package directions. Drain. Place in an 8-inch square baking pan that has been sprayed with a nonstick cooking spray.

Place turkey slices on top of broccoli.

Preheat oven to 400°.

In a small saucepan, melt margarine over medium-low heat. Stir in flour. Remove from heat.

Gradually stir in water, and then remaining ingredients. Stir until blended. Pour over turkey.

Bake, uncovered, 30 minutes, until hot and bubbly.

Each serving provides:

352 Calories

3	Protein Servings	35 g	Protein
1/2	Bread Serving	14 g	Fat
2	Vegetable Servings	21 g	Carbohydrate
2	Fat Servings	854 mg	Sodium
1/4	Milk Serving	70 mg	Cholesterol
28	Additional Calories		

Breaded Turkey Cutlets

One of our family's favorites! You'll love it, too!

Makes 4 servings

1-1/4 pounds turkey cutlets
2 tablespoons lemon juice
3/4 cup dry bread crumbs
1/8 teaspoon garlic powder
2 teaspoons dried oregano
1/4 teaspoon pepper
1/2 teaspoon salt
1/2 teaspoon poultry seasoning
2 tablespoons grated Parmesan cheese
2 tablespoons vegetable oil

Preheat oven to 350°.

Place turkey cutlets in a medium bowl. Cover with water. Add lemon juice.

In a shallow bowl, combine remaining ingredients, except oil. Mix well.

One at a time, take cutlets from water and dip into crumbs, turning once to coat both sides.

Place cutlets in a shallow baking pan that has been sprayed with a nonstick cooking spray.

Drizzle oil over breaded cutlets.

Bake 30 minutes, or until lightly browned.

Note: Extra servings make great sandwiches – hot or cold.

Each serving provides:

315 Calories

4	Protein Servings	37	g	Protein
1	Bread Serving	11	g	Fat
1-1/2	Fat Servings	16	g	Carbohydrate
15	Additional Calories	556	mg	Sodium
		91	mg	Cholesterol

Italian Turkey Burgers

A wonderful alternative to red meat!

Makes 4 servings

1-1/4 pounds ground turkey, uncooked
1 teaspoon dried oregano
1/2 teaspoon dried basil
1/8 teaspoon garlic powder
1 tablespoon minced onion flakes
Sauce
2 8-ounce cans tomato sauce
1 4-ounce can mushroom pieces, drained
1/4 teaspoon dried thyme
1/4 teaspoon garlic powder
1 tablespoon minced onion flakes
1 packet instant beef flavored broth mix

Preheat oven to 450°.

In a large bowl, combine turkey, oregano, basil, garlic powder and onion flakes. Mix well and shape into 8 patties. Place patties in a shallow baking pan that has been sprayed with a nonstick cooking spray. Bake 15 minutes, until burgers are no longer pink inside, turning once while cooking.

While burgers are cooking, prepare sauce:

Combine all sauce ingredients in a small saucepan. Heat over medium heat until mixture boils. Remove from heat.

Spoon mixture evenly over burgers. Return to oven for 5 minutes.

Spoon sauce over burgers when serving.

Each serving provides:

284 Calories

4 Protein Servings
1-1/2 Vegetable Servings
28 Additional Calories

28 g Protein
15 g Fat
11 g Carbohydrate
1030 mg Sodium
95 mg Cholesterol

Mock-Sausage and Peppers

Tastes just like the Italian specialty!

Makes 4 servings

1	tablespoon plus 1 teaspoon vegetable oil
1/2	cup finely minced green pepper
1/2	cup finely minced onions
1-1/4	pounds ground turkey, uncooked
1/4	teaspoon ground sage
1/4	teaspoon dried thyme
1/4	teaspoon dried marjoram
1/8	teaspoon ground savory
1/4	teaspoon pepper
1/2	teaspoon fennel seeds, crushed†
1/4	teaspoon salt

In a medium nonstick skillet, heat oil over medium heat. Add peppers and onions and cook until tender, about 10 minutes.

In a large bowl, combine turkey with peppers and onions. Add remaining ingredients and mix well. Refrigerate mixture 1 hour to blend flavors.

Form mixture into 8 thin patties. Cook on a nonstick skillet over medium heat, until lightly browned on both sides.

†Note: To crush seeds, roll between 2 layers of waxed paper with a rolling pin, or use a mortar and pestle.

Each serving provides:

284 Calories

4	Protein Servings	26	g Protein
1/2	Vegetable Serving	19	g Fat
1	Fat Serving	3	g Carbohydrate
		271	mg Sodium
		95	mg Cholesterol

Roast Turkey Breast with Peach Sauce

Makes 8 servings

1	7-pound turkey breast
1-1/2	teaspoons salt
1/4	teaspoon pepper
1/4	teaspoon dried thyme
1/2	teaspoon poultry seasoning

Sauce

1	tablespoon cornstarch
3/4	cup water
1	packet instant chicken flavored broth mix
1/4	cup reduced-calorie peach spread (16 calories per 2 teaspoons)
1-1/2	teaspoons sherry *or* brandy extract

Preheat oven to 325°.

Sprinkle top and bottom of turkey breast with salt, pepper, thyme and poultry seasoning. Place turkey, skin-side up, on a rack in a shallow roasting pan.

Roast 2-1/2 hours, or 20 minutes per pound. If using a meat thermometer, roast until the internal temperature reaches 190°.

Remove and discard skin before slicing. Serve desired amount.

Just before serving, prepare sauce:

Dissolve cornstarch in water in a small saucepan. Add broth mix and peach spread and mix well. Bring sauce to a boil over medium-low heat, stirring frequently. Boil 3 minutes, stirring constantly. Remove from heat and stir in extract.

Spoon over sliced turkey.

Each serving provides:

151 Calories

3	Protein Servings, or as desired (weigh before serving)	26	g Protein
		2	g Fat
		4	g Carbohydrate
16	Additional Calories in each 2 tablespoons of sauce	565	mg Sodium
		59	mg Cholesterol

Veal

Veal is a tender, lean meat that is low in fat and has a mild, delicate taste and texture.

In fact, we like it so much that we have devoted an entire section to veal. We have given you some of our favorite recipes, and we encourage you to let your imagination take over and substitute veal in your own favorite meat recipes.

Veal and Rosemary

A delicious combination of herbs and spices . . .

Makes 4 servings

1-1/4 pounds boneless veal, cut for scaloppine
1   cup sliced mushrooms
1/8   teaspoon garlic powder
1/2   cup dry white wine
1   teaspoon dried rosemary, crumbled
2   teaspoons Dijon mustard
1   cup plain lowfat yogurt

Preheat oven to 350°.

Place veal in a shallow baking pan that has been sprayed with a nonstick cooking spray. Cover with mushrooms.

Combine remaining ingredients in a small bowl. Mix well. Spread evenly over veal and mushrooms.

Bake, uncovered, 1 hour.

Each serving provides:

282 Calories

4	Protein Servings	31 g	Protein
1/2	Vegetable Serving	14 g	Fat
1/2	Milk Serving	7 g	Carbohydrate
25	Additional Calories	215 mg	Sodium
		104 mg	Cholesterol

Country Veal Loaf

An easy meatloaf with unusual flavor . . .

Makes 4 servings

1-1/4 pounds lean ground veal
1   large carrot, chopped into 1/4-inch pieces
1/2   cup chopped onions
1/2   cup chopped mushrooms
1/4   cup diced green pepper
2   tablespoons soy sauce
1/2   cup tomato sauce
      Salt and pepper to taste
1/8   teaspoon garlic powder

Preheat oven to 350°.
In a large bowl, combine veal with remaining ingredients. Mix
well. Shape into a loaf.
Place on a rack in a shallow baking pan.
Bake 1 hour, uncovered.

Each serving provides:

285 Calories

4   Protein Servings   29   g Protein
1-1/2 Vegetable Servings   16   g Fat
                                   8   g Carbohydrate
                                 925 mg Sodium
                                 101 mg Cholesterol

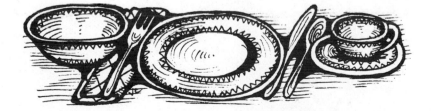

French Herbed Veal Roast

Makes 6 servings

1	teaspoon instant chicken bouillon granules
3/4	cup water
1/4	teaspoon dried rosemary, crumbled
1/4	teaspoon dried oregano
1/4	teaspoon dried thyme
1/8	teaspoon garlic powder
1/4	teaspoon salt
1	bay leaf
1/2	teaspoon pepper
1	2-1/4 pound boneless veal roast

In a small bowl, combine all ingredients except roast. Pour into a self-sealing plastic bag. Add meat to bag and seal. Refrigerate overnight, turning bag over several times.

Preheat oven to 450°.

Place roast on a rack in a shallow roasting pan. Place roast in oven and immediately reduce the heat to 300°. Bake, uncovered, 1-1/4 hours, or until done to taste. Baste often with marinade while baking.

Each serving provides:

188 Calories

3 Protein Servings, or as desired (weigh before serving)

23	g	Protein
10	g	Fat
1	g	Carbohydrate
332	mg	Sodium
86	mg	Cholesterol

Veal Chops Italiano

Makes 4 servings

4	6-ounce veal chops, each about 1-inch thick
	Salt and pepper to taste
1	tablespoon plus 1 teaspoon vegetable oil
2	cups sliced mushrooms
1/2	cup chopped onions
1/8	teaspoon garlic powder
2	green peppers, cut into strips
2	8-ounce cans tomato sauce
1/4	teaspoon dried oregano
1/4	teaspoon dried basil
1-1/2	teaspoons sherry extract
1	tablespoon lemon juice

Sprinkle chops with salt and pepper.

In a nonstick skillet over medium heat, heat oil. Add chops and brown on both sides.

Transfer chops to a shallow baking dish. Cover with mushrooms.

Preheat oven to 350°.

Place onions, garlic powder and green peppers in skillet. Cook until tender, about 5 minutes. Add remaining ingredients. Simmer 5 minutes.

Pour mixture evenly over chops. Bake, uncovered, 1 hour.

Each serving provides:

421 Calories

4	Protein Servings	34 g	Protein
3	Vegetable Servings	24 g	Fat
1	Fat Serving	15 g	Carbohydrate
25	Additional Calories	687 mg	Sodium
		115 mg	Cholesterol

Deviled Veal Chops

Tasty and tangy!

Makes 2 servings

1-1/2 teaspoons Worcestershire sauce
1/8   teaspoon garlic powder
1   tablespoon Dijon mustard
1   teaspoon vegetable oil
2   5-ounce veal chops

Preheat broiler.

Combine Worcestershire sauce, garlic powder, mustard and oil. Spread half of the mixture on one side of the chops.

Place veal on a broiler pan. Broil 3 inches from heat for 5 to 7 minutes, until brown.

Turn veal. Spread with remaining mixture. Broil 5 minutes more, or until done to taste.

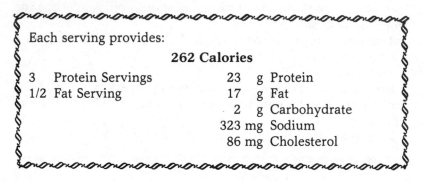

Each serving provides:

262 Calories

3	Protein Servings	23	g Protein
1/2	Fat Serving	17	g Fat
		2	g Carbohydrate
		323 mg	Sodium
		86 mg	Cholesterol

Italian Grilled Veal

Makes 2 servings

2	tablespoons reduced-calorie Italian dressing (16 calories per tablespoon)
2	tablespoons water
2	teaspoons vegetable oil
1/2	teaspoon dried oregano
10	ounces boneless veal, cut into 1-1/2 inch cubes
2	small zucchini, cubed
1	sweet red or green pepper, cut into squares

In a medium bowl, combine dressing, water, oil and oregano. Add veal. Marinate 2 to 3 hours, stirring occasionally.

Preheat broiler.

Remove veal from marinade. Alternately thread veal, zucchini and peppers on 2 skewers. Place on a broiler rack.

Broil 3 inches from heat for about 10 minutes, or until done to taste. Turn frequently and baste with any remaining marinade while broiling.

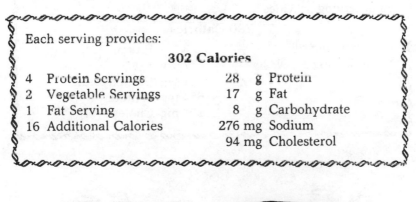

Each serving provides:

302 Calories

4	Protein Servings	28 g	Protein
2	Vegetable Servings	17 g	Fat
1	Fat Serving	8 g	Carbohydrate
16	Additional Calories	276 mg	Sodium
		94 mg	Cholesterol

French Veal Cutlets

Makes 4 servings

1-1/4 pounds boneless veal cutlets
1   teaspoon salt
1/2 teaspoon pepper
1   teaspoon dry mustard
1   tablespoon plus 1 teaspoon vegetable oil
2   tablespoons lemon juice
1   tablespoon dried chives
2   teaspoons Worcestershire sauce

With a mallet, flatten cutlets to 1/4-inch thick. Sprinkle each side with salt, pepper and dry mustard.

Heat oil in a nonstick skillet over medium-high heat. Add veal and cook 5 minutes, turning frequently. Reduce heat to medium.

Add lemon juice, chives and Worcestershire sauce. Cook, turning frequently, 5 minutes.

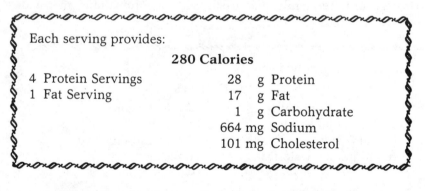

Each serving provides:

280 Calories

4 Protein Servings   28 g Protein
1 Fat Serving   17 g Fat
           1 g Carbohydrate
        664 mg Sodium
        101 mg Cholesterol

Veal in Dilled Cream Sauce

An unusual combination, but very tasty . . .

Makes 2 servings

12	ounces veal cutlets
1/2	cup plain lowfat yogurt
1/2	teaspoon dill seed
1/4	teaspoon salt
	Dash pepper
1	packet instant beef flavored broth mix
2	teaspoons minced onion flakes

Preheat oven to 350°.

Place veal in a shallow baking pan that has been sprayed with a nonstick cooking spray.

In a small bowl, combine remaining ingredients. Mix well. Spread evenly over veal.

Bake, uncovered, 1 hour.

Each serving provides:

324 Calories

4	Protein Servings	37	g Protein
1/2	Milk Serving	16	g Fat
5	Additional Calories	6	g Carbohydrate
		798	mg Sodium
		124	mg Cholesterol

Veal Oriental

Makes 4 servings

1   tablespoon plus 1 teaspoon vegetable oil
2   green peppers, cut into strips
1-1/4 pounds thinly sliced veal, fat and bone removed
1/2   teaspoon salt
2   tablespoons soy sauce
       Sweetener equivalent to 6 teaspoons sugar
2   teaspoons minced onion flakes
       Dash pepper
1   cup canned pineapple chunks (unsweetened)
1/4   cup juice from pineapple

Heat oil in a large nonstick skillet over medium heat. Add peppers and cook until tender.

Add veal. Brown on all sides. Reduce heat to low.

Add remaining ingredients.

Cover, and simmer until veal is tender, about 20 minutes.

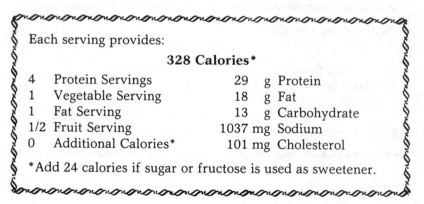

Each serving provides:

328 Calories*

4	Protein Servings	29	g Protein
1	Vegetable Serving	18	g Fat
1	Fat Serving	13	g Carbohydrate
1/2	Fruit Serving	1037	mg Sodium
0	Additional Calories*	101	mg Cholesterol

*Add 24 calories if sugar or fructose is used as sweetener.

Liver

Liver, an important source of iron, is neglected in so many diets. We've proven to you that liver can taste delicious. In our recipes we've combined liver with vegetables, sauces, and even pastas, and, in short, have created new ways to prepare old standbys.

Herbed Chicken Livers

A delicious combination of subtle flavors . . .

Makes 4 servings

1	tablespoon plus 1 teaspoon margarine
1-1/4	pounds chicken livers
1/2	teaspoon onion powder
2	teaspoons instant chicken bouillon granules
1/8	teaspoon ground nutmeg
1/4	teaspoon paprika
1/8	teaspoon pepper
1/8	teaspoon garlic powder
1/4	teaspoon salt
1/8	teaspoon dried thyme
1/8	teaspoon dried marjoram

Melt margarine in a nonstick skillet over medium heat. Add liver.

Combine remaining ingredients and sprinkle over liver. Cook, stirring frequently, until liver is brown on all sides and cooked through, about 10 minutes.

Each serving provides:

227 Calories

4 Protein Servings	29	g	Protein
1 Fat Serving	10	g	Fat
5 Additional Calories	5	g	Carbohydrate
	840	mg	Sodium
	787	mg	Cholesterol

Deviled Chicken Livers

Makes 4 servings

1	tablespoon plus 1 teaspoon all-purpose flour
2	teaspoons paprika
1-1/4	pounds chicken livers
2	tablespoons plus 2 teaspoons reduced-calorie margarine
1/2	cup chopped onions
1/2	teaspoon salt
	Dash pepper
1	teaspoon dry mustard
2	teaspoons Worcestershire sauce
3	tablespoons chili sauce
1	8-ounce can tomato sauce
1	cup water

In a small bowl, combine flour and paprika; sprinkle over livers.

Melt margarine in a large skillet over medium heat. Add onions; cook until golden.

Add liver. Cook, stirring frequently until liver is cooked through, about 10 minutes.

Add remaining ingredients. Heat through.

Each serving provides:

276 Calories

4	Protein Servings	30	g	Protein
1-1/4	Vegetable Servings	10	g	Fat
1	Fat Serving	17	g	Carbohydrate
22	Additional Calories	962	mg	Sodium
		787	mg	Cholesterol

Barbecued Beef Liver

The spicy sauce enhances the liver.

Makes 4 servings

1/4   cup ketchup
     Salt and pepper to taste
2   tablespoons minced onion flakes
1   tablespoon vinegar
1   tablespoon Worcestershire sauce
     Sweetener equivalent to 1 teaspoon sugar
1/8   teaspoon pepper
1   teaspoon prepared mustard
1/8   teaspoon chili powder
1   tablespoon water
1-1/4 pounds beef liver, thinly sliced

Preheat oven to 325°.
In a small bowl, combine all ingredients, except liver.
Arrange the liver slices in the bottom of a shallow baking pan that has been sprayed with a nonstick cooking spray.
Spoon sauce evenly over liver.
Bake, covered, 25 minutes.
Uncover and bake 10 minutes longer.

Each serving provides:

209 Calories*

4   Protein Servings   29   g Protein
15 Additional Calories*   5   g Fat
                              10   g Carbohydrate
                             253 mg Sodium
                           425 mg Cholesterol

*Add 4 calories if sugar or fructose is used as sweetener.

Piquant Livers and Noodles

A little imagination, a lot of flavor . . .

Makes 4 servings

1/4   cup reduced-calorie margarine
1   cup onions, thinly sliced
1   clove garlic, crushed
1-1/4   pounds chicken livers
  Dash ground allspice
1   bay leaf
1/4   teaspoon pepper
1/4   teaspoon salt
1/2   cup dry white wine
2   tablespoons lemon juice
2   teaspoons dried parsley flakes
2   cups cooked thin noodles
2   tablespoons plus 2 teaspoons grated Parmesan cheese

Melt margarine in a large nonstick skillet over medium heat. Add onions and garlic; cook until onions are lightly browned.

Add livers, allspice, bay leaf, pepper and salt. Cook 5 minutes, stirring frequently.

Add wine. Cover, reduce heat to low, and cook 5 minutes.

Add lemon juice and parsley. Simmer, uncovered, 5 minutes, adding water, if necessary to prevent drying.

Remove and discard bay leaf before serving.

Serve liver over noodles. Sprinkle with Parmesan cheese.

Each serving provides:

374 Calories

4	Protein Servings	34	g Protein
1	Bread Serving	13	g Fat
1/2	Vegetable Serving	29	g Carbohydrate
1-1/2	Fat Servings	446	mg Sodium
45	Additional calories	814	mg Cholesterol

Calves Liver Stroganoff

Liver never tasted so good!

Makes 4 servings

2	tablespoons plus 2 teaspoons reduced-calorie margarine
1-1/4	pounds calves liver, thinly sliced
1/2	cup chopped onions
1	cup chopped mushrooms
1/2	cup dry white wine
1	cup plain lowfat yogurt
1/2	teaspoon salt
1/4	teaspoon pepper
	Dash Worcestershire sauce
1	tablespoon imitation bacon bits
2	cups cooked noodles

Melt margarine in a nonstick skillet over medium-high heat. Add liver and cook until browned on all sides. Remove liver and keep warm in oven on a heated serving platter.

Add onions and mushrooms to skillet. Cook over medium heat until onions are tender, adding small amounts of water, if necessary to prevent drying.

Add wine. Bring to a boil.

Reduce heat to low and stir in yogurt, seasonings, Worcestershire sauce and bacon bits. Cook, stirring, until heated through.

To serve, divide noodles evenly onto 4 serving plates. Divide liver and place over noodles. Top with sauce.

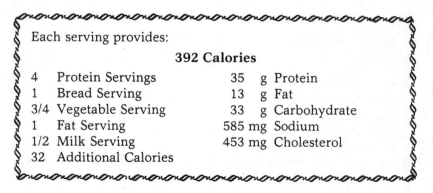

Each serving provides:

392 Calories

4	Protein Servings	35	g	Protein
1	Bread Serving	13	g	Fat
3/4	Vegetable Serving	33	g	Carbohydrate
1	Fat Serving	585	mg	Sodium
1/2	Milk Serving	453	mg	Cholesterol
32	Additional Calories			

Liver-Ka-Bobs

Polynesian flavoring makes this a delicious dish.

Makes 4 servings

1/4	cup soy sauce
1	teaspoon sherry extract
1/4	teaspoon garlic powder
1	teaspoon ground ginger
1	tablespoon water
1	pound chicken livers, cut in half
16	cherry tomatoes
12	fresh mushrooms

In a shallow bowl, combine soy sauce, sherry extract, garlic powder, ginger and water. Add livers. Marinate several hours in the refrigerator. Drain, reserving marinade.

Alternately thread livers, tomatoes and mushrooms on 4 skewers. Place in a shallow broiler pan. Pour marinade over them.

Broil in a preheated broiler, 4 inches from heat for 5 minutes. Turn. Broil 5 minutes longer, or until livers are cooked through.

Each serving provides:

196 Calories

3 Protein Servings	26	g Protein
1 Vegetable Serving	5	g Fat
	11	g Carbohydrate
	1438	mg Sodium
	629	mg Cholesterol

Chicken Livers and Pasta

A nice change of pace for liver . . .

Makes 4 servings

1	tablespoon plus 1 teaspoon reduced-calorie margarine
1-1/4	pounds chicken livers, cut into small pieces
1	cup sliced mushrooms
2	cups tomato sauce
2	teaspoons instant beef bouillon granules
1	teaspoon dried oregano
2	teaspoons sherry extract
3	ounces uncooked spaghetti or linguini

Melt margarine in a nonstick skillet over medium heat. Add livers and cook until brown on all sides, about 10 minutes.

Add mushrooms. Cook 3 minutes.

Add tomato sauce, bouillon and oregano. Reduce heat to low. Simmer 15 minutes, uncovered, stirring frequently. Stir in extract.

While liver is cooking, cook spaghetti according to package directions. Drain.

Serve liver over pasta.

Each serving provides:

339 Calories

4	Protein Servings	33	g	Protein
1	Bread Serving	8	g	Fat
1-1/2	Vegetable Servings	30	g	Carbohydrate
1/2	Fat Serving	1248	mg	Sodium
30	Additional Calories	787	mg	Cholesterol

Chicken Livers Provencal

Makes 2 servings

2   teaspoons margarine
1/4   cup chopped onions
10   ounces chicken livers
1   16-ounce can tomatoes, drained, chopped
1/8   teaspoon garlic powder
1/4   teaspoon salt
1/8   teaspoon pepper
1   4-ounce can mushroom pieces, drained

Melt margarine in a nonstick skillet over medium heat. Add onions and cook until tender.

Add liver. Cook, stirring, until brown on all sides, about 10 minutes.

Add remaining ingredients. Cook 2 minutes.

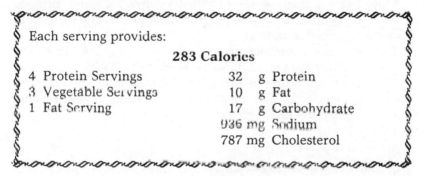

Each serving provides:

283 Calories

4 Protein Servings   32 g Protein
3 Vegetable Servings   10 g Fat
1 Fat Serving   17 g Carbohydrate
                           936 mg Sodium
                           787 mg Cholesterol

Paté en Aspic

The French favorite, made light . . .

Makes 8 servings

1-1/4 pounds chicken livers
1   cup water
1   envelope unflavored gelatin
1   packet instant chicken flavored broth mix
2   tablespoons minced onion flakes
1/2   teaspoon salt
1   teaspoon Dijon mustard
1/4   teaspoon pepper
1/4   teaspoon dried thyme
2   tablespoons dried parsley flakes
       Dash ground nutmeg
1   4-ounce can mushroom pieces, drained

Place livers in small saucepan with 3/4 cup of the water. Bring to a boil over medium heat. Cover, reduce heat to low, and simmer 10 minutes. Remove from heat.

In a small bowl, sprinkle gelatin over remaining 1/4 cup water. Let soften a few minutes. Add to livers. Stir to dissolve.

Place livers and water in a blender container with remaining ingredients. Blend until smooth. Pour into a 4 x 8-inch loaf pan that has been sprayed with a nonstick cooking spray.

Chill until firm.

Unmold to serve.

Each serving provides:

102 Calories

2   Protein Servings   15 g Protein
1/4 Vegetable Serving   3 g Fat
                                3 g Carbohydrate
                              367 mg Sodium
                              393 mg Cholesterol

Liver and Bacon Spread

Makes 2 servings

10   ounces chicken livers
1   4-ounce can mushroom pieces, drained
1   tablespoon imitation bacon bits
2   tablespoons reduced-calorie mayonnaise
     Salt and pepper to taste

In a nonstick skillet, cook livers over high heat until brown on all sides, about 5 minutes.

Place livers and remaining ingredients in a blender container or food processor. Process until smooth.

Chill.

Each serving provides:

246 Calories

4	Protein Servings	30	g Protein
1	Vegetable Serving	10	g Fat
1-1/2	Fat Servings	7	g Carbohydrate
15	Additional Calories	580	mg Sodium
		792	mg Cholesterol

Sherried Liver Spread

Easy to prepare and extra tasty . . .

Makes 4 servings

1-1/4	pounds chicken livers
2	tablespoons plus 2 teaspoons reduced-calorie margarine
1	teaspoon sherry extract
1	tablespoon dried parsley flakes
2	teaspoons minced onion flakes
3/4	teaspoon dried basil
1/2	teaspoon dried oregano
1/4	teaspoon pepper

In a nonstick skillet, cook livers over medium-high heat until brown on all sides, about 5 minutes.

Place liver in a blender container or food processor with remaining ingredients. Process until smooth.

Chill.

To serve, spread on toast or crackers.

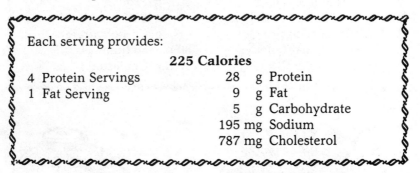

Each serving provides:

225 Calories

4	Protein Servings	28 g	Protein
1	Fat Serving	9 g	Fat
		5 g	Carbohydrate
		195 mg	Sodium
		787 mg	Cholesterol

Beef, Pork and Lamb

Although there's no need to give up meat when planning a healthy diet, we do recommend limiting the amount you eat, and balancing your diet with other sources of protein that offer lower fat content. In our beef, pork, and lamb recipes, we've lowered the fat content even more with our cooking methods, and increased the taste by emphasizing the use of herbs and spices. We know these dishes will delight the entire family.

Steak Diane

An epicurean delight with the calories lowered for you!

Makes 4 servings

1-1/4	pounds sirloin strip steaks, sliced 1/2-inch thick
	Salt and pepper to taste
1	teaspoon dry mustard
2	tablespoons margarine
2	tablespoons lemon juice
2	teaspoons dried chives
1	teaspoon Worcestershire sauce

With a meat mallet, pound steaks to 1/3-inch thick. Sprinkle each side with salt, pepper and a little of the dry mustard. Rub the seasoning into the meat.

Preheat broiler.

Place meat on a rack in a broiler pan. Broil until meat is lightly browned on each side, turning once. Place meat on a serving dish.

While meat is browning, heat remaining ingredients to boiling in a small skillet over low heat.

Pour over meat to serve.

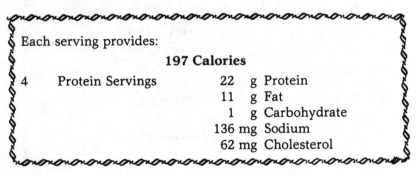

Each serving provides:

197 Calories

4	Protein Servings	22	g	Protein
		11	g	Fat
		1	g	Carbohydrate
		136	mg	Sodium
		62	mg	Cholesterol

Teriyaki Steak

This is our favorite for cookouts.

Makes 4   servings

1/4   cup soy sauce
2   teaspoons sherry extract
1/8   teaspoon garlic powder
1/4   teaspoon ground ginger
2   teaspoons honey
1-1/4   pounds boneless beef steak, fat removed
         (Veal steaks work well here, too.)

In a shallow pan, combine soy sauce, sherry extract, garlic powder, ginger and honey. Add steak. Marinate several hours, turning occasionally.

Preheat broiler or grill.

Place steak on a broiler pan or barbecue rack, reserving marinade. Broil, turning once and basting occasionally with reserved marinade, until done to taste.

Each serving provides:

270 Calories

4 Protein Servings	38	g Protein
10 Additional Calories	9	g Fat
	5	g Carbohydrate
	1464 mg	Sodium
	103 mg	Cholesterol

Meatloaf Florentine

Makes 4 servings

3/4	cup tomato sauce
1/2	teaspoon dried oregano
1/8	teaspoon garlic powder
1/4	teaspoon dried basil
1/8	teaspoon pepper
1	pound lean ground beef (or try ground veal or turkey)
1/4	cup plus 2 tablespoons seasoned Italian bread crumbs
1	10-ounce package frozen chopped spinach, thawed and drained well
4	ounces shredded Mozzarella cheese
1	tablespoon grated Parmesan cheese

Preheat oven to 350°.

In a small bowl, combine tomato sauce and spices.

In a large bowl, combine beef, crumbs, and 1/2 cup of the tomato sauce mixture. Mix well. Spread meat on a piece of wax paper, forming a rectangle about 8 x 10 inches.

Spread spinach over half of the meat. Top with Mozzarella cheese, still covering only half of the meat.

Fold meat over so that spinach and cheese are inside. Seal edges.

Transfer meat to a rack in a shallow baking pan. Top with remaining tomato sauce. Sprinkle with Parmesan cheese.

Bake 1 hour.

Each serving provides:

400 Calories

4	Protein Servings	30	g	Protein
1/2	Bread Serving	23	g	Fat
1-3/4	Vegetable Servings	15	g	Carbohydrate
8	Additional Calories	733	mg	Sodium
		110	mg	Cholesterol

Chili Meatloaf

This one is great!

Makes 4 servings

1-1/4   pounds lean ground beef (or veal)
1   tablespoon prepared mustard
2   tablespoons minced onion flakes
1   8-ounce can tomato sauce
1/8   teaspoon garlic powder
1/2   teaspoon dry mustard
1/2   teaspoon chili powder
        Salt and pepper to taste

Preheat oven to 350°.

In a large bowl, combine beef with remaining ingredients. Mix well.

Shape mixture into a loaf. Place on a rack in a shallow pan.

Bake, uncovered, 1 hour.

Each serving provides:

321 Calories

4 Protein Servings	26	g Protein
1 Vegetable Serving	21	g Fat
	6	g Carbohydrate
	412	mg Sodium
	96	mg Cholesterol

Barbecued Beef Loaf

Works just as well with ground veal or ground turkey . . .

Makes 6 servings

2   pounds lean ground beef
1   cup diced onions
1-1/2 teaspoons salt
1/4   teaspoon pepper
1/8   teaspoon garlic powder
2   teaspoons Worcestershire sauce
1   8-ounce can tomato sauce
      Sweetener equivalent to 2 tablespoons firmly-packed brown
       sugar
2   tablespoons prepared mustard
1   tablespoon vinegar

Preheat oven to 350°.

In a large bowl, combine beef, onions, salt, pepper, garlic powder, Worcestershire sauce, and 3/4 of the tomato sauce. Mix well.

Shape mixture into a loaf. Place on a rack in a shallow baking pan. Bake 20 minutes, uncovered.

Combine remaining tomato sauce, sweetener, mustard and vinegar. Pour over meat loaf.

Bake, uncovered, 40 minutes longer.

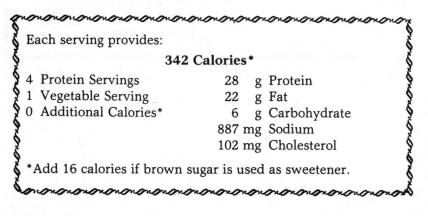

Each serving provides:

342 Calories*

4 Protein Servings   28   g Protein
1 Vegetable Serving   22   g Fat
0 Additional Calories*   6   g Carbohydrate
                      887 mg Sodium
                      102 mg Cholesterol

*Add 16 calories if brown sugar is used as sweetener.

Pepper Steak

Our variation of an old favorite . . .

Makes 4 servings

1-1/4 pounds round steak, sliced into 1/2-inch strips
1-1/2 teaspoons salt
1/8   teaspoon pepper
1   tablespoon plus 1 teaspoon vegetable oil
2   tablespoons chopped onions
1   clove garlic, minced
1   packet instant beef flavored broth mix
1-1/4 cups water
1   cup canned tomatoes, drained, chopped
2   green peppers, sliced into 1/2-inch strips
1   tablespoon plus 1 teaspoon cornstarch
2   teaspoons soy sauce

Sprinkle beef with salt and pepper.

Brown beef on a rack under broiler, turning once to brown on both sides.

In a large nonstick skillet, heat oil over medium-low heat. Add onions and garlic; cook, stirring, until onions are lightly browned.

Add cooked beef, broth mix and 1 cup of the water. Cover, reduce heat to low, and simmer 30 minutes, stirring occasionally.

Add tomatoes and peppers. Simmer 5 minutes.

Combine cornstarch, soy sauce and remaining 1/4 cup water. Stir until cornstarch is dissolved. Add to meat. Cook, uncovered, 5 minutes, stirring constantly.

Each serving provides:

240 Calories

4	Protein Servings	28	g Protein
1-1/2	Vegetable Servings	10	g Fat
1	Fat Serving	9	g Carbohydrate
12	Additional Calories	820	mg Sodium
		76	mg Cholesterol

Barbecued Franks

One of our children's favorites . . .

Makes 4 servings

8	ounces frankfurters, cut into 2-inch pieces (Use beef, turkey or chicken franks.)
1/4	cup sliced onions
2	tablespoons chopped celery
2	tablespoons chopped green pepper
1/2	cup tomato sauce
1/4	cup water
	Dash garlic powder
	Dash hot pepper sauce
2	teaspoons Worcestershire sauce
1	tablespoon prepared mustard
1	tablespoon vinegar
	Sweetener equivalent to 5 teaspoons firmly-packed brown sugar

Broil frankfurters on a rack, under the broiler, until brown on all sides.

In a large skillet, combine remaining ingredients. Cover and cook over medium-low heat until vegetables are tender, about 15 minutes. Uncover and cook 15 minutes longer. Stir in frankfurters. Heat through.

Each serving provides:

205 Calories

2	Protein Servings	7	g	Protein
3/4	Vegetable Serving	17	g	Fat
0	Additional Calories*	6	g	Carbohydrate
		812	mg	Sodium
		27	mg	Cholesterol

*Add 20 calories if brown sugar is used as sweetener.

Franks and Kraut

An easy, inexpensive family favorite . . .

Makes 4 servings

16   ounces beef, chicken or turkey frankfurters, sliced into 2-inch slices
1/2 cup chopped onions
2   small apples, coarsely shredded
1   16-ounce can sauerkraut, drained
1   16-ounce can tomatoes, chopped, undrained

Place franks on a rack in a broiler pan. Broil, turning occasionally, until brown on all sides.
Preheat oven to 350°.
In a 2-quart casserole, combine franks with remaining ingredients. Mix well.
Cover. Bake 45 minutes.

Each serving provides:

448 Calories

4   Protein Servings   15 g Protein
2-1/4   Vegetable Servings   34 g Fat
1/2   Fruit Serving   22 g Carbohydrate
                                  2158 mg Sodium
                                  54 mg Cholesterol

Hungarian Meatballs and Sauerkraut

A real "special" for a party . . .

Makes 4 servings

1-1/4 pounds lean ground beef (or ground veal or turkey)
     Salt and pepper to taste
1   cup diced onions
4   cups tomato juice
2   1-pound cans sauerkraut
1   tablespoon lemon juice
     Sweetener equivalent to 1 teaspoon sugar

Preheat oven to 350°.

Season meat with salt and pepper to taste. Shape meat into balls. Place on rack in a shallow baking pan. Bake, uncovered, 30 minutes, until brown.

Line the bottom of a large saucepan with diced onions. Add 1/2 cup of the tomato juice. Cook over medium heat until onions are tender, adding more tomato juice if necessary to prevent drying.

Layer meatballs and sauerkraut on onions.

Add lemon juice and sweetener to tomato juice and pour over meatballs.

Cover, reduce heat to low, and cook 1 hour.

Each serving provides:

394 Calories*

4	Protein Servings	30 g	Protein
1-1/2	Vegetable Servings	21 g	Fat
1	Fruit Serving	23 g	Carbohydrate
0	Additional Calories*	2239 mg	Sodium
		96 mg	Cholesterol

*Add 4 calories if sugar or fructose is used as sweetener.

Meat Sauce and Spaghetti Squash

Makes 2 servings

1/2	pound lean ground beef
	Salt and pepper to taste
1	tablespoon minced onion flakes
	Dash garlic powder
1	8-ounce can tomato sauce
1	teaspoon dried oregano
1/2	teaspoon dried basil
2	cups cooked, drained spaghetti squash†
1	tablespoon plus 1 teaspoon grated Parmesan cheese

Place beef on a broiler rack in a shallow pan. Sprinkle with salt and pepper to taste. Brown meat under broiler.

In a large saucepan, combine beef, onion flakes, garlic powder, tomato sauce, oregano and basil. Cook, covered, over medium heat for 10 minutes, stirring occasionally.

Preheat oven to 375°.

Add squash to beef mixture, toss to blend well. Pour mixture into a 2-quart casserole that has been sprayed with a nonstick cooking spray. Sprinkle with Parmesan cheese.

Bake, uncovered, 20 minutes.

†Note: To cook spaghetti squash – cut squash lengthwise, remove seeds, and place cut-side down in a shallow baking pan containing a small amount of water. Bake at 350° for 45 minutes. Drain. Pull strands free with a fork.

Each serving provides:

332 Calories

3	Protein Servings	24	g	Protein
3	Vegetable Servings	19	g	Fat
45	Additional Calories	19	g	Carbohydrate
		709	mg	Sodium
		79	mg	Cholesterol

Grilled Ham Steak

Makes 4 servings

1   ham slice, 1-pound, cut 1-1/2 inches thick
2   tablespoons margarine, melted
2   tablespoons plus 2 teaspoons reduced-calorie preserves or
          fruit spread, any flavor (16 calories per 2 teaspoons)
2   teaspoons dry mustard
1-1/2 teaspoons grated orange peel
1   tablespoon lemon juice

Place ham on a broiler rack or on a charcoal grill.
Combine remaining ingredients, mixing well.
Broil or grill ham 5 inches from heat for a total of 20 to 25
minutes, until done. Turn frequently while cooking, basting each
time meat is turned.
If any sauce is left, spread it on ham before serving.

Each serving provides:

237 Calories

4   Protein Servings   24   g Protein
1-1/2 Fat Servings   12   g Fat
16   Additional Calories   6   g Carbohydrate
                                       1431 mg Sodium
                                       60 mg Cholesterol

Ham Barbeque

Delicious over rice . . .

Makes 4 servings

1	tablespoon plus 1 teaspoon vegetable oil
1/2	cup chopped onions
2	cloves garlic, minced
1	teaspoon instant beef bouillon granules
1-1/2	cups tomato sauce
1-1/2	cups water
1/4	cup vinegar
2	tablespoons prepared mustard
1	tablespoon plus 1 teaspoon lemon juice
1	teaspoon Worcestershire sauce
	Sweetener equivalent to 2 tablespoons firmly-packed brown sugar
	Dash hot pepper sauce
16	ounces cooked ham, sliced paper-thin or shredded

Heat oil in a large nonstick skillet over medium heat. Add onions and garlic. Sauté until tender.

Add remaining ingredients, except ham. Cook on low heat until mixture has thickened slightly.

Stir in ham. Heat through.

Each serving provides:

263 Calories*

4	Protein Servings	26	g	Protein
1-1/4	Vegetable Servings	12	g	Fat
1	Fat Serving	13	g	Carbohydrate
18	Additional Calories*	2232	mg	Sodium
		60	mg	Cholesterol

*Add 24 calories if brown sugar is used as sweetener.

Roast Leg of Lamb

Delicious. The rosemary adds distinction.

Makes 8 servings

2   teaspoons seasoned salt
1   teaspoon dried rosemary, crumbled
1/4   teaspoon pepper
1   teaspoon dried thyme
1/2   teaspoon onion powder
       Dash garlic powder
1   6-pound leg of lamb

Preheat oven to 450°.
Combine seasonings and rub into meat, covering entire surface.
Place lamb on a rack in a shallow roasting pan and place in oven.
Reduce heat to 350°.
Roast 30 minutes per pound, or until done to taste.

Each serving provides:

213 Calories

4 Protein Servings, or as   33 g Protein
  desired (weigh   8 g Fat
  before serving)   1 g Carbohydrate
                                  387 mg Sodium
                                  113 mg Cholesterol

Lemony Lamb Chops

Makes 2 servings

12   ounces rib or loin lamb chops, 3/4-inch thick, fat removed
3   tablespoons water
1/8 teaspoon grated lemon peel
2   tablespoons lemon juice
2   teaspoons Worcestershire sauce
1/4 teaspoon salt
1/8 teaspoon dried oregano
1/8 teaspoon dried rosemary, crushed
     Pepper to taste

Broil chops on a rack under the broiler until brown on both sides.

Place browned chops in a medium nonstick skillet. Combine remaining ingredients and pour over lamb.

Cover. Cook on medium-low heat until chops are tender, about 30 minutes.

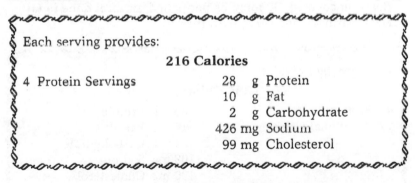

Each serving provides:

216 Calories

4 Protein Servings

28	g	Protein
10	g	Fat
2	g	Carbohydrate
426	mg	Sodium
99	mg	Cholesterol

Marinated Pork Roast

Makes 6 servings

2   tablespoons dry mustard
2   teaspoons dried thyme
1/2 cup dry red wine
1   teaspoon sherry extract
1/4 cup soy sauce
1/4 teaspoon garlic powder
1   teaspoon ground ginger
1   2-1/4 pound pork loin roast, boned, rolled and tied

In a small bowl, combine all ingredients, except pork. Pour into a self-sealing plastic bag. Add meat to bag and seal. Refrigerate 4 to 5 hours or overnight, turning bag over several times.

At cooking time, preheat oven to 450°.

Transfer roast to a rack in a shallow baking pan. Reserve marinade.

Place roast in oven and immediately reduce heat to 350°.

Roast, uncovered, 30 minutes per pound, or until done to taste.

Heat marinade and serve with roast.

Each serving provides:

335 Calories

4 Protein Servings
17 Additional Calories

35 g Protein
17 g Fat
4 g Carbohydrate
1108 mg Sodium
100 mg Cholesterol

Vegetables

Vegetables never had it so good! In these recipes we've taken into account the abundance of natural nutrients that vegetables provide, and the wide variety and tremendous assortment available to you. We've created ways to make garden vegetables "good enough for company," and yet easy to prepare.

Eat an abundance of vegetables every day. Remember, they fill you up, and not out.

Cooking Chart for Vegetables

Vegetable	Amount to Serve 4	Amount of Boiling Water	Cooking Time	Suggested Spices
Asparagus spears	2 lb.	1-inch	8 min.	lemon rind, basil, thyme
Beans, green or wax	1-1/2 lb.	1-inch	15 to 25 min.	basil, oregano, dill weed, thyme, rosemary
Beets, whole	2 lb.	to cover	1 to 1-1/2 hours	allspice, ginger, orange rind, cloves
Broccoli spears	2 lb.	1-inch	10 to 15 min.	dill weed, basil, thyme, lemon
Broccoli, flowerets	2 lb.	1-inch	5 min.	rind, tarragon
Brussels sprouts	1-1/4 lb.	1-inch	10 to 20 min.	same as broccoli
Cabbage wedges	1-1/2 lb.	2 to 3 inches	10 to 15 min.	savory, fennel, dill
Cabbage, shredded	1-1/2 lb.	2 inches	5 min.	
Carrots, sliced	1-1/2 lb.	1-inch	10 min.	cinnamon, allspice, nutmeg,
Carrots, whole	1-1/2 lb.	1-inch	20 min.	basil, orange rind
Cauliflower, whole	1 head	1-inch	20 to 30 min.	dill weed, basil, thyme, tarragon,
Cauliflower, flowerets	1 head	1-inch	8 to 10 min.	marjoram
Collards	2-1/2 lb.	1/2 inch	10 to 15 min.	lemon rind
Kale	2-1/2 lb.	1/2 inch	10 to 15 min.	marjoram, oregano mustard, nutmeg
Squash, zucchini, sliced	2 lb.	1-inch	8 to 10 min.	basil, marjoram, oregano
Squash, yellow, sliced	2 lb.	1-inch	8 to 10 min.	
Tomatoes, peeled, quartered	2 lb.	none	5 to 15 min.	bay leaves, oregano, basil, dill, marjoram
Turnips, peeled, whole	2 lb.	1-inch	30 min.	bay leaves, oregano, allspice

Basic Cooking Directions for Vegetables

Wash and trim vegetables before cooking. Bring water to a boil in a saucepan, over medium heat. Add vegetables, cover, and cook according to cooking time on chart (p. 226). Drain, sprinkle with any one of the suggested spices, and serve.

The weights and cooking times on the chart are approximate and may vary slightly with freshness of vegetables. The times given are for vegetables cooked to tender-crisp.

Eggplant Supreme

As an appetizer or side dish, it's the best!

Makes 8 servings

1	small eggplant, diced, unpeeled (3 cups)
1/2	cup chopped onions
1/2	cup chopped green peppers
1	4-ounce can mushroom pieces, drained
2	cloves garlic, minced
2	tablespoons plus 2 teaspoons vegetable oil
1	teaspoon salt
1/4	teaspoon pepper
1/2	teaspoon dried oregano
1	6-ounce can tomato paste
1/2	cup water
2	tablespoons red wine vinegar
8	stuffed olives, chopped
2	tablespoons plus 2 teaspoons sunflower seeds
	Sweetener equivalent to 1-1/2 teaspoons sugar

In a large nonstick skillet, combine eggplant, onions, green pepper, mushrooms, garlic and oil. Simmer, covered, over medium heat for 10 minutes, stirring occasionally. Add small amounts of water, if necessary, to prevent drying.

Add remaining ingredients. Reduce heat to low. Simmer, covered, for 30 minutes, stirring occasionally.

Place in bowl and chill thoroughly.

Serve cold.

Each serving provides:

99 Calories*

1-1/2	Vegetable Servings	3	g	Protein
1	Fat Serving	7	g	Fat
25	Additional Calories*	9	g	Carbohydrate
		594	mg	Sodium
		0	mg	Cholesterol

*Add 3 calories if sugar or fructose is used as sweetener.

Ratatouille

Makes 8 servings

1/4   cup vegetable oil
1   cup sliced onions
2   cloves garlic, minced
2   cups eggplant, peeled and cubed
2   cups zucchini, unpeeled, sliced thick
1   cup green pepper, cut into strips
2   cups canned tomatoes, drained (reserve juice)
1   teaspoon dried basil
1   teaspoon salt
1/2   teaspoon dried parsley
1/8   teaspoon pepper

In a large saucepan, heat the oil over medium heat. Sauté the onions and garlic until tender.

Add remaining ingredients. Cover and simmer 20 minutes, or until vegetables are tender.

Add the reserved tomato juice as necessary, to prevent drying.

Each serving provides:

98 Calories

2	Vegetable Servings	2	g	Protein
1-1/2	Fat Servings	7	g	Fat
		8	g	Carbohydrate
		352	mg	Sodium
		0	mg	Cholesterol

Italian Baked Spinach

This can also be made as a pie. Simply place mixture in a Bread Crumb Crust, page 413.

Makes 4 servings

1   tablespoon plus 1 teaspoon margarine
1/2   cup chopped onions
2   10-ounce packages frozen chopped spinach, thawed, drained well
1   ounce grated Parmesan cheese
3/4   cup part-skim ricotta cheese
1/4   teaspoon ground nutmeg
       Salt and pepper to taste
1/8   teaspoon garlic powder
1   8-ounce can tomato sauce
1/2   teaspoon dried oregano
1/2   teaspoon dried basil

Melt margarine in a large skillet over medium-high heat. Add onions and sauté until golden. Remove from heat.

Preheat oven to 350°.

Stir in spinach, Parmesan cheese, ricotta cheese, nutmeg, salt, pepper and garlic powder. Spoon mixture into a 9-inch pie pan that has been sprayed with a nonstick cooking spray. Smooth top of mixture with the back of a spoon.

Combine tomato sauce, oregano and basil. Spread evenly over spinach mixture.

Bake, uncovered, 25 minutes.

Let stand for 5 minutes before serving.

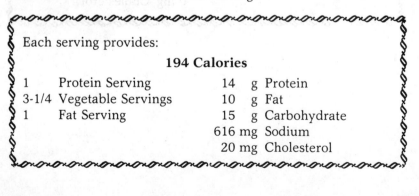

Each serving provides:

194 Calories

1   Protein Serving   14 g Protein
3-1/4   Vegetable Servings   10 g Fat
1   Fat Serving   15 g Carbohydrate
                                616 mg Sodium
                                 20 mg Cholesterol

Sweet and Sour Braised Onions

A unique blend of flavors . . .

Makes 4 servings

2   cups small white pearl onions, peeled†
1   cup canned tomatoes, chopped, drained
1   cup water
1   teaspoon instant chicken bouillon granules
1   teaspoon dry mustard
1-1/2 tablespoons wine vinegar
2   tablespoons vegetable oil
1/8   teaspoon pepper
1   bay leaf
1/4   teaspoon dried thyme
1   clove garlic, crushed
1/4   teaspoon salt
1/4   cup raisins
      Sweetener equivalent to 4 teaspoons sugar

Combine onions and all remaining ingredients in a medium saucepan over low heat. Cover and simmer 1 hour, or until onions are just tender. Serve hot or refrigerate and serve cold. Remove and discard bay leaf before serving.

†Note: To peel onions, drop them into a saucepan of boiling
    water. Boil 1 minute to loosen skin. Drain and peel.

Each serving provides:

133 Calories*

1-1/2 Vegetable Servings   2   g Protein
1-1/2 Fat Servings   7   g Fat
1/2   Fruit Serving   17 g Carbohydrate
2   Additional Calories*   502 mg Sodium
                              0   mg Cholesterol

*Add 16 calories if sugar or fructose is used as sweetener.

Almost-French-Fried Onion Rings

Makes 2 servings

1/4   cup plus 2 tablespoons dry bread crumbs
1/2   teaspoon salt
1/8   teaspoon pepper
1/2   large, sweet yellow onion, sliced 1/4-inch thick, separated
        into rings
1   egg white

Preheat oven to 450°.
Combine bread crumbs, salt and pepper in a small shallow bowl.
Dip each onion ring first in egg white, then in crumbs. Place on a
nonstick baking sheet.
Bake 10 minutes.

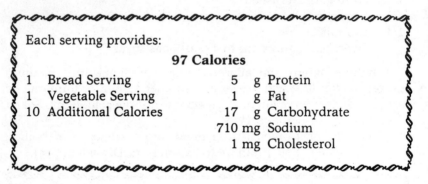

Each serving provides:

97 Calories

1 Bread Serving   5   g Protein
1 Vegetable Serving   1   g Fat
10 Additional Calories   17   g Carbohydrate
                            710 mg Sodium
                              1 mg Cholesterol

Green Beans and Tomatoes

A colorful blend of vegetables . . .

Makes 4 servings

1	10-ounce package frozen green beans
1	16-ounce can tomatoes, chopped, with juice
1/8	teaspoon garlic powder
1/2	teaspoon dried oregano
1/4	teaspoon salt

Cook beans in a medium saucepan according to package directions. Drain.

Add remaining ingredients. Heat through.

Each serving provides:

43 Calories

2 Vegetable Servings

2	g	Protein
0	g	Fat
9	g	Carbohydrate
282	mg	Sodium
0	mg	Cholesterol

Carrot Loaf

Makes 4 servings

1	1-pound bag of carrots, shredded (about 4 cups)
1	small onion, grated
2	slices white or whole wheat bread, crumbled
4	eggs
1	tablespoon soy sauce
1	packet instant chicken flavored broth mix
2	tablespoons all-purpose flour

Preheat oven to 350°.

Place shredded carrots and onion in a large bowl.

In a blender container, combine remaining ingredients. Blend until smooth. Pour over carrots. Mix well.

Place mixture in a 4 x 8-inch loaf pan that has been sprayed with a nonstick cooking spray.

Bake 50 minutes, until set and lightly browned.

Let loaf cool 5 minutes before serving.

Each serving provides:

169 Calories

1	Protein Serving	9	g	Protein
1/2	Bread Serving	6	g	Fat
2-1/4	Vegetable Servings	20	g	Carbohydrate
18	Additional Calories	693	mg	Sodium
		274	mg	Cholesterol

Apricot-Glazed Carrots

(shown on cover)

A nice side-dish for chicken or turkey . . .

Makes 4 servings

1	tablespoon plus 1 teaspoon margarine, melted
3	tablespoons reduced-calorie apricot spread (16 calories per 2 teaspoons)
1/4	teaspoon salt
1/4	teaspoon grated orange rind
1/4	teaspoon ground nutmeg
2	teaspoons lemon juice
4	cups carrots, sliced 1/4-inch thick

In a small bowl, combine margarine, apricot spread, salt, orange rind, nutmeg and lemon juice.

Place carrots in a medium saucepan. Cover with water. Bring to a boil. Cook over medium heat, covered, 2 minutes. Drain. Place in a serving bowl.

Spoon sauce over carrots. Toss and serve.

Each serving provides:

100 Calories

2	Vegetable Servings	1 g	Protein
1	Fat Serving	4 g	Fat
18	Additional Calories	16 g	Carbohydrate
		232 mg	Sodium
		0 mg	Cholesterol

Beets á l'Orange

Makes 4 servings

2   cups canned, small whole beets, undrained
2   teaspoons vinegar
2   tablespoons grated orange rind
2   tablespoons lime juice (*or* lemon juice)
1   cup orange juice (unsweetened)
1/2   teaspoon ground nutmeg
3   tablespoons cornstarch

Drain beets, reserving juice. Add water to juice, if necessary, to equal 1 cup.

In a medium saucepan, combine beet juice, vinegar, orange rind, lime juice, orange juice, nutmeg and cornstarch. Simmer over medium heat, stirring, until sauce is thick enough to coat a metal spoon.

Add beets. Heat through.

Each serving provides:

99 Calories

1 Vegetable Serving	2 g Protein	
1/2 Fruit Serving	0 g Fat	
15 Additional Calories	23 g Carbohydrate	
	295 mg Sodium	
	0 mg Cholesterol	

Mushrooms, Onions and Peppers

Makes 4 servings

2   tablespoons vegetable oil
1   cup thinly sliced green pepper
1   cup thinly sliced onions
2   cups sliced mushrooms
    Salt and pepper to taste

Heat oil in a large nonstick skillet over medium heat. Add green pepper and onions, and cook until vegetables are tender, about 5 minutes.

Add mushrooms. Cook, stirring frequently, until vegetables are tender-crisp, about 5 minutes.

Add salt and pepper to taste.

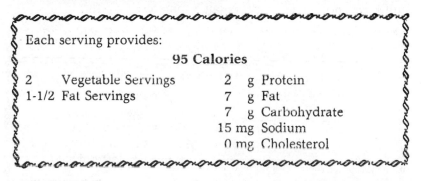

Each serving provides:

95 Calories

2	Vegetable Servings	2	g	Protein
1-1/2	Fat Servings	7	g	Fat
		7	g	Carbohydrate
		15	mg	Sodium
		0	mg	Cholesterol

Snow Peas Surprise

Simple to do and so delicious . . .

Makes 4 servings

2-1/2 cups fresh snow pea pods
2   tablespoons plus 2 teaspoons reduced-calorie margarine
1/2   cup chopped onions
1/2   teaspoon salt
1   teaspoon dried oregano
1   tablespoon soy sauce

Wash pods. Trim ends and remove strings.

Melt margarine in a large skillet over medium heat. Add onions and cook until tender, about 5 minutes.

Add pods, salt, oregano and soy sauce. Cook, stirring frequently, until pods are tender-crisp, about 5 minutes.

Each serving provides:

91 Calories

1-1/2 Vegetable Servings	3 g	Protein
1 Fat Serving	4 g	Fat
	13 g	Carbohydrate
	693 mg	Sodium
	0 mg	Cholesterol

Tomato Pie

Makes 6 servings

2   pounds fresh, ripe tomatoes, peeled
6   slices white or whole wheat bread, crumbled
2   tablespoons grated Parmesan cheese
2   tablespoons minced onion flakes
2   teaspoons dried oregano
     Salt and pepper to taste
     Sweetener equivalent to 1 teaspoon sugar
2   egg whites
1   tablespoon dry bread crumbs

Preheat oven to 375°.

In a blender container, combine tomatoes, bread, Parmesan cheese, onion flakes, oregano, salt, pepper, and sweetener. Blend until smooth. Pour into a large bowl.

In a medium bowl, beat egg whites on high speed of an electric mixer until stiff. Fold into tomato mixture gently, but thoroughly.

Pour mixture into a 9-inch pie pan that has been sprayed with a nonstick cooking spray. Sprinkle evenly with bread crumbs.

Bake 40 minutes, or until set and lightly browned. Let pie stand for 10 minutes before cutting.

This pie is also delicious chilled and served cold.

Each serving provides:

117 Calories*

1	Bread Serving	6	g Protein
1-1/2	Vegetable Servings	2	g Fat
22	Additional Calories*	21	g Carbohydrate
		178	mg Sodium
		2	mg Cholesterol

*Add 3 calories if sugar or fructose is used as sweetener.

Tomatoes Provençal

A delicious and colorful side dish . . .

Makes 4 servings

1   tablespoon plus 1 teaspoon margarine
1   cup chopped onions
1   cup fresh mushrooms, sliced
     Dash garlic powder
1   teaspoon seasoned salt
1   tablespoon all-purpose flour
1   tablespoon imitation bacon bits
2   pounds fresh tomatoes, cut into 1/2-inch slices
2   tablespoons grated Parmesan cheese

Preheat oven to 350°.

Melt margarine in a large nonstick skillet over medium heat. Add onions and mushrooms. Cook until onions are tender, about 5 minutes. Stir in garlic powder, seasoned salt, flour and bacon bits.

Place half of tomato slices in the bottom of a baking dish that has been sprayed with a nonstick cooking spray.

Spread mushroom mixture evenly over tomatoes.

Sprinkle with half of the Parmesan cheese, top with remaining tomatoes, and then sprinkle with remaining cheese.

Bake, covered, 30 to 40 minutes, until hot and bubbly.

Each serving provides:

131 Calories

2   Vegetable Servings   5   g Protein
1   Fat Serving   5   g Fat
30 Additional Calories   17 g Carbohydrate
                               483 mg Sodium
                               2 mg Cholesterol

Best Stewed Tomatoes

Makes 4 servings

3   cups canned tomatoes, undrained, cut into chunks
1/2   cup minced celery
1/2   teaspoon dried oregano
1/4   teaspoon dried basil
1   tablespoon minced onion flakes
1/2   teaspoon salt
2   teaspoons margarine
      Sweetener equivalent to 2 teaspoons sugar
      Dash pepper

Combine all ingredients in a medium saucepan. Cover and cook over medium-low heat until celery is tender, about 10 minutes. Stir frequently while cooking.

Each serving provides:

60 Calories*

1-3/4	Vegetable Servings	2	g Protein
1/2	Fat Serving	2	g Fat
0	Additional Calories*	9	g Carbohydrate
		544 mg	Sodium
		0 mg	Cholesterol

*Add 8 calories if sugar or fructose is used as sweetener.

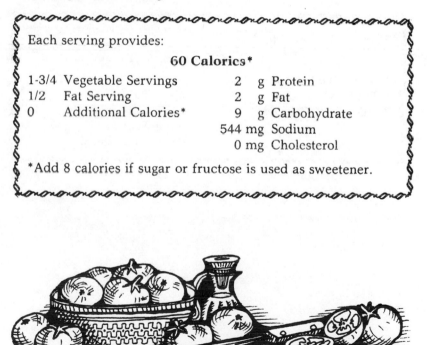

Savory Sprouts

Makes 4 servings

1	10-ounce package frozen Brussels sprouts
1	tablespoon plus 1 teaspoon margarine
1/8	teaspoon ground savory
1/4	teaspoon dried basil
1	packet instant chicken flavored broth mix
1/8	teaspoon pepper
	Dash nutmeg

Cook Brussels sprouts according to package directions. Drain.
While sprouts are cooking, melt margarine in a small saucepan
over medium heat. Add remaining ingredients and pour over
sprouts.
Toss and serve.

Each serving provides:

62 Calories

1 Vegetable Serving	3	g	Protein
1 Fat Serving	4	g	Fat
2 Additional Calories	6	g	Carbohydrate
	264	mg	Sodium
	0	mg	Cholesterol

Simmered Sauerkraut

Makes 4 servings

2 cups sauerkraut, drained
1 small apple, peeled, chopped
1 tablespoon minced onion flakes
1 teaspoon instant beef flavored broth mix
2 cups canned tomatoes, undrained, cut into small pieces
  Sweetener equivalent to 4 teaspoons firmly-packed brown sugar

In a medium saucepan, combine all ingredients. Cover. Bring to a boil over medium heat. Reduce heat to low. Simmer 30 minutes.

Each serving provides:

67 Calories*

2   Vegetable Servings   3 g Protein
1/4 Fruit Serving   1 g Fat
2   Additional Calories*   15 g Carbohydrate
                         1278 mg Sodium
                            0 mg Cholesterol

*Add 16 calories if brown sugar is used as sweetener

Mock Mashed Potatoes

Amazing! You'll make this over and over again.

Makes 4 servings

2	10-ounce packages frozen cauliflower
1	packet instant chicken flavored broth mix
1/8	teaspoon pepper
1	tablespoon minced onion flakes
1	tablespoon plus 1 teaspoon reduced-calorie margarine

Cook cauliflower according to package directions. Continue cooking until very tender. Drain.

Preheat oven to 375°.

Combine cauliflower and remaining ingredients in a blender container or food processor. Process until mixture is puréed.

Place mixture in a 1-1/2 quart baking dish that has been sprayed with a nonstick cooking spray.

Bake, uncovered, 10 minutes, or until hot.

Each serving provides:

53 Calories

2	Vegetable Servings	3	g	Protein
1/2	Fat Serving	2	g	Fat
2	Additional Calories	7	g	Carbohydrate
		271	mg	Sodium
		0	mg	Cholesterol

Lemon Broccoli

Makes 4 servings

2	10-ounce packages frozen broccoli spears or 1 pound fresh broccoli†
1/4	cup reduced-calorie margarine
1/4	cup chopped green onions
1/4	cup chopped celery
1	tablespoon plus 1 teaspoon lemon juice
1/4	teaspoon grated lemon rind

Cook broccoli according to package directions. Drain.

While broccoli is cooking, melt margarine in a small saucepan. Add onions and celery. Cook until tender. Stir in lemon juice.

Place broccoli in a serving dish. Pour onion mixture over broccoli. Sprinkle with lemon rind.

†Note: If using fresh broccoli, cook in 1-inch of boiling water, covered, until tender, about 10 to 15 minutes.

Each serving provides:

96 Calories

2-1/4 Vegetable Servings   5 g Protein
1-1/2 Fat Servings   6 g Fat
    9 g Carbohydrate
    174 mg Sodium
    0 mg Cholesterol

Cabbage with Mustard Sauce

Our favorite way to serve cabbage . . .

Makes 4 servings

1   small head cabbage, cut into 4 wedges
3   tablespoons reduced-calorie margarine
1   tablespoon minced onion flakes, reconstituted in a small amount of water
1   tablespoon plus 1 teaspoon flour
2   tablespoons water
1/4   teaspoon salt
     Pepper to taste
1/2   cup evaporated skim milk
1/2   cup water
2   teaspoons prepared horseradish
1   tablespoon prepared mustard

In a medium saucepan, bring 2 inches of water to a boil. Add cabbage, cover, and cook until tender-crisp, about 10 to 15 minutes. Drain.

While cabbage is cooking, melt margarine in a small saucepan. Stir in onion flakes.

Blend flour with 2 tablespoons water. Add to margarine, stirring. Add salt, pepper, milk and 1/2 cup water.

Cook, stirring, until mixture is thickened and bubbly. Stir in horseradish and mustard.

Place cabbage in 4 small serving bowls. Spoon sauce evenly over cabbage.

Each serving provides:

106 Calories

1-1/2	Vegetable Servings	5	g Protein
3/4	Fat Serving	5	g Fat
1/4	Milk Serving	13	g Carbohydrate
10	Additional Calories	351	mg Sodium
		1	mg Cholesterol

Zucchini-Mozzarella Casserole

An Italian-flavored delight . . .

Makes 4 servings

1	tablespoon plus 1 teaspoon margarine
4	cups thinly sliced zucchini, unpeeled
1/2	cup chopped onions
2	tablespoons dried parsley flakes
1/8	teaspoon garlic powder
1/2	teaspoon dried oregano
1/4	teaspoon dried basil
	Salt and pepper to taste
2	eggs, slightly beaten
6	ounces Mozzarella cheese, shredded
1	teaspoon Dijon mustard

Melt margarine in a large nonstick skillet over medium heat. Add zucchini and onions and cook 10 minutes, stirring frequently, until vegetables are tender-crisp. Remove from heat.

Preheat oven to 350°.

Stir parsley, garlic powder, oregano, basil, salt and pepper into zucchini.

In a large bowl, combine eggs, Mozzarella cheese and mustard. Add zucchini mixture and stir until mixture is combined. Pour into a casserole dish that has been sprayed with a nonstick cooking spray.

Bake, uncovered, 35 minutes, until lightly browned.

Each serving provides:

227 Calories

2	Protein Servings	13	g	Protein
1-1/4	Vegetable Servings	16	g	Fat
1	Fat Serving	9	g	Carbohydrate
		282	mg	Sodium
		170	mg	Cholesterol

Mealtime Zucchini Fritters

Makes 2 servings

2	eggs
2/3	cup lowfat cottage cheese
2	slices white or whole wheat bread, crumbled
1/4	teaspoon salt
1/8	teaspoon pepper
1/2	teaspoon double-acting baking powder
2	teaspoons vegetable oil
1/16	teaspoon garlic powder
1/4	teaspoon dried marjoram, crumbled
1/4	teaspoon dried thyme, crumbled
1	tablespoon minced onion flakes
1	cup finely shredded zucchini, unpeeled

In a blender container, combine all ingredients, except zucchini. Blend until smooth. Pour mixture into a bowl.

Drain zucchini on paper towels. Stir into egg mixture.

Preheat a nonstick griddle or skillet over medium-high heat. Drop batter onto griddle with a large spoon, making 4-inch fritters. Turn fritters carefully when edges appear dry. Brown lightly on both sides.

Divide evenly.

(To make turning the fritters easier, spray spatula with a nonstick cooking spray.)

Each serving provides:

253 Calories

2 Protein Servings	18	g Protein
1 Bread Serving	12	g Fat
1 Vegetable Serving	18	g Carbohydrate
1 Fat Serving	863	mg Sodium
	278	mg Cholesterol

Dessert Zucchini Fritters

A great way to get the children to eat vegetables . . .

Makes 2 servings

2	eggs
2/3	cup lowfat cottage cheese
2	slices white or whole wheat bread, crumbled
	Sweetener equivalent to 6 teaspoons sugar
	Dash salt
1/2	teaspoon double-acting baking powder
2	teaspoons vegetable oil
1	teaspoon vanilla extract
1/2	teaspoon ground cinnamon
1/4	teaspoon ground nutmeg
1/8	teaspoon ground allspice
2	tablespoons raisins
1	cup finely shredded zucchini, unpeeled

In a blender container, combine all ingredients, *except* raisins and zucchini. Blend until smooth. Pour mixture into a bowl. Drain zucchini on paper towels. Stir zucchini and raisins into egg mixture. Preheat a nonstick griddle, or skillet, over medium-high heat. Drop batter onto griddle with a large spoon, making 4-inch fritters. Turn fritters carefully when edges appear dry. Brown lightly on both sides. (To make turning the fritters easier, spray spatula with a nonstick cooking spray.) Divide evenly.

Each serving provides:

286 Calories*

2	Protein Servings	18	g	Protein
1	Bread Serving	12	g	Fat
1	Vegetable Serving	25	g	Carbohydrate
1	Fat Serving	659	mg	Sodium
1/2	Fruit Serving	278	mg	Cholesterol
0	Additional Calories*			

*Add 48 calories if sugar or fructose is used as sweetener.

Italian Baked Spaghetti Squash

Makes 4 servings

2 cups cooked, drained spaghetti squash†
1 8-ounce can tomato sauce
1/2 teaspoon dried oregano
1/8 teaspoon garlic powder
1 tablespoon plus 1 teaspoon grated Parmesan cheese

Preheat oven to 375°.

Place spaghetti squash in a 1-quart casserole that has been sprayed with a nonstick cooking spray.

Combine tomato sauce, oregano, and garlic powder and pour evenly over squash.

Sprinkle with Parmesan cheese.

Bake 20 minutes, or until hot and bubbly.

†Note: To cook squash, cut in half lengthwise. Remove seeds. Bake, cut-side-down in baking pan containing 1 to 2 inches of water, for 45 minutes at 350°. Drain. Pull strands free with a fork.

Each serving provides:

47 Calories

2 Vegetable Servings
10 Additional Calories

2 g Protein
1 g Fat
9 g Carbohydrate
330 mg Sodium
1 mg Cholesterol

Dilled Squash

A unique way to serve squash . . .

Makes 4 servings

2	tablespoons plus 2 teaspoons vegetable oil
1	cup chopped onions
1	clove garlic, minced
4	cups yellow summer squash, sliced 1/2-inch thick
1/2	teaspoon salt
1/8	teaspoon pepper
1	teaspoon dill weed

Heat oil in a large nonstick skillet over medium heat. Add onions and garlic; cook until onions start to brown.

Add squash and mix well with onions. Sprinkle salt, pepper and dill over squash.

Cover and cook, stirring frequently, for 10 minutes, or until squash is just tender-crisp.

Each serving provides:

122 Calories

2-1/2	Vegetable Servings	2	g	Protein
2	Fat Servings	9	g	Fat
		9	g	Carbohydrate
		275	mg	Sodium
		0	mg	Cholesterol

Baked Squash — Southern Style

This has been a family favorite for years.

Makes 4 servings

2   10-ounce packages frozen yellow summer squash
1   tablespoon minced onion flakes
2   tablespoons plus 2 teaspoons reduced-calorie margarine
2   egg whites
    Sweetener equivalent to 1-1/2 teaspoons sugar
1/2 teaspoon salt
1/8 teaspoon pepper
3   tablespoons dry bread crumbs

Cook squash according to package directions. Drain.
Preheat oven to 350°.
Place squash in a large bowl and mash well.
Add onion flakes, 2 tablespoons of the margarine, egg whites, sweetener, salt, pepper, and half of the crumbs. Mix well.
Pour mixture into a 1-quart baking dish that has been sprayed with a nonstick cooking spray. Sprinkle with remaining crumbs.
Dot with remaining margarine.
Bake, uncovered, 45 minutes, or until set and lightly browned.

Each serving provides:

90 Calories*

1/4	Bread Serving	4	g Protein
2	Vegetable Servings	4	g Fat
1	Fat Serving	10	g Carbohydrate
10	Additional Calories*	426	mg Sodium
		0	mg Cholesterol

*Add 6 calories if sugar or fructose is used as sweetener.

Italian Stuffed Squash

Squash never tasted so good.

Makes 4 servings

2 yellow or zucchini squash, about 8-ounces each
1 tablespoon plus 1 teaspoon margarine
1/2 cup minced onions
2 teaspoons grated Parmesan cheese
1 tablespoon plus 1-1/2 teaspoons dry bread crumbs
1/2 teaspoon dried oregano
1/4 teaspoon dried basil
Dash garlic powder
Dash pepper

Steam whole squash in 1-inch of boiling water for 5 minutes. Drain.

Cut squash in half, lengthwise. Carefully scoop out pulp with a spoon, leaving about 1/2-inch shell.

Chop pulp.

Heat margarine in a small skillet over medium heat. Add onions and sauté until lightly browned.

Preheat oven to 350°.

In a small bowl, combine onions, squash pulp and remaining ingredients. Mix well.

Pile mixture into squash shells. Place in a shallow baking dish that has been sprayed with a nonstick cooking spray.

Bake 30 minutes, or until lightly browned.

Each serving provides:

74 Calories

1 Vegetable Serving
1 Fat Serving
17 Additional Calories

2 g Protein
4 g Fat
8 g Carbohydrate
81 mg Sodium
1 mg Cholesterol

Starchy Vegetables

Starchy vegetables, while higher in calories than other vegetables, still offer us many essential nutrients. When eaten in place of a bread serving, a serving from our unique selection of recipes will add to your taste, but not to your waist.

Baked Orange Squash

A delicious way to serve squash . . .

Makes 4 servings

2   cups cooked, mashed butternut or acorn squash
1/4   cup frozen orange juice concentrate (unsweetened), thawed
        Dash ground ginger
1/8   teaspoon ground cinnamon
1/2   teaspoon grated orange peel
1   tablespoon plus 1 teaspoon reduced-calorie margarine
        Sweetener equivalent to 4 teaspoons firmly-packed brown
          sugar

Preheat oven to 375°.
In a medium bowl, combine all ingredients, mixing well.
Place mixture in a 1-quart baking dish that has been sprayed
with a nonstick cooking spray.
Bake, uncovered, 20 minutes.

Each serving provides:

94 Calories*

1	Bread Serving	2 g	Protein
1/2	Fat Serving	2 g	Fat
1/2	Fruit Serving	19 g	Carbohydrate
0	Additional Calories*	48 mg	Sodium
		0 mg	Cholesterol

*Add 16 calories if brown sugar is used as sweetener.

Pineapple Acorn Squash

A delicious blend of flavors . . .

Makes 4 servings

2   acorn squash, 10-ounces each
1   cup canned crushed pineapple (unsweetened)
1   teaspoon ground cinnamon
1/4   teaspoon imitation butter flavor
      Sweetener equivalent to 4 teaspoons sugar

Preheat oven to 400°.

Cut squash in half, lengthwise. Remove seeds. Place squash, cut side down, in a shallow baking pan. Pour hot water around squash to a depth of 1/2-inch.

Bake, uncovered, 40 minutes, until soft.

Carefully remove pulp from squash with a spoon. Place pulp in a small bowl and mash with remaining ingredients.

Pile mixture gently back into shells. Return squash to pan of water.

Bake, uncovered, 10 minutes.

Each serving provides:

85 Calories*

1	Bread Serving	2	g Protein
1/2	Fruit Serving	0	g Fat
0	Additional Calories*	22	g Carbohydrate
		2	mg Sodium
		0	g Cholesterol

*Add 16 calories if sugar or fructose is used as sweetener.

Whipped Spiced Parsnips

Makes 4 servings

12   ounces parsnips
     Sweetener equivalent to 2 teaspoons firmly-packed brown
     sugar
1/4 teaspoon grated orange peel
1/4 cup orange juice (unsweetened)
2   teaspoons margarine
     Dash salt
     Dash ground allspice
1/4 cup canned crushed pineapple (unsweetened)

Peel and slice parsnips. Cook, covered, in a small amount of boiling water until tender, about 15 to 20 minutes. Drain.

Preheat oven to 350°.

Mash parsnips in a bowl or food processor. Add sweetener, orange peel, orange juice, margarine, salt and allspice. Mix well.

Stir in pineapple.

Place mixture in a 1-quart baking dish that has been sprayed with a nonstick cooking spray.

Bake, uncovered, 15 minutes, until hot.

Each serving provides:

89 Calories*

1	Bread Serving	1 g	Protein
1/2	Fat Serving	2 g	Fat
1/4	Fruit Serving	17 g	Carbohydrate
0	Additional Calories*	63 mg	Sodium
		0 mg	Cholesterol

*Add 8 calories if brown sugar is used as sweetener.

Peas New Orleans

A colorful and tasty side dish . . .

Makes 4 servings

1   10-ounce package frozen green peas
2   tablespoons plus 2 teaspoons reduced-calorie margarine
1/4   cup chopped onions
1/4   cup chopped green pepper
1   16-ounce can tomatoes
        Salt and pepper to taste
        Sweetener equivalent to 1 teaspoon sugar
2   teaspoons cornstarch

Cook peas according to package directions. Drain.

In a medium saucepan, melt margarine over medium heat. Add onions and green pepper; cook until tender.

Drain and chop tomatoes, reserving liquid. Add tomatoes to saucepan.

Stir in peas, salt, pepper and sweetener.

In a small bowl, stir a few tablespoons of the tomato liquid into the cornstarch, stirring to dissolve the cornstarch. Add cornstarch mixture and remaining tomato liquid to peas.

Cook, stirring, until hot and bubbly.

Each serving provides:

120 Calories*

1	Bread Serving	5	g Protein
1-1/4	Vegetable Servings	4	g Fat
1	Fat Serving	17	g Carbohydrate
5	Additional Calories*	335	mg Sodium
		0	mg Cholesterol

*Add 4 calories if sugar or fructose is used as sweetener.

Peas and Mushrooms

Makes 4 servings

1   10-ounce package frozen green peas
1   4-ounce can mushroom pieces, drained
1   teaspoon onion powder
1   tablespoon plus 1 teaspoon reduced-calorie margarine
1/4 teaspoon dried savory, crushed
     Salt and pepper to taste

Cook peas according to package directions. Add mushrooms and heat through. Drain.
Add onion powder, margarine, savory, salt and pepper.
Toss and serve.

Each serving provides:

75 Calories

1 Bread Serving	4 g Protein
1/2 Vegetable Serving	2 g Fat
1/2 Fat Serving	10 g Carbohydrate
	252 mg Sodium
	0 mg Cholesterol

Potato Kugel

Mama will be envious!

Makes 4 servings

12   ounces potatoes, peeled
2   eggs, separated
1   small onion, grated
2   tablespoons all-purpose flour
1   tablespoon plus 1 teaspoon vegetable oil
1   teaspoon salt
1/4   teaspoon pepper
1   teaspoon double-acting baking powder

Preheat oven to 375°.

Grate the potatoes. Drain well.

Combine grated potatoes in a bowl with egg yolks, onion, flour, oil, salt, pepper, and baking powder. Mix well.

Beat egg whites in another bowl until stiff. Fold them into the potato mixture, gently, but thoroughly.

Spoon the mixture into a 1-1/2 quart baking dish that has been sprayed with a nonstick cooking spray.

Bake, uncovered, 1 hour, until set and lightly browned.

Each serving provides:

167 Calories

1/2	Protein Serving	6	g Protein
1	Bread Serving	7	g Fat
1/4	Vegetable Serving	20	g Carbohydrate
1	Fat Serving	679	mg Sodium
15	Additional Calories	137	mg Cholesterol

Buttermilk Potatoes

So creamy!

Makes 4 servings

12	ounces baking potatoes, peeled and quartered
1	tablespoon minced onion flakes
1/8	teaspoon garlic powder
1	8-ounce can mushroom pieces, drained
	Salt to taste
1/4	teaspoon pepper
1/4	teaspoon dried thyme
1/4	cup buttermilk
1	tablespoon plus 1 teaspoon wheat germ, *or* dry bread crumbs
2	tablespoons plus 2 teaspoons reduced-calorie margarine

Cook potatoes, covered, in boiling water, until tender, about 20 minutes. Drain.

Preheat oven to 400°.

In a medium bowl, mash potatoes. Add onion flakes, garlic powder, mushrooms, salt, pepper, thyme and buttermilk. Mix well.

Place mixture in a 1-quart baking dish that has been sprayed with a nonstick cooking spray.

Sprinkle with wheat germ.

Dot with margarine.

Bake, uncovered, 15 minutes, until hot and lightly browned.

Each serving provides:

126 Calories

1	Bread Serving	4	g Protein
1	Vegetable Serving	4	g Fat
1	Fat Serving	19	g Carbohydrate
18	Additional Calories	340	mg Sodium
		1	mg Cholesterol

Our Own Potatoes

A great lo-cal version of our favorite French Fries . . .

Makes 4 servings

2   6-ounce baking potatoes
2   teaspoons vegetable oil
       Salt to taste

Preheat oven to 450°.
Peel potatoes and cut them into strips. Place strips in a medium bowl. Drizzle with oil and toss to coat evenly.
Place potatoes on a nonstick baking sheet, in a single layer.
Bake 15 minutes. Turn potatoes; bake 15 minutes longer, or until desired crispness is reached.

Each serving provides:

72 Calories

1	Bread Serving	1	g Protein
1/2	Fat Serving	2	g Fat
		12	g Carbohydrate
		2 mg	Sodium
		0 mg	Cholesterol

Potato Latkes (Pancakes)

You'll love them topped with applesauce.

Makes 4 servings

6	ounces raw potatoes, peeled, cut into small cubes
2	slices white or whole wheat bread, crumbled
2	eggs
1	tablespoon plus 1 teaspoon minced onion flakes
1/2	teaspoon salt
1/8	teaspoon pepper

In a blender container, combine all ingredients. Blend until smooth.

Drop mixture by spoonfuls onto a hot, nonstick griddle or skillet that has been preheated over medium heat. (Makes eight 4-inch latkes.)

Brown latkes on both sides, turning carefully when edges appear dry.

Serve hot.

Each serving provides:

106 Calories

1/2	Protein Serving	5 g	Protein
1	Bread Serving	3 g	Fat
		14 g	Carbohydrate
		363 mg	Sodium
		137 mg	Cholesterol

Sweet Potatoes and Apples

Makes 4 servings

12   ounces cooked sweet potatoes, peeled, sliced lengthwise into thin slices

2   small, sweet apples, peeled, cut in half, and then cut into thin slices

1/4   cup frozen orange juice concentrate (unsweetened), thawed

1/4   cup water

      Sweetener equivalent to 6 teaspoons sugar

1/8   teaspoon ground ginger

1/4   teaspoon ground cinnamon

1/8   teaspoon ground nutmeg

1   tablespoon plus 1 teaspoon margarine

Preheat oven to 350°.

Arrange alternate slices of sweet potatoes and apples in a baking dish that has been sprayed with a nonstick cooking spray.

Combine orange juice concentrate, water, sweetener and spices. Pour mixture evenly over sweet potatoes and apples.

Dot with margarine.

Bake, uncovered, 1 hour.

Each serving provides:

183 Calories*

1 Bread Serving   2   g   Protein
1 Fat Serving   4   g   Fat
1 Fruit Serving   36   g   Carbohydrate
0 Additional Calories*   86 mg   Sodium
                         0 mg   Cholesterol

*Add 24 calories if sugar or fructose is used as sweetener.

Island Sweet Potato Pudding

Makes 4 servings

12   ounces cooked sweet potatoes, peeled, cut into chunks
1   medium, ripe banana, mashed
      Sweetener equivalent to 3 teaspoons firmly-packed brown
      sugar
2   tablespoons plus 2 teaspoons reduced-calorie margarine
1/4   teaspoon ground nutmeg
1   teaspoon rum extract
1   egg white

Preheat oven to 350°.

In a large bowl, combine sweet potatoes, banana, sweetener, margarine, nutmeg and rum extract. Beat on low speed of an electric mixer until mixture is smooth. Add a small amount of water, if necessary, to get a smooth consistency.

In a separate bowl, beat egg white until stiff. Fold into sweet potato mixture.

Spoon mixture into a casserole that has been sprayed with a non-stick cooking spray.

Bake, uncovered, 45 to 50 minutes, until lightly browned.

Each serving provides:

162 Calories*

1	Bread Serving	3 g	Protein
1	Fat Serving	4 g	Fat
1/2	Fruit Serving	28 g	Carbohydrate
5	Additional Calories*	147 mg	Sodium
		0 mg	Cholesterol

*Add 12 calories if brown sugar is used as sweetener.

Corn Soufflé

So creamy and rich-tasting . . .

Makes 4 servings

2   eggs, separated
1   1-pound can cream-style corn
1/2 cup skim milk
3   tablespoons all-purpose flour
     Sweetener equivalent to 2 teaspoons sugar
1   teaspoon minced onion flakes
1/2 teaspoon dry mustard

Preheat oven to 350°.

In a medium bowl, beat egg yolks until light. Stir in corn, milk, flour, sweetener, onion flakes and mustard.

In another bowl, beat egg whites until stiff. Fold whites into corn mixture.

Pour mixture into a 2-quart soufflé or baking dish that has been sprayed with a nonstick cooking spray.

Bake, uncovered, 45 minutes.

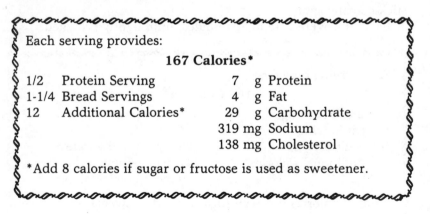

Each serving provides:

167 Calories*

1/2   Protein Serving   7 g Protein
1-1/4 Bread Servings   4 g Fat
12   Additional Calories*   29 g Carbohydrate
                              319 mg Sodium
                              138 mg Cholesterol

*Add 8 calories if sugar or fructose is used as sweetener.

Mexi-Corn

Makes 4 servings

1	tablespoon plus 1 teaspoon margarine
1/4	cup minced green pepper
2	tablespoons minced onion
2	tablespoons minced pimiento
1/4	cup water
2	cups cooked corn
	Salt and pepper to taste

Melt margarine in a medium saucepan over medium heat. Add green pepper and onion; cook until tender, about 10 minutes.

Add remaining ingredients. Heat through.

Each serving provides:

106 Calories

1	Bread Serving	3 g	Protein
1/4	Vegetable Serving	4 g	Fat
1	Fat Serving	17 g	Carbohydrate
		48 mg	Sodium
		0 mg	Cholesterol

Breads and Grains

Breads and grains provide essential nutrition. So, in keeping with this fact, we've provided a special grouping of breads and grains that offer the sound nutrition we all require, along with different textures and flavors that will add variety and pleasure to your meals.

Enjoy grains, such as cracked wheat and kasha and unusual breads, such as beer bread and scones. And, they've all been made lite for you.

Cooking Chart For Grains*

Grain	Number of Servings	Uncooked Amount	Amount of Water	Cooking Time	Cooked Amount
Barley	4	1/2 cup (4 oz.)	3 cups	50-60 min.	2 cups
Buckwheat	4	2/3 cup (4 oz.)	1-1/3 c.	8-10 min.	2 cups
Bulgur	4	3/4 cup (4 oz.)	1-1/2 c.	15-20 min.	2 cups
Brown rice	4	2/3 cup (4 oz.)	1-2/3 c.	50 min.	2 cups
Converted rice	4	2/3 cup (4 oz.)	1-2/3 c.	20 min.	2 cups
White rice	4	2/3 cup (4 oz.)	1-2/3 c.	20-30 min.	2 cups

BASIC COOKING DIRECTIONS FOR GRAINS

Rinse raw grain in cold water; drain.

Bring water to a boil in a saucepan over medium-high heat. Make sure that the saucepan is large enough to allow for the expansion of the grain during cooking.

Add grain and stir. Return to a boil, reduce heat to low, cover, and cook according to chart.

Drain and serve, or use in your favorite recipe.

(If grain is not soft enough, add a small amount of hot water and cook a little longer.)

Note: Some recipes call for baking as an alternative method of cooking grains. If using one of these recipes, do not boil grains first.

*These weights and measures are approximate and may vary with the size and quality of grains.

Raisin Rice Patties

Makes 4 servings

1/2 cup part-skim ricotta cheese
2 eggs
2 teaspoons vanilla extract
   Sweetener equivalent to 4 teaspoons sugar
2 teaspoons vegetable oil
1/4 teaspoon ground cinnamon
1 teaspoon double-acting baking powder
1 tablespoon all-purpose flour
1 cup cooked white or brown rice
1/4 cup raisins

In a blender container, combine all ingredients, *except* rice and raisins. Blend until smooth; pour mixture into a bowl.

Stir in rice and raisins.

Preheat a nonstick griddle or skillet over medium-high heat.

Drop mixture onto griddle, using about 2 tablespoons of batter for each patty. When the tops of the patties are slightly dry and bubbly, turn them carefully, browning both sides.

(Makes twelve 4-inch patties.)

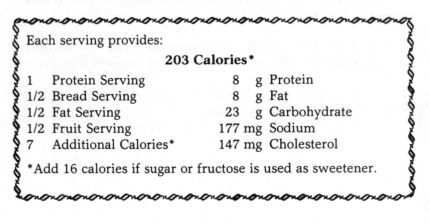

Each serving provides:

203 Calories*

1 Protein Serving   8 g Protein
1/2 Bread Serving   8 g Fat
1/2 Fat Serving   23 g Carbohydrate
1/2 Fruit Serving   177 mg Sodium
7 Additional Calories* 147 mg Cholesterol

*Add 16 calories if sugar or fructose is used as sweetener.

Oriental Fried Rice

In fine Chinese style . . .

Makes 4 servings

1	tablespoon plus 1 teaspoon vegetable oil
2	cups cooked white or brown rice
2	tablespoons soy sauce
	Dash garlic powder
	Dash ground ginger
1/2	cup sliced green onions
6	ounces cooked shrimp or chicken, diced
2	eggs, beaten

Heat oil in a large nonstick skillet over medium heat. Add rice, soy sauce, garlic powder, and ginger. Cook, stirring, until rice is hot.

Stir in onions. Cook, stirring, until onions are tender.

Add shrimp or chicken. Cook until heated through, still stirring.

Slowly stir in egg, a little at a time. Cook, stirring, until egg is set.

Each serving provides:

269 Calories

2	Protein Servings	17	g	Protein
1	Bread Serving	9	g	Fat
1/4	Vegetable Serving	27	g	Carbohydrate
1	Fat Serving	747	mg	Sodium
		187	mg	Cholesterol

Favorite Rice Casserole

A long-time family favorite . . .

Makes 8 servings

1/4	cup margarine
8	ounces uncooked white rice
1	8-ounce can mushroom pieces, drained
2	packets instant beef flavored broth mix
2	tablespoons minced onion flakes
2	cups water

Preheat oven to 350°.

Melt margarine in a 1-1/2-quart ovenproof saucepan or casserole over medium heat. Stir in rice. Cook, stirring, until rice is lightly browned. Remove from heat.

Add remaining ingredients.

Cover and bake 1 hour, stirring once after 45 minutes of cooking.

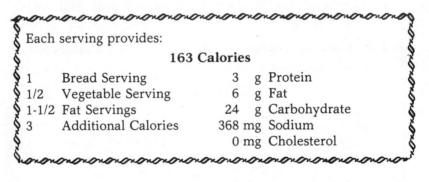

Each serving provides:

163 Calories

1	Bread Serving	3	g	Protein
1/2	Vegetable Serving	6	g	Fat
1-1/2	Fat Servings	24	g	Carbohydrate
3	Additional Calories	368	mg	Sodium
		0	mg	Cholesterol

Barley-Cheddar Sauté

An unusual and nutritious combination . . .

Makes 4 servings

1	tablespoon plus 1 teaspoon margarine
1/2	cup chopped green pepper
1/2	cup chopped onions
1	clove garlic, minced
2	cups cooked barley
1/2	small eggplant, peeled and cubed (about 1 cup)
1	small zucchini, cubed (about 1 cup)
1	teaspoon dried oregano
	Salt and pepper to taste
1	1-pound can tomatoes, chopped, drained slightly
4	ounces grated Cheddar cheese

Melt margarine in a large nonstick skillet over medium heat. Add green pepper, onions and garlic. Cook until tender, about 10 minutes.

Stir barley into onion mixture.

Add eggplant and zucchini. Cook, stirring, for 2 minutes.

Add oregano, salt, pepper, and tomatoes. Cook, stirring frequently, until eggplant and zucchini are tender-crisp, about 10 minutes.

Stir in cheese. Cook, stirring, until cheese is melted.

Serve hot.

Each serving provides:

283 Calories

1	Protein Serving	12	g	Protein
1	Bread Serving	14	g	Fat
2-1/2	Vegetable Servings	29	g	Carbohydrate
1	Fat Serving	375	mg	Sodium
		30	mg	Cholesterol

Buckwheat-Cheese Bake

Hearty and satisfying . . .

Makes 4 servings

1-1/3 cups lowfat cottage cheese
4   eggs
       Salt and pepper to taste
1   teaspoon dried parsley flakes
2   teaspoons minced onion flakes
1/2   teaspoon dried basil
1/2   teaspoon dried thyme
1   packet instant chicken flavored broth mix
2   teaspoons vegetable oil
1   tablespoon all-purpose flour
2   cups cooked buckwheat groats (kasha)

Preheat oven to 375°.

In a blender container, combine all ingredients, *except* buckwheat. Blend until smooth.

Stir in buckwheat; mix thoroughly.

Pour mixture into an 8-inch square baking pan that has been sprayed with a nonstick cooking spray.

Bake 30 minutes, until lightly browned. Cut into squares and serve hot.

Each serving provides:

255 Calories

2	Protein Servings	19 g	Protein
1	Bread Serving	9 g	Fat
1/2	Fat Serving	25 g	Carbohydrate
10	Additional Calories	581 mg	Sodium
		277 mg	Cholesterol

Baked Cracked Wheat

Makes 4 servings

1	tablespoon plus 1 teaspoon margarine
1/2	cup chopped onions
1	clove garlic, minced
4	ounces cracked wheat (bulgur)
1/4	teaspoon dried marjoram
1-1/2	cups water
2	packets instant beef flavored broth mix
1	4-ounce can mushroom pieces, drained

Preheat oven to 350°.

Melt margarine in a small skillet over medium heat. Add onions and garlic; cook until onions are lightly browned.

In a 1-quart casserole that has been sprayed with a nonstick cooking spray, combine onion mixture with bulgur.

Stir in remaining ingredients.

Cover and bake 30 minutes, or until liquid has been absorbed.

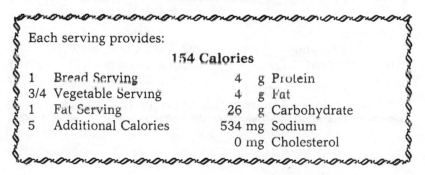

Each serving provides:

154 Calories

1	Bread Serving	4	g	Protein
3/4	Vegetable Serving	4	g	Fat
1	Fat Serving	26	g	Carbohydrate
5	Additional Calories	534	mg	Sodium
		0	mg	Cholesterol

Strawberries 'n Creme Breakfast Cereal

A delicious change-of-pace way to have your breakfast cereal . . .

Makes 1 serving

1/2   cup plain lowfat yogurt
1/2   teaspoon vanilla extract
       Sweetener equivalent to 2 teaspoons sugar
1/2   cup sliced strawberries, fresh or frozen (If frozen, thaw before using.)
3/4   ounce corn flakes, or any other dry, unsweetened breakfast cereal

In a serving bowl, combine yogurt, vanilla and sweetener. Stir in strawberries and cereal.

Enjoy.

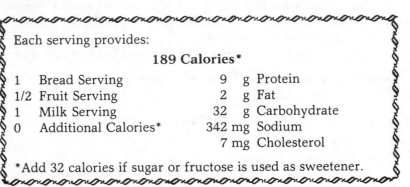

Each serving provides:

189 Calories*

1	Bread Serving	9 g	Protein
1/2	Fruit Serving	2 g	Fat
1	Milk Serving	32 g	Carbohydrate
0	Additional Calories*	342 mg	Sodium
		7 mg	Cholesterol

*Add 32 calories if sugar or fructose is used as sweetener.

Grape-Nuts® Raisin Pudding

A nice way to start the day . . .

Makes 2 servings

1   cup water
1-1/2 ounces Grape-Nuts® cereal
1   tablespoon plus 1 teaspoon quick-cooking tapioca
1/4   teaspoon maple extract
1/4   cup raisins, chopped
1   teaspoon vanilla extract
      Sweetener equivalent to 6 teaspoons firmly-packed brown
      sugar
      Ground cinnamon

Combine all ingredients, *except* cinnamon, in the top of a double
boiler over boiling water. Cook, stirring constantly, until mixture
thickens, about 5 minutes.
      Sprinkle with cinnamon.
      Serve warm.

Each serving provides:

165 Calories*

1	Bread Serving	3	g	Protein
1	Fruit Serving	0	g	Fat
20	Additional Calories*	38	g	Carbohydrate
		150	mg	Sodium
		0	mg	Cholesterol

*Add 48 calories if brown sugar is used as sweetener.

Apple Kugel

As good as the fattening kind!

Makes 4 servings

2/3 cup lowfat cottage cheese
2   eggs
1   tablespoon plus 1 teaspoon margarine, melted
1/2 teaspoon ground cinnamon
2/3 cup nonfat dry milk
1-1/2 cups water
     Sweetener equivalent to 6 teaspoons sugar
2   teaspoons lemon juice
1-1/2 teaspoons vanilla extract
2   cups cooked thin or medium noodles
2   small, sweet apples, peeled, coarsely chopped

Preheat oven to 350°.

In a blender container, combine all ingredients, *except* noodles and apples. Blend until smooth. Pour into a bowl and stir in noodles and apples.

Pour mixture into an 8-inch square baking dish that has been sprayed with a nonstick cooking spray. Sprinkle with additional cinnamon.

Bake, uncovered, 45 minutes, until set and lightly browned.

Each serving provides:

279 Calories*

1 Protein Serving	15 g Protein
1 Bread Serving	8 g Fat
1 Fat Serving	34 g Carbohydrate
1/2 Fruit Serving	300 mg Sodium
1/2 Milk Serving	165 mg Cholesterol
0 Additional Calories*	

*Add 24 calories if sugar or fructose is used as sweetener.

Pineapple Kugel For One

Go ahead, you're worth it!

Makes 1 serving

1	egg
1/3	cup lowfat cottage cheese
	Sweetener equivalent to 3 teaspoons sugar
1/4	cup plain lowfat yogurt
1	teaspoon vanilla extract
1/2	teaspoon vanilla butternut flavor
1/8	teaspoon ground cinnamon
1/2	cup canned crushed pineapple (unsweetened)
1/2	cup cooked thin noodles

Preheat oven to 325°.

In a blender container, combine egg, cottage cheese, sweetener, yogurt, vanilla, vanilla butternut, and cinnamon. Blend until smooth.

Add pineapple; blend 2 seconds.

Add noodles to mixture; mix gently.

Pour mixture into a small baking dish that has been sprayed with a nonstick cooking spray. Sprinkle with additional cinnamon, if desired.

Bake, uncovered, 40 minutes.

Serve hot or cold.

Each serving provides:

367 Calories*

2	Protein Servings	22	g Protein
1	Bread Serving	9	g Fat
1	Fruit Serving	45	g Carbohydrate
1/2	Milk Serving	411	mg Sodium
0	Additional Calories*	305	mg Cholesterol

*Add 48 calories if sugar or fructose is used as sweetener.

Parmesan Noodles

Makes 4 servings

3   ounces medium noodles
2   tablespoons margarine
1/16   teaspoon garlic powder
2   teaspoons dried parsley flakes
2   tablespoons grated Parmesan cheese

Cook noodles according to package directions; drain. Place noodles in a bowl and add remaining ingredients. Toss until well blended.

Serve warm.

Each serving provides:

146 Calories

1	Bread Serving	4	g Protein
1-1/2	Fat Servings	7	g Fat
15	Additional Calories	16	g Carbohydrate
		116	mg Sodium
		22	mg Cholesterol

Macaroni Parmesan

Makes 4 servings

2   cups cooked elbow macaroni
1/2 teaspoon salt
1/8 teaspoon pepper
1/8 teaspoon dried oregano
2   tablespoons minced onion flakes
4   ounces Cheddar cheese, shredded
2   tablespoons grated Parmesan cheese
1   cup evaporated skim milk
2   tablespoons dry bread crumbs
1/8 teaspoon dried basil
2   teaspoons margarine

Preheat oven to 375°.

Place half of the macaroni in a 1-quart baking dish that has been sprayed with a nonstick cooking spray.

On top of the macaroni, sprinkle half *each* of the salt, pepper, oregano, and onion flakes; then half *each* of the Cheddar and Parmesan cheese.

Pour half of the milk evenly over all.

Repeat.

Sprinkle with bread crumbs and basil.

Dot with margarine.

Bake, uncovered, 30 minutes.

Each serving provides:

290 Calories

1	Protein Serving	16	g Protein
1	Bread Serving	13	g Fat
1/2	Fat Serving	28	g Carbohydrate
1/2	Milk Serving	613	mg Sodium
30	Additional Calories	34	mg Cholesterol

Pasta á Pesto

Our favorite pasta dish . . .

Makes 4 servings

1/4	teaspoon salt
1/4	cup grated Parmesan cheese
1/8	teaspoon ground nutmeg
2	tablespoons plus 2 teaspoons vegetable oil
1	small clove garlic
1	tablespoon dried parsley flakes
1	tablespoon dried basil
2	cups cooked elbow macaroni

In a blender container, combine all ingredients, *except* macaroni. Blend until smooth.

Place macaroni in a bowl. Add Parmesan mixture and toss until blended.

Chill several hours.

To serve, bring pasta to room temperature and mix gently.

Each serving provides:

188 Calories

1	Bread Serving	5 g	Protein
2	Fat Servings	11 g	Fat
30	Additional Calories	18 g	Carbohydrate
		230 mg	Sodium
		4 mg	Cholesterol

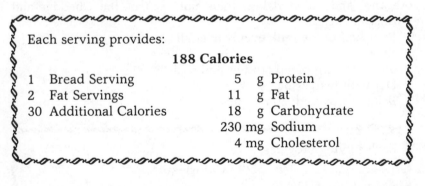

Pineapple Cheese Bread Pudding

Tastes almost like cheesecake . . .

Makes 4 servings

4	slices white or whole wheat bread, cut into cubes
1	cup canned crushed pineapple (unsweetened)
2	eggs
1/2	cup part-skim ricotta cheese
2	teaspoons vanilla extract
1	teaspoon lemon extract
1/2	teaspoon ground cinnamon
2	cups skim milk
	Sweetener equivalent to 8 teaspoons sugar

Preheat oven to 350°.

Place bread cubes in an 8-inch square baking pan that has been sprayed with a nonstick cooking spray. Spread pineapple evenly over the bread.

In a blender container, combine remaining ingredients. Blend until smooth. Pour mixture evenly over bread and pineapple. Let stand 5 minutes. Sprinkle with additional cinnamon, if desired.

Bake, uncovered, 35 to 40 minutes, until set.

Chill and cut into squares to serve.

Each serving provides:

240 Calories*

1	Protein Serving	13	g Protein
1	Bread Serving	6	g Fat
1/2	Fruit Serving	29	g Carbohydrate
1/2	Milk Serving	255	mg Sodium
0	Additional Calories*	150	mg Cholesterol

*Add 32 calories if sugar or fructose is used as sweetener.

Banana Bran Muffins

How can healthy taste so good?

Makes 6 servings

3/4   cup all-purpose flour
1/2   teaspoon baking soda
1   teaspoon double-acting baking powder
1-1/2   ounces bran cereal flakes, slightly crushed
2   tablespoons vegetable oil
1   egg, slightly beaten
1   teaspoon vanilla extract
1-1/2   medium, ripe bananas, mashed
        Sweetener equivalent to 9 teaspoons sugar

Preheat oven to 375°.

In a medium bowl, sift flour, baking soda, and baking powder. Stir in cereal.

In a larger bowl, combine remaining ingredients. Beat with a fork or wire whisk until well blended.

Stir dry ingredients into wet mixture. Stir just until all ingredients are moistened.

Spoon batter evenly into 6 nonstick muffin cups, or ones that have been sprayed well with a nonstick cooking spray.

Bake 20 to 30 minutes, until lightly browned. Remove muffins to a rack to cool, or serve hot.

Each serving provides:

164 Calories*

1	Bread Serving	4	g	Protein
1	Fat Serving	6	g	Fat
1/2	Fruit Serving	25	g	Carbohydrate
8	Additional Calories*	165	mg	Sodium
		46	mg	Cholesterol

*Add 24 calories if sugar or fructose is used as sweetener.

Multi-Grain Apple Muffins

(shown on cover)

Makes 8 servings

1-1/2 ounces uncooked quick-cooking oats
3/4   cup all-purpose flour
1-1/2 ounces bran flakes cereal, slightly crushed
1-1/2 teaspoons double-acting baking powder
1/2   teaspoon ground cinnamon
1/4   teaspoon salt
       Sweetener equivalent to 6 teaspoons firmly-packed brown
       sugar
1   egg
1/4   cup plus 2 tablespoons skim milk
2   tablespoons plus 2 teaspoons vegetable oil
1   tablespoon honey
1   small, sweet apple, peeled, chopped into 1/4-inch pieces
1/4   cup plus 2 tablespoons raisins

Preheat oven to 400°. In a medium bowl, combine oats, flour, bran flakes, baking powder, cinnamon and salt. Mix well with a fork. In a larger bowl, combine sweetener, egg, milk, oil and honey. Beat with a fork or wire whisk until blended. Stir in apple and raisins. Add dry ingredients to wet mixture, stirring until all ingredients are moistened. Divide mixture evenly into 8 muffin cups that have been sprayed with a nonstick cooking spray. Press batter down gently with the back of a spoon.

Bake 12 to 15 minutes, until lightly browned. Remove muffins to a rack to cool, or serve hot.

Each serving provides:

173 Calories*

1	Bread Serving	4	g Protein
1	Fat Serving	6	g Fat
1/2	Fruit Serving	27	g Carbohydrate
19	Additional Calories*	210	mg Sodium
		34	mg Cholesterol

*Add 12 calories if brown sugar is used as sweetener.

Cheddar 'n Onion Muffins

The subtle onion flavor makes this a favorite.

Makes 4 servings

2   slices white or whole wheat bread, crumbled
1/3   cup nonfat dry milk
2   eggs
2   ounces shredded Cheddar cheese
1   tablespoon plus 1 teaspoon reduced-calorie margarine
2   teaspoons double-acting baking powder
1   tablespoon plus 1-1/2 teaspoons minced onion flakes
      Sweetener equivalent to 2 teaspoons sugar

Preheat oven to 350°.
In a blender container, combine all ingredients. Blend 1 minute.
Divide mixture evenly into 4 nonstick muffin cups.
Bake 15 minutes, until golden.
Cool muffins in pan 10 minutes. Remove to a rack to finish cooling, or serve warm.

Each serving provides:

171 Calories*

1	Protein Servings	10	g Protein
1/2	Bread Serving	10	g Fat
1/2	Fat Serving	11	g Carbohydrate
1/4	Milk Serving	465	mg Sodium
0	Additional Calories*	154	mg Cholesterol

*Add 8 calories if sugar or fructose is used as sweetener.

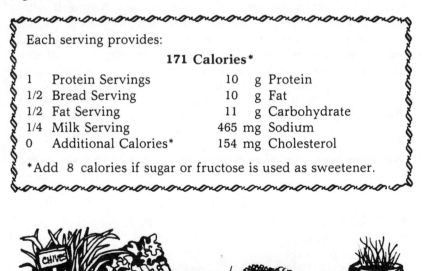

Zucchini Muffins

A family favorite for years . . .

Makes 8 servings

3/4   cup all-purpose flour
1/2   teaspoon double-acting baking powder
3/4   teaspoon ground cinnamon
1/4   teaspoon ground nutmeg
1/2   teaspoon baking soda
1/8   teaspoon salt
       Sweetener equivalent to 8 teaspoons sugar
1/2   teaspoon vanilla extract
2   tablespoons water
1   tablespoon plus 1 teaspoon vegetable oil
2   eggs
1   cup shredded, unpeeled zucchini
1/4   cup raisins

Preheat oven to 350°.

In a small bowl, combine flour, baking powder, cinnamon, nut-meg, baking soda, and salt. Mix well with a fork. In a larger bowl, combine sweetener, vanilla, water, oil and eggs. Beat on low speed of an electric mixer until blended. Add dry ingredients, beating on low speed until all ingredients are just moistened. Stir in zucchini and raisins. Spoon mixture evenly into 8 nonstick muffin cups.

Bake 15 to 17 minutes, until lightly browned.

Cool muffins in pan 10 minutes. Then remove to a rack to finish cooling, or serve warm.

Each serving provides:

102 Calories*

1/4	Protein Serving	3	g Protein
1/2	Bread Serving	4	g Fat
1/4	Vegetable Serving	14	g Carbohydrate
1/2	Fat Serving	93	mg Sodium
1/4	Fruit Serving	69	mg Cholesterol
0	Additional Calories*		

*Add 16 calories if sugar or fructose is used as sweetener.

Pumpkin Apple Muffins

Makes 6 servings

1	cup plus 2 tablespoons all-purpose flour
1/2	teaspoon double-acting baking powder
1/4	teaspoon baking soda
1/8	teaspoon salt
1/2	teaspoon ground cinnamon
1/4	teaspoon ground nutmeg
1/4	teaspoon ground cloves
1/8	teaspoon ground ginger
	Sweetener equivalent to 12 teaspoons sugar
2	tablespoons margarine, melted
1	egg, slightly beaten
1/2	teaspoon vanilla extract
1/2	teaspoon vanilla butternut flavor
1/2	cup canned pumpkin
1	small, sweet apple, peeled, coarsely shredded.
1/4	cup raisins

Preheat oven to 350°. In a medium bowl, stir together flour, baking powder, baking soda, salt and spices. In a larger bowl, combine sweetener, margarine, egg, vanilla, and vanilla butternut. Beat with a fork or wire whisk until blended. Beat in pumpkin. Add dry ingredients to pumpkin mixture; mix until all ingredients are moistened. (Batter will be dry.) Add apple and raisins. Mix thoroughly. Divide mixture evenly into 6 nonstick muffin cups.

Bake 35 minutes, until browned. Remove muffins to a rack to cool.

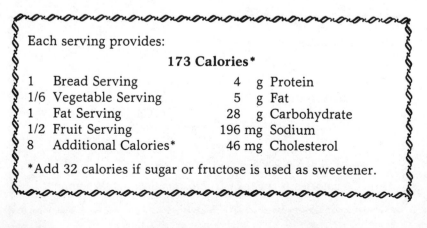

Each serving provides:

173 Calories*

1	Bread Serving	4 g	Protein
1/6	Vegetable Serving	5 g	Fat
1	Fat Serving	28 g	Carbohydrate
1/2	Fruit Serving	196 mg	Sodium
8	Additional Calories*	46 mg	Cholesterol

*Add 32 calories if sugar or fructose is used as sweetener.

Cinnamon Yogurt Muffins

Makes 8 servings

1-1/2 cups all-purpose flour
1-1/2 teaspoons double-acting baking powder
3/4   teaspoon baking soda
2   teaspoons ground cinnamon
1/4   teaspoon ground nutmeg
1/8   teaspoon salt
1   egg
1/2   cup plain lowfat yogurt
2   tablespoons plus 2 teaspoons margarine, melted
1-1/2 teaspoons vanilla extract
       Sweetener equivalent to 10 teaspoons sugar

Preheat oven to 400°.

In a medium bowl, sift flour, baking powder, baking soda, cinnamon, nutmeg and salt.

In a larger bowl, combine remaining ingredients. Beat on low speed of an electric mixer until blended.

Stir in dry ingredients. Mix by hand until all ingredients are moistened. (Batter will be stiff.)

Divide batter evenly into 8 nonstick muffin cups, or ones that have been sprayed with a nonstick cooking spray.

Bake 12 minutes, until lightly browned. Remove muffins to a rack to cool, or serve hot for best flavor.

Each serving provides:

146 Calories*

1	Bread Serving	4	g	Protein
1	Fat Serving	5	g	Fat
18	Additional Calories*	20	g	Carbohydrate
		196	mg	Sodium
		35	mg	Cholesterol

*Add 20 calories if sugar or fructose is used as sweetener.

Jelly Muffins

The jelly's inside the muffin!

Makes 4 servings

3/4   cup all-purpose flour
       Sweetener equivalent to 4 teaspoons sugar
1/4   teaspoon baking soda
1/4   teaspoon salt
1/2   cup plain lowfat yogurt
1   tablespoon plus 1 teaspoon margarine, melted
4   teaspoons reduced-calorie jelly or preserves, any flavor (16
       calories per 2 teaspoons)

Preheat oven to 400°.

In a medium bowl, combine flour, sweetener, baking soda and salt. Add yogurt and melted margarine, stirring until dry ingredients are just moistened.

Using half the batter, fill 4 nonstick muffin cups about half full. With your thumb, make a dent in the center of each muffin. Place 1 teaspoon of the jelly in the center of each.

Divide remaining batter evenly over jelly.

Bake 20 minutes, until lightly browned.

Cool in pan 10 minutes. Run a knife carefully around the edge of each muffin, and remove to a rack to finish cooling. For best flavor, serve warm.

Each serving provides:

147 Calories*

1	Bread Serving	4	g Protein
1	Fat Serving	4	g Fat
1/4	Milk Serving	22	g Carbohydrate
8	Additional Calories*	213	mg Sodium
		2	mg Cholesterol

*Add 16 calories if sugar or fructose is used as sweetener.

Pumpkin Bread

Too delicious to be so easy!

Makes 8 servings

1	cup canned pumpkin
4	eggs
2	slices whole wheat bread, crumbled
2	teaspoons vegetable oil
1-1/3	cups nonfat dry milk
1-1/2	teaspoons double-acting baking powder
1	teaspoon vanilla extract
1/2	teaspoon orange extract
1	teaspoon ground cinnamon
1/4	teaspoon ground cloves
1/4	teaspoon ground ginger
1/2	teaspoon ground nutmeg
	Sweetener equivalent to 12 teaspoons sugar

Preheat oven to 350°.

In a blender container, combine pumpkin, eggs, bread and oil. Blend until smooth.

Add remaining ingredients. Blend until all ingredients are moistened. Continue to blend for 1 minute.

Pour batter into a 4 x 8-inch nonstick loaf pan, or one that has been sprayed with a nonstick cooking spray.

Bake 35 to 40 minutes, until brown.

Cool in pan.

Each serving provides:

123 Calories*

1/2	Protein Serving	8	g Protein
1/4	Bread Serving	4	g Fat
1/4	Vegetable Serving	12	g Carbohydrate
1/2	Milk Serving	281 mg	Sodium
12	Additional Calories*	139 mg	Cholesterol

*Add 24 calories if sugar or fructose is used as sweetener.

Orange Raisin Bread

Makes 5 servings

1/4   cup boiling water
1/2   cup raisins
1   small orange
      Sweetener equivalent to 9 teaspoons sugar
1   egg white
1   teaspoon vanilla extract
2-1/2 teaspoons vegetable oil
1   cup *minus* 1 tablespoon all-purpose flour
1/2   teaspoon double-acting baking powder
1/2   teaspoon baking soda
1/8   teaspoon salt
1/2   teaspoon ground cinnamon
1/4   teaspoon ground nutmeg
1/4   teaspoon ground ginger

Preheat oven to 325°. Pour boiling water over raisins in a small bowl; set aside. Grate the orange, saving the rind. Peel off and discard the white membrane. Cut up orange pulp. Place the orange pulp, raisins and water in a blender container. Blend for a few seconds, until raisins are just chopped. Do not purée. In a large bowl, combine raisin mixture, orange rind, sweetener, egg white, vanilla and oil. Mix with a spoon. Sift flour, baking powder, baking soda, salt and spices. Add to wet ingredients, stirring until moistened. Place batter in a 4 x 8-inch nonstick loaf pan, or one that has been sprayed with a nonstick cooking spray. Bake 35 minutes, until lightly browned. Cool in pan 10 minutes. Remove to a rack to finish cooling. Serve warm or cool.

Each serving provides:

169 Calories*

1	Bread Serving	4	g Protein
1/2	Fat Serving	3	g Fat
1	Fruit Serving	34	g Carbohydrate
4	Additional Calories*	132	mg Sodium
		0	mg Cholesterol

*Add 28 calories if sugar or fructose is used as sweetener.

Skillet Cheese Corn Bread

Great on a cold morning . . .

Makes 4 servings

3	ounces cornmeal
1	teaspoon double-acting baking powder
1/4	teaspoon salt
1	tablespoon plus 1 teaspoon reduced-calorie margarine
1/2	cup plain lowfat yogurt
2	eggs, slightly beaten
2	ounces grated Cheddar cheese
2	teaspoons vegetable oil

Preheat oven to 400°.

In a medium bowl, combine cornmeal, baking powder, and salt. Add the margarine, yogurt, eggs and cheese. Stir until blended.

Heat the oil in a large cast iron skillet over medium heat. Pour the hot oil into the cornmeal mixture; stir until combined. Pour mixture into the skillet.

Bake 20 minutes, until lightly browned.

Cut into wedges and serve hot.

Each serving provides:

203 Calories

1	Protein Serving	9	g Protein
1	Bread Serving	12	g Fat
1	Fat Serving	14	g Carbohydrate
1/4	Milk Serving	426	mg Sodium
		154	mg Cholesterol

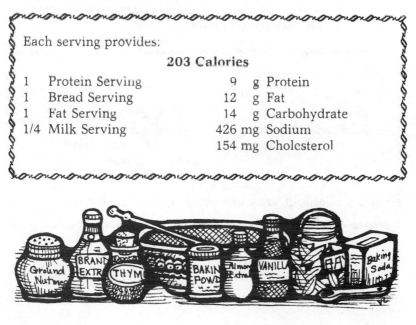

Beer Bread

The texture is divine!

Makes 12 servings

2-1/4 cups all-purpose flour
2-1/4 teaspoons double-acting baking powder
1   teaspoon salt
       Sweetener equivalent to 6 teaspoons sugar
1   12-ounce can beer, at room temperature

Preheat oven to 375°.

In a large bowl, sift flour, baking powder, salt and sweetener. (If using a liquid sweetener, add it with the beer.)

Add beer. Stir until foam subsides and all ingredients are moistened.

Place dough in a 4 x 8-inch loaf pan that has been sprayed with a nonstick cooking spray. (Dough will be loose.)

Bake 45 to 50 minutes, until golden brown.

Cool bread in pan 5 minutes. Then remove to a rack to finish cooling.

Variation: For a delicious rye bread, add 1/8 teaspoon garlic powder to dry ingredients, and stir 1 teaspoon caraway seeds in with the beer.

Each serving provides:

93 Calories*

1	Bread Serving	3	g Protein
12	Additional Calories*	0	g Fat
		20	g Carbohydrate
		259	mg Sodium
		0	mg Cholesterol

*Add 8 calories if sugar or fructose is used as sweetener.

Scones

A Scottish treat . . .

Makes 8 servings

1/4   cup raisins
1-1/2   cups all-purpose flour
1/8   teaspoon salt
1   teaspoon double-acting baking powder
1/2   teaspoon baking soda
2   tablespoons plus 2 teaspoons margarine
1   egg, slightly beaten
1/2   cup plain lowfat yogurt
1/4   teaspoon grated lemon peel
        Sweetener equivalent to 6 teaspoons sugar

Preheat oven to 400°.

Place raisins in a bowl and sprinkle with 1-1/2 teaspoons of the flour. Stir to coat raisins. Set aside. Sift remaining flour, salt, baking powder, and baking soda. Add margarine, cutting it into the flour with 2 knives, until mixture resembles coarse crumbs. Combine egg, yogurt, lemon peel and sweetener, mixing well. Stir in raisins. Add egg mixture to dry ingredients, mixing until all ingredients are moistened. Divide mixture evenly into 8 portions. Wetting your hands slightly to keep dough from sticking, shape each section into a ball. Place on a nonstick baking sheet, or one that has been sprayed with a nonstick cooking spray. Flatten each ball to 1/2-inch thick with the palm of your hand.

Bake 12 to 15 minutes, until golden. Remove to a rack.

Serve warm for best flavor.

Each serving provides:

154 Calories*

1	Bread Serving	4	g Protein
1	Fat Serving	5	g Fat
1/4	Fruit Serving	23	g Carbohydrate
18	Additional Calories*	164	mg Sodium
		35	mg Cholesterol

*Add 12 calories if sugar or fructose is used as sweetener.

Quick Onion Biscuits

1-2-3 done!

Makes 5 servings

2-1/2 teaspoons margarine, melted
2-1/2 teaspoons minced onion flakes
1   5-ounce package refrigerator biscuits (5 biscuits)

Preheat oven to 450°.
Combine margarine and onion flakes in a small bowl.
Place biscuits on a nonstick baking sheet. With your finger, make a large dent in the center of each biscuit. Fill the dents with the onion mixture, dividing it evenly.
Bake 8 to 10 minutes, until golden.
Remove from pan immediately and serve hot.

Each serving provides:

97 Calories

1	Bread Serving	2 g	Protein
1/2	Fat Serving	4 g	Fat
		14 g	Carbohydrate
		269 mg	Sodium
		0 mg	Cholesterol

Onion Rolls

Makes 6 servings

1	cup plus 2 tablespoons all-purpose flour
3/4	teaspoon baking soda
1	packet instant beef flavored broth mix
1	tablespoon minced onion flakes
2	tablespoons margarine, melted
1	egg
2	teaspoons honey
1/4	cup plus 2 tablespoons plain lowfat yogurt

Preheat oven to 375°.

In a small bowl, combine flour, baking soda, broth mix and onion flakes.

In a larger bowl, combine remaining ingredients, beating with a fork until blended.

Add dry ingredients to wet mixture. Mix with a spoon until all ingredients are moistened. Knead dough a few times until it holds together.

Divide dough evenly into 6 nonstick muffin cups.

Bake 12 minutes, until golden. Remove rolls to a rack to cool, or serve hot.

Each serving provides:

154 Calories

1	Bread Serving	5	g	Protein
1	Fat Serving	5	g	Fat
30	Additional Calories	22	g	Carbohydrate
		219	mg	Sodium
		47	mg	Cholesterol

Onion Bread

Makes 12 servings

Preheat oven to 375°.

Prepare dough for Onion Rolls on page 297, *doubling* all ingredients.

Spoon dough into a 4 x 8-inch nonstick loaf pan.

Bake 35 minutes, until crusty and brown.

Remove bread to a rack to cool.

To serve, slice into 12 thick slices or 24 thin slices.

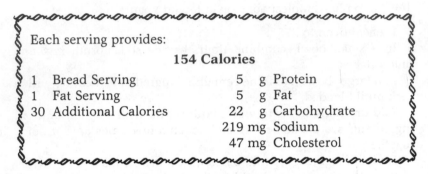

Each serving provides:

154 Calories

1	Bread Serving	5 g	Protein
1	Fat Serving	5 g	Fat
30	Additional Calories	22 g	Carbohydrate
		219 mg	Sodium
		47 mg	Cholesterol

Sweet Potato Rolls

Unique and delicious . . .

Makes 8 servings

1   cup plus 2 tablespoons all-purpose flour
1-1/2 teaspoons double-acting baking powder
1/4   teaspoon salt
1/2   teaspoon grated lemon peel
1/4   teaspoon baking soda
1/4   teaspoon dried basil
1/4   teaspoon dried thyme
2   tablespoons dried chives
1   egg
6   ounces finely shredded, peeled, sweet potato
1/2   cup plain lowfat yogurt
1   tablespoon plus 1 teaspoon margarine, melted

Preheat oven to 425°.

In a large bowl, stir together flour, baking powder, salt, lemon peel, baking soda, basil, thyme, and chives.

In another bowl, combine egg, sweet potato, yogurt and margarine. Add this mixture to dry ingredients; stir until moistened.

Divide dough evenly into 8 nonstick muffin cups.

Bake 20 minutes, until browned.

Remove muffins to a rack to cool, or, for best flavor, serve hot.

Each serving provides:

127 Calories

1	Bread Serving	4	g	Protein
1/2	Fat Serving	3	g	Fat
19	Additional Calories	21	g	Carbohydrate
		194	mg	Sodium
		35	mg	Cholesterol

Yogurt Biscuits

Try 'em while they're hot!

Makes 6 servings

1	cup plus 2 tablespoons all-purpose flour
1-1/2	teaspoons double-acting baking powder
1/4	teaspoon baking soda
1/2	teaspoon salt
2	tablespoons margarine
	Sweetener equivalent to 1 teaspoon sugar
1/2	cup plain lowfat yogurt
1/2	teaspoon skim milk

Preheat oven to 450°.

In a large bowl, combine flour, baking powder, baking soda, and salt. Add margarine. Using a fork or pastry blender, mix until mixture resembles coarse crumbs.

Stir sweetener into yogurt; add to flour mixture. Stir until all ingredients are moistened. Knead dough a few times until mixture is smooth and holds together.

Roll or pat dough into a rectangle, about 1-inch thick, on a nonstick baking sheet. With a sharp knife, cut into the dough, forming 6 even biscuits, but do not separate them.

Drizzle with milk, and rub it evenly over the top of the biscuits, using your fingertips.

Bake 12 to 15 minutes, until golden.

Serve hot, or remove to a rack to finish cooling.

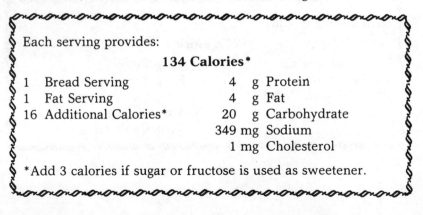

Each serving provides:

134 Calories*

1	Bread Serving	4	g	Protein
1	Fat Serving	4	g	Fat
16	Additional Calories*	20	g	Carbohydrate
		349	mg	Sodium
		1	mg	Cholesterol

*Add 3 calories if sugar or fructose is used as sweetener.

Cheese Pinwheels

Makes 6 servings

1   recipe Yogurt Biscuits, page 300
3   ounces Cheddar cheese, shredded

Prepare dough for Yogurt Biscuits, as directed.
Preheat oven to 425°.
Roll dough into a rectangle 1/4-inch thick between 2 sheets of wax paper. Sprinkle evenly with cheese.
Starting with 1 long side, roll dough tightly into a log. Cut into 18 even slices. Place slices, cut-side-down, on a nonstick baking sheet.
Bake 12 minutes, until lightly browned.
Remove from pan immediately and cool on a rack, or serve hot.

Each serving provides:

192 Calories*

1/2	Protein Serving	7	g	Protein
1	Bread Serving	9	g	Fat
1	Fat Serving	20	g	Carbohydrate
16	Additional Calories*	437	mg	Sodium
		16	mg	Cholesterol

*Add 3 calories if sugar or fructose is used as sweetener.

Legumes and Tofu

Those of you who already have a passion for natural foods will find pleasant surprises among our legume recipes. We offer unique combinations of ingredients and new ways to serve interesting, good-tasting meals. If you're not committed to natural foods as a lifestyle, try these creative recipes for variety and a change of pace.

Tofu is a little-known food that offers incredible variety. The curd from the soybean, tofu "becomes" whatever it is placed with. In pancakes, cheesecakes, puddings, or "meatballs," tofu is prepared in ways that will teach you how really unique natural foods can be.

It is important to note that legumes and tofu add protein to your diet without adding high levels of fat. So, enjoy our tasty selections of good nutrition.

302

Basic Cooking Directions for Legumes

Bring water to a boil in a saucepan over medium-high heat. (Use 3 to 4 cups of water for each cup of legumes.) Add legumes to water slowly, so that water continues to boil.

Reduce heat to low, cover, and cook until legumes are soft. This will generally take from 1-1/2 to 3 hours. Stir occasionally while cooking, and add more water, if necessary, to keep legumes covered.

Legumes may be soaked overnight in water before cooking. This will shorten cooking time.

Note: Generally 1 cup of dry legumes will yield 2 to 3 cups cooked. One cup of cooked legumes will weigh approximately 6 ounces. The yield and amount of cooking time will vary with the size and quality of the legumes, and the mineral content of the water being used.

Prairie Bean Tortillas

Makes 4 servings

2   tablespoons vegetable oil
1   cup diced onions
1   clove garlic, minced
16   ounces cooked pink beans or cooked red kidney beans
2   tablespoons water
1   4-ounce can chopped green chilies, drained
1/4   teaspoon salt
       Pepper to taste
1/4   cup tomato sauce
1/4   teaspoon dried oregano
4   6-inch corn tortillas
1   cup shredded lettuce
4   ounces grated Cheddar cheese

In a medium saucepan, heat oil over medium heat. Add onions and garlic; cook until onions are tender, about 10 minutes, stirring occasionally.

Add beans, water, chilies, salt, pepper, tomato sauce, and oregano. Cook 5 minutes, stirring occasionally, and mashing beans slightly with a spoon.

Steam tortillas according to package directions.

Place each tortilla on a serving plate. Top with shredded lettuce.

Divide bean mixture evenly over lettuce. Top with Cheddar cheese. Roll up tortilla.

Each serving provides:

381 Calories

3	Protein Servings	18	g Protein
1	Bread Serving	17	g Fat
1-3/4	Vegetable Servings	41	g Carbohydrate
1-1/2	Fat Servings	400	mg Sodium
		30	mg Cholesterol

Bean-Stuffed Eggplant

A real gourmet dish that's easy on the budget . . .

Makes 4 servings

2	medium eggplants
1	tablespoon plus 1 teaspoon vegetable oil
2	cloves garlic, minced
1	cup chopped onions
16	ounces cooked kidney beans
2	cups cooked white or brown rice
1/4	teaspoon dried thyme
1	teaspoon dried basil
1	teaspoon dried oregano
4	ounces Cheddar cheese, grated
2/3	cup nonfat dry milk
1/2	cup water
2	teaspoons sesame seeds
1	tablespoon grated Parmesan cheese

Cut eggplants in half, lengthwise. Scoop out pulp, leaving 1/4-inch-thick shells. Chop pulp. Heat oil in a large nonstick skillet over medium heat. Add eggplant, garlic and onions. Cook, covered, until vegetables are tender. Reduce heat to low. Preheat oven to 350°. Stir in remaining ingredients, *except* sesame seeds and Parmesan cheese. Heat, stirring, until cheese is melted. Remove from heat. Fill eggplant shells with bean mixture. Sprinkle evenly with sesame seeds and Parmesan cheese. Place eggplants in a shallow baking dish that has been sprayed with a nonstick cooking spray. Bake 30 minutes, uncovered.

Each serving provides:

530 Calories

3	Protein Servings	26	g	Protein
1	Bread Serving	16	g	Fat
3-1/2	Vegetable Servings	72	g	Carbohydrate
1	Fat Serving	281	mg	Sodium
1/2	Milk Serving	33	mg	Cholesterol
17	Additional Calories			

Cheesy Beans and Rice

A hearty family supper dish . . .

Makes 4 servings

2	tablespoons vegetable oil
1/2	cup chopped onions
1/2	cup chopped carrot
1/2	cup chopped celery
1	tablespoon dried basil
1/2	teaspoon dried oregano
1/8	teaspoon garlic powder
12	ounces cooked red kidney beans
	Salt and pepper to taste
1	cup chopped fresh tomato
2	ounces grated Cheddar cheese
2	cups cooked white or brown rice

Heat oil in a large nonstick skillet over medium heat. Add onions, carrot, celery, basil, oregano and garlic powder. Cook, stirring frequently, until vegetables are tender, about 10 minutes. Reduce heat to low.

Stir in beans, salt, pepper, and tomato. Heat through.

Stir in cheese and rice. Heat, stirring, until cheese is melted and mixture is hot.

Each serving provides:

362 Calories

2	Protein Servings	14	g	Protein
1	Bread Serving	12	g	Fat
1-1/4	Vegetable Servings	51	g	Carbohydrate
1-1/2	Fat Servings	120	mg	Sodium
		15	mg	Cholesterol

Herbed Chick Pea Patties

Makes 4 servings

12   ounces canned chick peas, drained
3   tablespoons dry bread crumbs
2/3   cup nonfat dry milk
2   teaspoons vegetable oil
2   eggs
1/8   teaspoon garlic powder
1/8   teaspoon dried basil
1/4   teaspoon dried oregano
1/2   teaspoon dry mustard
1   teaspoon Worcestershire sauce
      Salt and pepper to taste

In a blender container or food processor, combine all ingredients. Process until smooth.

Preheat a nonstick skillet or griddle over medium-high heat.
Drop mixture onto griddle, making twelve 3-inch patties. Cook until brown on both sides, turning once.

Each serving provides:

227 Calories

2   Protein Servings   14 g Protein
1/4 Bread Serving   7 g Fat
1/2 Milk Serving   28 g Carbohydrate
1/2 Fat Serving   443 mg Sodium
                             139 mg Cholesterol

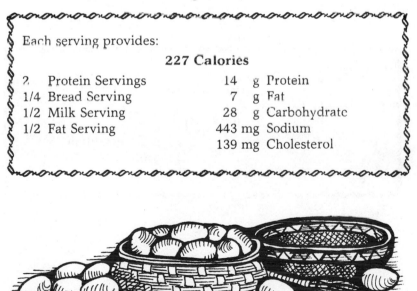

Soybean Soufflé

Makes 4 servings

12 ounces cooked soybeans
4 eggs, separated
1 tablespoon minced onion flakes
1 tablespoon parsley flakes
  Salt and pepper to taste
1/2 teaspoon dried thyme
1/4 teaspoon dried marjoram
1/2 cup water

Preheat oven to 350°.

In a medium bowl, combine soybeans, egg yolks, onion flakes, parsley, salt, pepper, thyme, marjoram and water. Place mixture, half at a time, into a blender container. Blend to a paste. Place mixture in a large bowl.

In another bowl, beat egg whites on high speed of an electric mixer until stiff. Fold into soybean mixture, gently, but thoroughly.

Place mixture in a soufflé or baking dish that has been sprayed with a nonstick cooking spray.

Bake 30 to 40 minutes, until set.

Each serving provides:

197 Calories

2-1/2 Protein Servings

16 g Protein
11 g Fat
11 g Carbohydrate
73 mg Sodium
274 mg Cholesterol

Bean Stroganoff

Hearty and delicious . . .

Makes 4 servings

2	tablespoons vegetable oil
1	cup sliced onions
3	cups chopped mushrooms
3	tablespoons all-purpose flour
1	cup water
1	packet instant beef-flavored broth mix
2	teaspoons sherry extract
1/2	teaspoon salt
2	teaspoons Worcestershire sauce
1	teaspoon dry mustard
	Dash ground nutmeg
16	ounces cooked soybeans
1	cup plain lowfat yogurt
2	cups cooked noodles

Heat oil in a large nonstick skillet over medium heat. Add onions and mushrooms; cook until onions are tender, separating them into rings.

Stir in flour. Cook 2 minutes, stirring constantly. Stir in water, broth mix, sherry extract, salt, Worcestershire sauce, mustard and nutmeg. Cook, stirring, until thickened. Reduce heat to low. Stir in soybeans. Heat through, stirring frequently. Remove from heat. Stir in yogurt.

Serve over noodles.

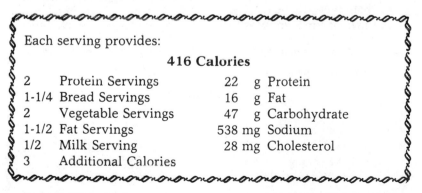

Each serving provides:

416 Calories

2	Protein Servings	22 g	Protein
1-1/4	Bread Servings	16 g	Fat
2	Vegetable Servings	47 g	Carbohydrate
1-1/2	Fat Servings	538 mg	Sodium
1/2	Milk Serving	28 mg	Cholesterol
3	Additional Calories		

Mushroom Soy Loaf Supreme

Makes 4 servings

10	ounces cooked soybeans
3	eggs
2	teaspoons vegetable oil
2	packets instant chicken flavored broth mix
1/2	cup water
1	tablespoon minced onion flakes
1/8	teaspoon garlic powder
	Salt and pepper to taste
1	slice whole wheat bread, crumbled
1	8-ounce can mushroom pieces, drained
1/2	cup minced celery

Sauce

1	8-ounce can tomato sauce
1	teaspoon Worcestershire sauce
1/4	teaspoon dried basil
1/4	teaspoon dried oregano

Preheat oven to 375°.

In a blender container, combine soybeans, eggs, oil, broth mix, water, onion flakes, garlic powder, salt, pepper, and bread. Blend to a smooth paste. Stir in mushrooms and celery.

Pour mixture into a 4 x 8-inch loaf pan that has been sprayed with a nonstick cooking spray.

Bake 30 to 35 minutes, until set and lightly browned.

While loaf is baking, combine sauce ingredients in a small saucepan. Heat over low heat.

Let loaf sit for 5 minutes before slicing. Serve sauce over slices.

Each serving provides:

230 Calories

2	Protein Servings	16	g	Protein
1/4	Bread Serving	11	g	Fat
1-3/4	Vegetable Servings	19	g	Carbohydrate
1/2	Fat Serving	1058	mg	Sodium
5	Additional Calories	206	mg	Cholesterol

Easiest Bean Salad

So zesty and good . . .

Makes 8 servings

2   1-pound cans cut green beans, drained
12   ounces cooked red kidney beans
12   ounces cooked chick peas
1   tablespoon plus 1 teaspoon sweet pickle relish
1/2   cup chopped onions
1/4   cup chopped green pepper
1   tablespoon dried parsley flakes
1/2   cup reduced-calorie Italian dressing (6 calories per tablespoon)

In a large bowl, combine all ingredients. Toss until blended. Chill several hours to combine flavors. Mix several times while chilling.

Each serving provides:

163 Calories

1-1/2 Protein Servings	9	g Protein
1-1/4 Vegetable Servings	2	g Fat
10 Additional Calories	29	g Carbohydrate
	779	mg Sodium
	0	mg Cholesterol

Roman Tuna Salad

Makes 4 servings

8   ounces cooked red kidney beans
8   ounces canned chick peas, drained
4   ounces canned tuna, drained and flaked
2   tablespoons vegetable oil
1/4   cup red wine vinegar
1/2   teaspoon dried marjoram
1/2   teaspoon dried basil
1/2   teaspoon dried oregano
1   teaspoon dried parsley flakes
1/8   teaspoon garlic powder
      Salt and pepper to taste

In a large bowl, combine all ingredients. Toss until well blended.
Chill several hours to blend flavors, mixing occasionally.

Each serving provides:

231 Calories

3   Protein Servings   16 g Protein
1-1/2   Fat Servings   8 g Fat
                                   25 g Carbohydrate
                                  315 mg Sodium
                                   17 mg Cholesterol

Pepper-Bean Casserole

An easy casserole with an unusual flavor . . .

Makes 4 servings

2	10-ounce packages frozen lima beans
1	tablespoon plus 1 teaspoon vegetable oil
2	green peppers, cut into 1/4-inch strips
1	tablespoon imitation bacon bits
3/4	teaspoon dry mustard
2	teaspoons molasses
1/4	teaspoon dried oregano
2	teaspoons minced onion flakes
1	16-ounce can tomatoes, chopped, undrained
	Sweetener equivalent to 2 teaspoons firmly-packed brown sugar

Cook beans according to package directions. Drain. Place in a 1-1/2-quart casserole.

In a medium nonstick skillet, heat oil over medium heat. Add green peppers and cook until tender, about 10 minutes. Add peppers to beans and toss until combined.

Preheat oven to 325°.

Combine remaining ingredients. Pour mixture over beans and peppers.

Cover and bake 35 minutes.

Each serving provides:

239 Calories*

2-1/2	Protein Servings	11 g	Protein
2	Vegetable Servings	5 g	Fat
1	Fat Serving	38 g	Carbohydrate
17	Additional Calories*	409 mg	Sodium
		0 mg	Cholesterol

*Add 8 calories if brown sugar is used as sweetener.

Barbecued Black-Eyed Peas

Makes 4 servings

16   ounces cooked black-eyed peas
2   cups tomato purée
1   tablespoon plus 1 teaspoon minced onion flakes
1/2   teaspoon paprika
1/2   teaspoon Worcestershire sauce
1   teaspoon dry mustard
       Dash garlic powder
       Salt and pepper to taste
       Sweetener equivalent to 2 tablespoons firmly-packed brown
           sugar

Preheat oven to 350°.
Combine all ingredients. Place in a 1-1/2-quart baking dish that
has been sprayed with a nonstick cooking spray.
Bake, uncovered, 1 hour.

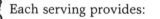

Each serving provides:

143 Calories*

2	Protein Servings	8 g	Protein
1	Vegetable Serving	1 g	Fat
25	Additional Calories*	28 g	Carbohydrate
		512 mg	Sodium
		0 mg	Cholesterol

*Add 24 calories if brown sugar is used as sweetener.

Baked Lentils and Tomatoes

Makes 4 servings

2	tablespoons vegetable oil
1/2	cup chopped onions
1/2	cup chopped celery
1/2	cup chopped green pepper
1	16-ounce can tomatoes, chopped, drained
1/2	teaspoon dried oregano
	Dash garlic powder
	Salt and pepper to taste
16	ounces cooked lentils
2	tablespoons dry bread crumbs or wheat germ
1	tablespoon grated Parmesan cheese

Heat oil in a medium nonstick skillet over medium heat. Add onions, celery and green pepper; cook until vegetables are tender, stirring frequently.

Preheat oven to 350°

In a 1-1/2-quart baking dish that has been sprayed with a nonstick cooking spray, combine onion mixture with tomatoes, oregano, garlic powder, salt, pepper and lentils. Mix well.

Sprinkle with bread crumbs and Parmesan cheese.

Bake, uncovered, 30 minutes.

Each serving provides:

238 Calories

2	Protein Servings	12	g	Protein
1-1/2	Vegetable Servings	8	g	Fat
1-1/2	Fat Servings	33	g	Carbohydrate
22	Additional Calories	233	mg	Sodium
		1	mg	Cholesterol

Tangy Baked Kidney Beans

An unusual taste treat . . .

Makes 4 servings

1	tablespoon plus 1 teaspoon vegetable oil
1/2	cup chopped onions
1	teaspoon instant chicken bouillon granules
1	small apple, unpeeled, shredded
1/4	cup tomato paste
1/2	teaspoon dry mustard
2	tablespoons vinegar
1/4	teaspoon dried oregano
2	teaspoons honey
12	ounces cooked red or white kidney beans
	Salt and pepper to taste

Heat oil in a medium nonstick skillet over medium heat. Add onions, bouillon and apple. Cook, stirring frequently, until onions are tender, about 10 minutes.

Preheat oven to 350°.

In a 1-1/2 quart casserole that has been sprayed with a nonstick cooking spray, combine onion mixture with remaining ingredients. Mix well.

Cover and bake 40 minutes.

Each serving provides:

194 Calories

1-1/2	Protein Servings	8	g	Protein
1/2	Vegetable Serving	5	g	Fat
1	Fat Serving	31	g	Carbohydrate
1/4	Fruit Serving	416	mg	Sodium
12	Additional Calories	0	mg	Cholesterol

Kidney Beans Provençal

Makes 2 servings

12   ounces cooked red or white kidney beans, drained
1   cup canned tomatoes, drained, chopped
1/2 cup chopped onions
1   tablespoon imitation bacon bits
1   tablespoon grated Parmesan cheese
1   tablespoon dry bread crumbs
1   tablespoon plus 1 teaspoon reduced-calorie margarine

Preheat oven to 350°.

Combine beans, tomatoes, onions and bacon bits in a small baking dish that has been sprayed with a nonstick cooking spray.

Combine Parmesan cheese and bread crumbs and sprinkle over bean mixture. Dot with margarine. Bake, uncovered, 30 minutes.

Each serving provides:

307 Calories

3	Protein Servings	17	g Protein
1-1/2	Vegetable Servings	7	g Fat
1	Fat Serving	47	g Carbohydrate
45	Additional Calories	472 mg	Sodium
		2 mg	Cholesterol

Pink Bean "Pumpkin" Pie

Close your eyes and you'll think it's pumpkin pie!
(Thanks for this one, Bubbie!)   *Makes 6 servings*

Crust
1   cup plus 2 tablespoons all-purpose flour
1/4   cup plus 2 tablespoons reduced-calorie margarine
3   tablespoons cold water
Filling
14   ounces cooked pink beans†
1-1/2   cups evaporated skim milk
2   eggs
1/4   teaspoon salt
1-1/4   teaspoons ground cinnamon
1/2   teaspoon ground cloves
1/2   teaspoon ground nutmeg
1/8   teaspoon ground ginger
        Sweetener equivalent to 18 teaspoons sugar

Preheat oven to 400°. Blend flour, margarine and water with a fork to form a dough. Shape into a ball. Roll dough between 2 pieces of wax paper to an 11-inch circle, 1/8-inch thick. Fit dough into a 9-inch pie plate, leaving a 1-inch overhang. Bend edges under and flute with a fork. Prick the bottom and sides of crust about 30 times with a fork. Bake 10 minutes. Remove from oven. Reduce oven temperature to 375°.

In a blender container, combine all filling ingredients. Blend until smooth. Pour mixture into crust. Bake 30 minutes, until set. Cool slightly. Chill.

†Note: Pinto beans may be substituted for pink beans.

Each serving provides:

295 Calories*

1-1/2	Protein Servings	15	g Protein
1	Bread Serving	8	g Fat
1-1/2	Fat Servings	41	g Carbohydrate
1/2	Milk Serving	330	mg Sodium
0	Additional Calories*	94	mg Cholesterol

*Add 48 calories if sugar or fructose is used as sweetener.

Surprise Apple Bean Cake

A moist, delicious, hi-protein dessert . . .

Makes 8 servings

1/3   cup margarine, softened
        Sweetener equivalent to 18 teaspoons sugar
1   egg
1/2   cup applesauce (unsweetened)
6   ounces cooked pinto beans
1-1/2   cups all-purpose flour
2   teaspoons double-acting baking powder
1/8   teaspoon salt
1   teaspoon ground cinnamon
1/2   teaspoon ground nutmeg
1/4   teaspoon each: ground cloves and ground allspice
1   small, sweet apple, peeled, diced into 1/4-inch pieces
1/4   cup raisins

Preheat oven to 350°. In a large bowl, cream margarine and sweetener on low speed of an electric mixer. Add egg and beat until mixture is light in color. In a blender container, combine applesauce and beans. Blend until smooth. Add to first mixture, beating on low speed until mixture is well blended.

Into another bowl, sift flour, baking powder, salt, cinnamon, nutmeg, cloves and allspice. Add to batter, beating on low speed until blended. Stir in apples and raisins, mixing well. Spoon mixture into a Bundt pan or tube pan that has been sprayed with a non-stick cooking spray. Bake 35 minutes, until a toothpick inserted in the cake comes out clean. Cool in pan 10 minutes. Then invert cake onto a rack to finish cooling.

Each serving provides:

218 Calories*

1/2	Protein Serving	5 g	Protein
1	Bread Serving	9 g	Fat
2	Fat Servings	31 g	Carbohydrate
1/2	Fruit Serving	236 mg	Sodium
0	Additional Calories*	34 mg	Cholesterol

*Add 36 calories if sugar or fructose is used as sweetener.

Oriental Tofu Fish Cakes

An unusually tasty combo!

Makes 4 servings

12	ounces flounder or sole fillets, cooked and flaked
15	ounces tofu, sliced, drained well
2	tablespoons minced onion flakes
1/4	teaspoon garlic powder
1/4	cup soy sauce
1/4	teaspoon ground ginger
1/4	teaspoon sherry extract
2	slices white or whole wheat bread, crumbled
1	egg, slightly beaten
2	teaspoons honey
3	tablespoons dry bread crumbs
1	tablespoon plus 1 teaspoon vegetable oil

Sauce

3	tablespoons reduced-calorie grape spread (16 calories per 2 teaspoons)
2	teaspoons vinegar

Preheat oven to 400°.

Combine all ingredients, *except* grape spread and vinegar, in a large bowl. Mix well, mashing ingredients with a fork until well blended. Shape into 8 patties, pressing firmly.

Dip each patty in bread crumbs and place on a nonstick baking sheet. Bake 20 minutes.

Heat grape spread and vinegar in a small saucepan over low heat, until hot. Serve over patties.

Each serving provides:

301 Calories

4-1/2	Protein Servings	27	g	Protein
3/4	Bread Serving	12	g	Fat
1	Fat Serving	23	g	Carbohydrate
28	Additional Calories	1505	mg	Sodium
		112	mg	Cholesterol

Italian Tofu "Meatballs"

They'll ask for this one again and again.

Makes 2 servings

15 ounces firm tofu
2 tablespoons minced onion flakes
1/4 teaspoon dried oregano
1/4 teaspoon salt
1/8 teaspoon pepper
    Dash garlic powder
2 slices white or whole wheat bread, crumbled
1 egg
1 tablespoon dried parsley flakes
Sauce
1 8-ounce can tomato sauce
1/4 teaspoon *each* dried oregano and dried basil
1/8 teaspoon *each* garlic powder, salt and pepper
1 tablespoon grated Parmesan cheese

Preheat oven to 375°.

Slice tofu and drain well between layers of paper towels, squeezing gently to remove water. In a large bowl, combine tofu, onion flakes, oregano, salt, pepper, garlic powder, bread, egg and parsley. Mix well with a fork, mashing to blend ingredients. Shape mixture into balls, squeezing tightly.

Place "meatballs" in a single layer in a shallow baking pan that has been sprayed with a nonstick cooking spray.

In a small bowl, combine sauce ingredients. Spoon over "meatballs." Sprinkle with Parmesan cheese.

Bake, uncovered, 20 minutes.

Each serving provides:

320 Calories

3	Protein Servings	25 g	Protein
1	Bread Serving	14 g	Fat
1	Vegetable Serving	29 g	Carbohydrate
40	Additional Calories	1224 mg	Sodium
		140 mg	Cholesterol

Tofu Cheddar Squares

One of our quickest, easiest favorites . . .

Makes 4 servings

2	tablespoons margarine
1/4	cup plus 1 tablespoon dry bread crumbs
12	ounces tofu, soft or firm
4	eggs
4	ounces Cheddar cheese, grated or cubed
1	tablespoon all-purpose flour
2	tablespoons minced onion flakes
2	teaspoons honey
1/2	teaspoon dry mustard
	Salt and pepper to taste
1	teaspoon dried parsley flakes

Preheat oven to 350°.

Melt 4 teaspoons of the margarine and spread in the bottom of an 8-inch square baking pan. Sprinkle evenly with 3 tablespoons of the bread crumbs. Bake 8 minutes. Remove from oven.

In a blender container, combine tofu, eggs, cheese, flour, onion flakes, honey, dry mustard, salt and pepper. Blend until smooth. Pour mixture over the baked crumbs.

Sprinkle evenly with remaining crumbs and parsley flakes. Dot with remaining margarine.

Bake 25 to 30 minutes, until lightly browned.

Cool 5 minutes. Cut into squares. Serve hot.

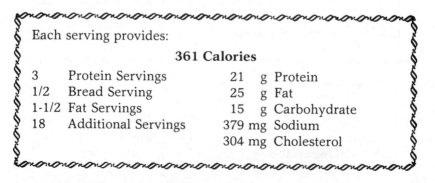

Each serving provides:

361 Calories

3	Protein Servings	21	g	Protein
1/2	Bread Serving	25	g	Fat
1-1/2	Fat Servings	15	g	Carbohydrate
18	Additional Servings	379	mg	Sodium
		304	mg	Cholesterol

Cauliflower-Tofu Bake

Makes 2 servings

1   10-ounce package frozen cauliflower
6   ounces tofu, drained and mashed
2   ounces grated Cheddar cheese
1/4 cup reduced-calorie Italian dressing (6 calories per table-
     spoon)

Cook cauliflower according to package directions. Drain. Place cauliflower in a 1-quart baking dish that has been sprayed with a nonstick cooking spray.

Preheat oven to 375°.

In a small bowl, combine tofu, Cheddar cheese and dressing. Mix well. Spoon over cauliflower.

Bake, uncovered, 20 minutes.

Each serving provides:

220 Calories

2	Protein Servings	17	g Protein
2	Vegetable Servings	15	g Fat
12	Additional Calories	9	g Carbohydrate
		639	mg Sodium
		30	mg Cholesterol

Tofu Parmigiana

A favorite way to enjoy tofu . . .

Makes 4 servings

1/4	cup plus 2 tablespoons dry bread crumbs
2	teaspoons dried oregano
	Salt and pepper to taste
12	ounces firm tofu, sliced 1/4-inch thick
1	tablespoon plus 1 teaspoon vegetable oil
1	8-ounce can tomato sauce
1/2	teaspoon dried basil
	Dash garlic powder
4	ounces shredded Provolone *or* Mozzarella cheese
3	tablespoons grated Parmesan cheese

In a small, shallow bowl, combine bread crumbs, 1 teaspoon of the oregano, salt and pepper.

Place tofu slices in a bowl of water. One at a time, dip slices in crumb mixture. Pat with a fork to press crumbs to tofu.

Heat 2 teaspoons of the oil in a medium nonstick skillet over medium heat. Cook tofu slices until crisp on one side. Drizzle with remaining oil, turn and brown on the other side.

Preheat oven to 400°.

Combine tomato sauce, basil, garlic powder and remaining oregano. Place a thin layer of sauce in an 8-inch square baking pan. Top with tofu slices. Spoon remaining sauce over tofu.

Top with cheese.

Bake, uncovered, 20 minutes.

Each serving provides:

280 Calories

2	Protein Servings	18	g	Protein
1/2	Bread Serving	18	g	Fat
1	Vegetable Serving	15	g	Carbohydrate
1	Fat Serving	696	mg	Sodium
22	Additional Calories	23	mg	Cholesterol

Tofu Rice Pudding

Makes 2 servings

3   ounces tofu, soft or firm
1/2   envelope unflavored gelatin
1/2   cup water
      Sweetener equivalent to 4 teaspoons sugar
1/4   teaspoon ground cinnamon
1   teaspoon vanilla extract
1   teaspoon vanilla butternut flavor
1/3   cup nonfat dry milk
1/2   cup cooked white or brown rice
2   tablespoons raisins
      Ground cinnamon
      Dash ground nutmeg

Slice tofu and drain well between layers of paper towels.

Sprinkle gelatin over water in a small saucepan and let soften a few minutes. Heat over low heat until gelatin is completely dissolved, stirring frequently.

In a blender container, combine gelatin mixture, tofu, sweetener, cinnamon, vanilla extract, vanilla butternut flavor and dry milk. Blend until smooth. Pour into a bowl and chill until firm, about 45 minutes.

Beat chilled pudding on low speed of an electric mixer until smooth. Stir in rice and raisins and pour mixture into a serving bowl.

Sprinkle with cinnamon and a dash of nutmeg. Chill.

Each serving provides:

184 Calories*

1/2	Protein Serving	11	g Protein
1/2	Bread Serving	2	g Fat
1/2	Fruit Serving	27	g Carbohydrate
1/2	Milk Serving	71	mg Sodium
0	Additional Calories*	2	mg Cholesterol

*Add 32 calories if sugar or fructose is used as sweetener.

Tofu Chocolate Pudding

Makes 2 servings

1   teaspoon unflavored gelatin
1/2   cup water
3   ounces tofu, soft or firm
1   teaspoon vanilla butternut flavor
1/4   teaspoon chocolate extract
1/3   cup nonfat dry milk
1-1/2   teaspoons cocoa (unsweetened)
        Sweetener equivalent to 5 teaspoons sugar

Sprinkle gelatin over water in a small saucepan. Heat on low heat until gelatin is completely dissolved, stirring frequently.

Slice tofu and drain well between layers of paper towels.

In a blender container, combine gelatin mixture with remaining ingredients. Blend until smooth.

Divide evenly into 2 bowls. Chill until firm.

Variation: Add 1/4 teaspoon almond *or* rum extract before blending.

Each serving provides:

95 Calories*

1/2 Protein Serving   10   g Protein
1/2 Milk Serving   2   g Fat
3   Additional Calories*   8   g Carbohydrate
                            69 mg Sodium
                             2 mg Cholesterol

*Add 40 calories if sugar or fructose is used as sweetener.

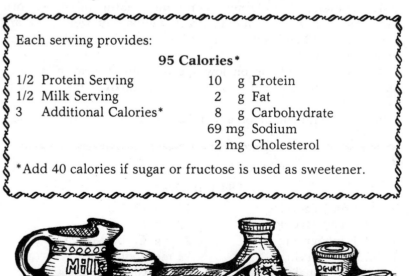

Tofu Banana Fritters

Sure to become a breakfast favorite . . .

Makes 2 servings

3	ounces tofu, soft or firm
1/3	cup nonfat dry milk
1	egg
3	tablespoons all-purpose flour
1/2	teaspoon double-acting baking powder
1	teaspoon vanilla extract
1/4	teaspoon banana extract
1/2	medium, ripe banana, sliced
2	teaspoons reduced-calorie margarine
	Sweetener equivalent to 3 teaspoons sugar

Slice tofu and drain well between layers of paper towels.

Place all ingredients in a blender container. Blend until smooth.

Pour mixture onto a preheated nonstick griddle or skillet over medium heat, making eight 4-inch pancakes. Turn pancakes carefully when edges are dry and bubbles have formed on top. Brown on both sides.

Each serving provides:

210 Calories*

1	Protein Serving	12 g	Protein
1/2	Bread Serving	7 g	Fat
1/2	Fat Serving	24 g	Carbohydrate
1/2	Fruit Serving	252 mg	Sodium
1/2	Milk Serving	139 mg	Cholesterol
0	Additional Calories*		

*Add 24 calories if sugar or fructose is used as sweetener.

Tofu, Peanut Butter and Banana Spread

You have to try this to believe it!

Makes 2 servings

3	ounces tofu, soft or firm
1	tablespoon peanut butter
1/2	medium, ripe banana, mashed
1	teaspoon lemon juice
1	teaspoon honey
1	teaspoon vanilla extract
	Sweetener equivalent to 2 teaspoons sugar
	Ground cinnamon

Slice tofu and drain well between layers of paper towels.

In a small bowl, mash tofu. Add remaining ingredients. Mix well.

Chill.

To serve, spread on toast or crackers, or eat as a pudding. Sprinkle with cinnamon before serving.

Each serving provides:

126 Calories*

1	Protein Serving	6	g	Protein
1/2	Fruit Serving	6	g	Fat
1/2	Fat Serving	12	g	Carbohydrate
10	Additional Calories*	53	mg	Sodium
		0	mg	Cholesterol

*Add 16 calories if sugar or fructose is used as sweetener.

Chocolate Tofu Cheese Pie

Tofu never tasted so good!

Makes 6 servings

Crust
Prepare "Extra-Thick Graham Crust," page 410.

Filling

1-1/2	envelopes unflavored gelatin
1-1/2	cups water
9	ounces tofu, sliced
	Sweetener equivalent to 15 teaspoons sugar
1	tablespoon vanilla butternut flavor
3/4	teaspoon chocolate extract
1	cup nonfat dry milk
3/4	cup part-skim ricotta cheese
2	tablespoons cocoa (unsweetened)
3/4	teaspoon almond extract (optional)

Prepare "Extra-Thick Graham Crust." Cool completely.

In a small saucepan, sprinkle gelatin over water and let soften a few minutes. Heat on low heat until gelatin is completely dissolved, stirring frequently.

Drain tofu well on paper towels.

In a blender container, combine gelatin mixture and tofu with remaining ingredients. Blend until smooth. Pour mixture into cooled crust. Chill until firm.

Each serving provides:

246 Calories*

1	Protein Serving	15	g Protein
1	Bread Serving	12	g Fat
1-1/2	Fat Servings	20	g Carbohydrate
1/2	Milk Serving	271	mg Sodium
5	Additional Calories*	12	mg Cholesterol

*Add 40 calories if sugar or fructose is used as sweetener.

Tofu Banana Cream Pie

Makes 6 servings

Crust

8   2-1/2-inch graham cracker squares, crushed (2 ounces graham cracker crumbs)
2   tablespoons margarine, melted

Filling

9   ounces tofu, soft or firm
3   eggs
1   cup lowfat cottage cheese
1-1/2 teaspoons vanilla butternut flavor
1   teaspoon banana extract
1   tablespoon all-purpose flour
      Sweetener equivalent to 12 teaspoons sugar
1-1/2 medium, ripe bananas, cut into chunks

Preheat oven to 350°.

In a 9-inch pie pan, combine graham cracker crumbs and margarine. Mix until all crumbs are moistened. Press crumbs into bottom and sides of pan to form a crust.

Bake 8 minutes.

Slice tofu and drain well between layers of paper towels.

In a blender container, combine tofu with remaining ingredients. Blend until smooth. Pour into crust.

Bake 30 to 35 minutes, until set.

Cool slightly and then chill.

Each serving provides:

234 Calories*

1-1/2	Protein Servings	12	g Protein
3/4	Bread Serving	14	g Fat
1	Fat Serving	12	g Carbohydrate
1/2	Fruit Serving	209	mg Sodium
5	Additional Calories*	170	mg Cholesterol

*Add 32 calories if sugar or fructose is used as sweetener.

Peanut Butter

Almost everyone loves peanut butter, but so many people avoid it because they think of it as "fattening." However, this nutritionally valuable food can be a real and economical contribution to your diet. It is a delicious source of protein, and can bring a welcome change from meat and cheese.

In each of our recipes the choice is yours to use crunchy or smooth peanut butter. When used in the right way, and counted as part of your daily protein and fat allotment, peanut butter can now be enjoyed by all.

Chocolate Peanut Butter Log

So rich and delicious . . .

Makes 2 servings

3   tablespoons peanut butter
3/4   ounce quick-cooking oats
2   teaspoons cocoa (unsweetened)
1   teaspoon vanilla extract
2   tablespoons plus 1-1/2 teaspoons water
      Sweetener equivalent to 3 teaspoons sugar
1/3   cup nonfat dry milk

In a small bowl, combine all ingredients and mix well. Place mixture on wax paper and shape into a log. Roll up wax paper and chill log in the refrigerator at least 30 minutes.

Each serving provides:

240 Calories*

1-1/2	Protein Servings	14	g Protein
1/2	Bread Serving	13	g Fat
1-1/2	Fat Servings	18	g Carbohydrate
1/2	Milk Serving	213 mg	Sodium
5	Additional Calories*	2 mg	Cholesterol

*Add 24 calories if sugar or fructose is used as sweetener.

Honey Crunch Peanut Spread

Makes 2 servings

3/4 ounce toasted oats†
2 tablespoons peanut butter
1 tablespoon honey

In a small bowl, combine all ingredients. Mix well.

Use as a spread for toast or crackers, or on sliced apples or vegetable sticks.

†Note: To toast oats, place uncooked quick-cooking oats in a single layer on an ungreased cookie sheet. Bake in a preheated 350° oven 15 to 20 minutes, until lightly browned.

Each serving provides:

167 Calories

1	Protein Serving	6	g Protein
1/2	Bread Serving	9	g Fat
1	Fat Serving	19	g Carbohydrate
30	Additional Calories	99	mg Sodium
		0	mg Cholesterol

Peanut Butter Pineapple Spread

Makes 2 servings

1/4   cup peanut butter
1/2   cup canned crushed pineapple (unsweetened), drained
2   tablespoons juice from pineapple
      Dash ground cinnamon

Combine all ingredients in a small bowl. Mix well.
Makes a great sandwich!

Each serving provides:

223 Calories

2	Protein Servings	9	g Protein
2	Fat Servings	16	g Fat
1/2	Fruit Serving	15	g Carbohydrate
		195	mg Sodium
		0	mg Cholesterol

Peanut Butter Corn Muffins

A change-of-pace hi-protein muffin!

Makes 8 servings

3	ounces cornmeal
3/4	cup all-purpose flour
1	teaspoon double-acting baking powder
1/4	teaspoon salt
3	tablespoons peanut butter
2	tablespoons honey
1	egg, beaten
1/2	cup skim milk
1/4	cup water
1	teaspoon vegetable oil

Preheat oven to 425°.

In a large bowl, combine cornmeal, flour, baking powder and salt. Set aside.

Combine remaining ingredients in another bowl, and mix well with a fork until blended.

Stir wet mixture into dry ingredients, stirring until moistened.

Divide batter evenly into 8 nonstick muffin cups.

Bake 12 minutes, until lightly browned. Remove muffins to a rack to cool, or serve warm for best flavor.

Each serving provides:

154 Calories

1/2 Protein Serving	5	g Protein
1 Bread Serving	5	g Fat
1/2 Fat Serving	24	g Carbohydrate
21 Additional Calories	172 mg	Sodium
	35 mg	Cholesterol

Chocolate Peanut Butter Bars

Easy enough for the children to make . . .

Makes 4 servings

2　　tablespoons peanut butter
2/3　cup nonfat dry milk
2　　teaspoons cocoa (unsweetened)
　　　Sweetener equivalent to 5 teaspoons sugar
1/4　cup water
1-1/2 ounces unsweetened breakfast cereal, such as corn or oat
　　　flakes
2　　tablespoons raisins

In a small bowl, combine peanut butter, dry milk, cocoa, sweetener and water. Mix well with a spoon until well blended.
Stir in cereal and raisins.
Press mixture into the bottom of a nonstick 4 x 8-inch loaf pan.
Chill 30 minutes or longer.
To serve, cut into bars.

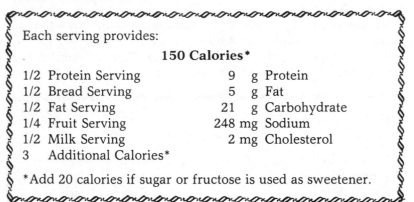

Each serving provides:

150 Calories*

1/2	Protein Serving	9	g Protein
1/2	Bread Serving	5	g Fat
1/2	Fat Serving	21	g Carbohydrate
1/4	Fruit Serving	248	mg Sodium
1/2	Milk Serving	2	mg Cholesterol
3	Additional Calories*		

*Add 20 calories if sugar or fructose is used as sweetener.

Peanut Butter Bread

Different and delicious! Tastes great toasted and spread with jelly!

Makes 8 servings

3/4	cup all-purpose flour
1	teaspoon double-acting baking powder
1/4	teaspoon salt
1/4	teaspoon ground cinnamon
1/8	teaspoon ground mace
	Sweetener equivalent to 6 teaspoons sugar
1/4	cup plus 3 tablespoons peanut butter
1	egg, slightly beaten
1	teaspoon vegetable oil
1	teaspoon vanilla extract
1/2	cup skim milk

Preheat oven to 350°.

In a medium bowl, sift flour, baking powder, salt, cinnamon and mace.

Add sweetener, peanut butter, egg and oil. Mix well with a fork until well blended. (Mixture will be dry.)

Add vanilla to milk. Gradually add milk to peanut butter mixture, mixing well with a fork until mixture is well blended.

Place in a nonstick 4 x 8-inch loaf pan.

Bake 30 minutes, until lightly browned.

Cool in pan on rack. Slice to serve.

Each serving provides:

149 Calories*

1	Protein Serving	6	g	Protein
1/2	Bread Serving	8	g	Fat
1	Fat Serving	13	g	Carbohydrate
6	Additional Calories*	221	mg	Sodium
		35	mg	Cholesterol

*Add 12 calories if sugar or fructose is used as sweetener.

Peanut Butter Cookies

Makes 10 servings
(4 cookies each serving)

1   cup minus 1 tablespoon all-purpose flour
1/2   teaspoon baking soda
1/4   teaspoon salt
1/2   cup plus 1 tablespoon peanut butter
       Sweetener equivalent to 18 teaspoons sugar
2   tablespoons margarine, melted
1   egg
1   teaspoon vanilla extract
2   tablespoons skim milk

Preheat oven to 375°.

In a small bowl, combine flour, baking soda and salt.

In another bowl, combine remaining ingredients. Beat on low speed of an electric mixer until blended.

Stir dry mixture into peanut butter mixture, mixing well with a spoon.

Roll mixture into 1-inch balls. Place on a nonstick cookie sheet 2 inches apart. Flatten each to 1/4-inch thick with a fork, using a crisscross pattern.

Bake 10 to 12 minutes, until lightly browned.

Remove cookies from pan and cool on a rack.

Each serving provides:

158 Calories*

1	Protein Serving	6 g	Protein
1/2	Bread Serving	10 g	Fat
1-1/2	Fat Servings	12 g	Carbohydrate
2	Additional Calories*	187 mg	Sodium
		27 mg	Cholesterol

*Add 29 calories if sugar or fructose is used as sweetener.

Chocolate Peanut Butter Pudding

A creamy, rich pudding . . .

Makes 2 servings

2   teaspoons cocoa (unsweetened)
1   tablespoon cornstarch
1   cup skim milk
1   tablespoon peanut butter
     Sweetener equivalent to 3 teaspoons sugar†
1   teaspoon vanilla extract
1/2 teaspoon chocolate extract

In a small saucepan, combine cocoa and cornstarch. Gradually stir in milk.

Add remaining ingredients.

Cook over medium-low heat, stirring constantly, until mixture comes to a boil. Boil 1 minute, stirring.

Pour into 2 small bowls or custard cups.

Chill.

†Note: If using aspartame as sweetener, it can be added after
pudding is cooked. Cool for a few minutes before adding.

Each serving provides:

126 Calories*

1/2 Protein Serving   8 g Protein
1/2 Fat Serving   5 g Fat
1/2 Milk Serving   12 g Carbohydrate
5   Additional Calories*   114 mg Sodium
                             2 mg Cholesterol

*Add 24 calories if sugar or fructose is used as sweetener.

Peanut Butter and Raisin Muffins

Makes 8 servings

1/2	cup raisins
	Boiling water
3/4	cup all-purpose flour
1/4	teaspoon salt
1/2	teaspoon double-acting baking powder
1/2	teaspoon baking soda
1/3	cup nonfat dry milk
1/4	teaspoon ground cinnamon
3	tablespoons peanut butter
1	tablespoon margarine, melted
1	egg
1/2	cup plain lowfat yogurt
	Sweetener equivalent to 6 teaspoons sugar

Preheat oven to 400°. Pour boiling water over raisins to cover. Set aside. In a large bowl, combine flour, salt, baking powder, baking soda, dry milk and cinnamon.

In another bowl, combine peanut butter, margarine, egg, yogurt and sweetener. Beat with a fork or wire whisk until blended. Stir peanut butter mixture into dry ingredients until just moistened. Drain raisins. Stir into batter.

Divide batter evenly into 8 nonstick muffin cups. Bake 12 minutes, until brown. Cool in pan 5 minutes. Remove to a rack to finish cooling, or serve warm.

Each serving provides:

148 Calories*

1/2	Protein Serving	6	g	Protein
1/2	Bread Serving	6	g	Fat
3/4	Fat Servings	20	g	Carbohydrate
1/2	Fruit Serving	196	mg	Sodium
1/4	Milk Serving	36	mg	Cholesterol
0	Additional Calories*			

*Add 12 calories if sugar or fructose is used as sweetener.

Peanut Butter Fruit Candy

You'll love this rich, fruitty candy.

Makes 2 servings

2	tablespoons peanut butter
2	dried apricot halves, chopped†
1	tablespoon raisins, chopped†
1	teaspoon honey
1/8	teaspoon ground cinnamon
1/3	cup nonfat dry milk
2	tablespoons water
1	teaspoon vanilla extract
2	2-1/2-inch graham crackers, crushed (or 1/2-ounce graham cracker crumbs)

In a small bowl, combine all ingredients. Mix well with a spoon.
Roll into 1-inch balls.
Chill.

†Note: An easy way to "chop" dried fruit is to snip it into pieces
with kitchen shears.

Each serving provides:

205 Calories

1	Protein Serving	10	g	Protein
1/2	Bread Serving	9	g	Fat
1	Fat Serving	23	g	Carbohydrate
1/2	Fruit Serving	212	mg	Sodium
1/2	Milk Serving	2	mg	Cholesterol
10	Additional Calories			

Peanut Butter-Scotch Bars

Makes 6 servings

3/4   cup all-purpose flour
1-1/2   ounces uncooked quick-cooking oats
1/4   teaspoon baking soda
1/4   teaspoon salt
1/4   cup plus 1 tablespoon peanut butter
        Sweetener equivalent to 12 teaspoons sugar
1   egg
1   tablespoon plus 1 teaspoon margarine, melted
1/2   teaspoon vanilla extract
1/2   teaspoon vanilla butternut flavor
2   tablespoons water

Preheat oven to 350°.

In a small bowl, combine flour, oats, baking soda and salt. Mix well.

In a large bowl, cream peanut butter, sweetener, egg, margarine, extracts and water on low speed of an electric mixer.

Add dry mixture to peanut butter mixture. Beat on low speed until well blended.

Spread mixture in an 8-inch square baking pan that has been sprayed with a nonstick cooking spray, patting mixture in the pan with your fingertips.

Bake 15 minutes, until lightly browned.

Cool in pan on rack. Cut into squares to serve.

Each serving provides:

202 Calories*

1	Protein Serving	8	g Protein
1	Bread Serving	11	g Fat
1-1/2	Fat Servings	19	g Carbohydrate
0	Additional Calories*	222 mg	Sodium
		46 mg	Cholesterol

*Add 32 calories if sugar or fructose is used as sweetener.

Peanut Butter French Toast

You must try this!

Makes 1 serving

1   egg
1   tablespoon water
1   teaspoon vanilla extract
    Sweetener equivalent to 1 teaspoon sugar
2   slices thin-sliced white or whole wheat bread (80 calories
    per 2 slices)
1   tablespoon peanut butter
1   tablespoon raisins

In a shallow bowl, combine egg, water, vanilla and sweetener. Beat with a fork.

Make a sandwich with the bread, peanut butter and raisins. Dip the sandwich in the egg mixture, turning carefully until the egg is absorbed.

Cook sandwich on a preheated nonstick griddle or skillet over medium heat, turning occasionally, until brown on both sides.

Each serving provides:

294 Calories*

2	Protein Servings	13	g	Protein
1	Bread Serving	14	g	Fat
1	Fat Serving	25	g	Carbohydrate
1/2	Fruit Serving	312	mg	Sodium
0	Additional Calories*	275	mg	Cholesterol

*Add 16 calories if sugar or fructose is used as sweetener.

Peanut Butter Fudge

A tasty confection fit for royalty . . .

Makes 2 servings

2   tablespoons peanut butter
1/3   cup nonfat dry milk
1   teaspoon honey
1   tablespoon water

In a small bowl, combine all ingredients. Mix well with a spoon until well blended.

Place mixture on a sheet of wax paper, and shape into a rectangle, about 1/2-inch high. Press firmly in place.

Chill at least 30 minutes.

To serve, cut into squares.

Each serving provides:

147 Calories

1	Protein Serving	9	g	Protein
1	Fat Serving	8	g	Fat
1/2	Milk Serving	12	g	Carbohydrate
10	Additional Calories	163	mg	Sodium
		2	mg	Cholesterol

Peanut Butter-Banana Squares

A favorite flavor combo!

Makes 8 servings

3/4	cup all-purpose flour
1/2	teaspoon ground cinnamon
1/4	teaspoon salt
1/2	teaspoon double-acting baking powder
2	eggs
1/4	cup plus 2 tablespoons peanut butter
1	medium, ripe banana, chopped
2	tablespoons honey
1	teaspoon vanilla extract
2	teaspoons vegetable oil

Preheat oven to 350°.

In a medium bowl, combine flour, cinnamon, salt and baking powder.

Add remaining ingredients. Beat on low speed of an electric mixer until dry ingredients are just moistened.

Spread mixture in an 8-inch square baking pan that has been sprayed with a nonstick cooking spray.

Bake 15 to 17 minutes, until top of cake is dry.

Cool in pan.

To serve, cut into squares.

Each serving provides:

176 Calories

1	Protein Serving	6	g Protein
1/2	Bread Serving	9	g Fat
1	Fat Serving	19	g Carbohydrate
1/4	Fruit Serving	184	mg Sodium
15	Additional Calories	69	mg Cholesterol

Peanut Butter-Dressed Fruit Salad

Makes 2 servings

1/2   medium, ripe banana, sliced
1/2   cup canned pineapple tidbits (unsweetened)
2   tablespoons juice from pineapple
1/4   cup peanut butter
1/4   cup evaporated skim milk
2   teaspoons shredded coconut (unsweetened)

In a small bowl, combine banana and pineapple.

In another bowl, stir pineapple juice into peanut butter until blended. Stir in evaporated milk. Mix well with a spoon until smooth.

Divide fruit evenly into 2 serving bowls. Spoon dressing evenly over fruit. Sprinkle with coconut.

Each serving provides:

283 Calories

2	Protein Servings	12	g Protein
2	Fat Servings	17	g Fat
1	Fruit Serving	26	g Carbohydrate
1/4	Milk Serving	232	mg Sodium
10	Additional Calories	1	mg Cholesterol

Peanut Butter Date Spread

Makes 1 serving

2 tablespoons peanut butter
1 date, chopped†
1 tablespoon lowfat cottage cheese

Combine all ingredients in a small bowl.
Use as a spread for toast or crackers, or on carrot or celery sticks.
†Note: An easy way to cut dates is to snip them with kitchen
  shears.

Each serving provides:

220 Calories

2	Protein Servings	11	g Protein
2	Fat Servings	16	g Fat
1/2	Fruit Serving	12	g Carbohydrate
9	Additional Calories	253	mg Sodium
		1	mg Cholesterol

Fruit

Fruit is a sweet, natural gift from Mother Nature. Its versatility is endless, whether used as an appetizer, main dish, dessert, or as an in-between-meal snack.

In preparing fruit recipes, always choose varieties of fruits that are naturally sweet. The sweeter the fruit, the less sweetener you'll need to use. So, enjoy exploring the many culinary possibilities we've created here for you, and browse through our other sections too, to find fruit uniquely combined with milk, eggs and cheese, and as an added bonus in many of our cakes and pies.

Company Fruit Compote

One of our quick and easy favorites!

Makes 4 servings

1/2 cup canned, sliced peaches (unsweetened), with 2 table-
     spoons juice
1/2 cup frozen dark sweet cherries (unsweetened)
1/2 cup canned, sliced pears (unsweetened), with 2 tablespoons
     juice
1/2 cup canned pineapple chunks (unsweetened), with 2 table-
     spoons juice
     Sweetener equivalent to 4 teaspoons firmly packed brown
     sugar
1/2 teaspoon vanilla extract
1/4 teaspoon maple extract
1/8 teaspoon grated lemon peel
1/4 teaspoon ground cinnamon
1   tablespoon plus 1 teaspoon cornstarch
1   tablespoon plus 1 teaspoon margarine

Preheat oven to 350°.

Drain fruits, reserving designated amounts of juices.

In an oven-proof casserole, combine fruits, sweetener, extracts,
lemon peel and cinnamon. Mix well.

In a small bowl, combine cornstarch with the reserved fruit
juices. Stir to dissolve. Pour mixture over fruit.

Dot with margarine.

Bake, uncovered, 15 to 20 minutes, until hot and bubbly.

Serve hot.

Each serving provides:

96 Calories*

1	Fat Serving	1 g Protein
1	Fruit Serving	4 g Fat
10	Additional Calories*	15 g Carbohydrate
		46 mg Sodium
		0 mg Cholesterol

*Add 16 calories if brown sugar is used as sweetener.

Chewy Fruit Squares

Kids of all ages love this chewy treat!

Makes 4 servings

3   envelopes unflavored gelatin
1   cup water
1/2 cup frozen orange juice concentrate (unsweetened), thawed

Sprinkle gelatin over water in a medium saucepan. Let soften a few minutes.

Heat, stirring frequently, over low heat, until gelatin is completely dissolved. Remove from heat.

Stir in orange juice concentrate.

Pour mixture into a 4 x 8-inch loaf pan. Chill several hours.

To serve, cut into squares.

Variation: Substitute grape juice concentrate for the orange juice. (Makes 6 servings.)

Each serving provides:

75 Calories

1   Fruit Serving

5 g Protein
0 g Fat
14 g Carbohydrate
6 mg Sodium
0 mg Cholesterol

Blueberry Bread 'n Butter Pudding

A stupendous creation!

Makes 4 servings

2   cups blueberries, fresh or frozen (unsweetened)
1/4   cup plus 2 tablespoons water
1/4   teaspoon ground cinnamon
       Sweetener equivalent to 9 teaspoons sugar
2   tablespoons plus 2 teaspoons reduced-calorie margarine
8   slices thin-sliced bread (80 calories per 2 slices)

In a small bowl, combine blueberries, water and cinnamon.
Bring to a boil over medium heat, reduce heat to low, and boil gently for 10 minutes. Remove from heat and stir in sweetener.

Spread margarine on both sides of each bread slice, using 1/2 teaspoon of margarine per side. Cut each slice of bread into 5 or 6
triangular-shaped pieces.

Line the bottom of a 9-inch cake pan with half of the slices, ar-
ranging them to fit like a jigsaw puzzle.

Pour about 3/4 of the blueberries evenly over the bread.

Arrange remaining bread over berries and top evenly with remaining berries.

Cover pan with plastic wrap and top with a dish or paper plate.
Place weights, such as several 1-pound cans of food, on top of plate.
Refrigerate overnight.

To serve, loosen pudding with a spatula and unmold onto a serving platter.

Each serving provides:

155 Calories*

1   Bread Serving   4   g Protein
1   Fat Serving   5   g Fat
1   Fruit Serving   25   g Carbohydrate
0   Additional Calories*   242   mg Sodium
                               1   mg Cholesterol

*Add 36 calories if sugar or fructose is used as sweetener.

Blueberry Clafouti

Makes 2 servings

1   cup blueberries, fresh or frozen (unsweetened)
2   slices white or whole wheat bread, crumbled
1   teaspoon double-acting baking powder
1/3   cup nonfat dry milk
1/3   cup water
2   teaspoons margarine
1   teaspoon vanilla extract
      Sweetener equivalent to 6 teaspoons sugar

Preheat oven to 375°.

Place blueberries in the bottom of small, shallow baking pan that has been sprayed with a nonstick cooking spray.

Combine remaining ingredients in a blender container. Blend 1 minute. Pour evenly over berries.

Bake, uncovered, 25 minutes, until golden.

Let stand 5 minutes.

Serve hot or cold.

Variation: Cherries or thinly-sliced fresh peaches make a delicious substitute for the blueberries.

Each serving provides:

189 Calories*

1	Bread Serving	7	g Protein
1	Fat Serving	5	g Fat
1	Fruit Serving	28	g Carbohydrate
1/2	Milk Serving	435	mg Sodium
0	Additional Calories*	3	mg Cholesterol

*Add 48 calories if sugar or fructose is used as sweetener.

Orange Tapioca

Makes 2 servings

1   cup orange juice (unsweetened)
1   tablespoon plus 1 teaspoon quick-cooking tapioca
1/8 teaspoon lemon extract
     Sweetener equivalent to 2 teaspoons firmly-packed brown
     sugar

In a small saucepan, combine orange juice, tapioca and lemon
extract. Mix and let stand 5 minutes.

Bring mixture to a boil over medium heat, stirring frequently.
Remove from heat. Stir in sweetener and cinnamon.

Cool mixture in pan 20 minutes. Stir. Pour into 2 custard cups.
Chill.

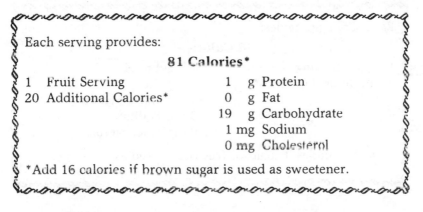

Each serving provides:

81 Calories*

1 Fruit Serving   1 g Protein
20 Additional Calories*   0 g Fat
                         19 g Carbohydrate
                         1 mg Sodium
                         0 mg Cholesterol

*Add 16 calories if brown sugar is used as sweetener.

Grape Gelatin Dessert

As simple to prepare as the commercial product, and so tasty . . .

Makes 6 servings

2   cups grape juice (unsweetened)
1   envelope unflavored gelatin
       Sweetener equivalent to 6 teaspoons sugar

Sprinkle gelatin over grape juice in a small saucepan. Let soften a few minutes.

Heat, stirring frequently, over low heat, until gelatin is completely dissolved. Remove from heat. Stir in sweetener.

Pour mixture into 1 bowl, or divide among 6 small dessert bowls. Chill until firm.

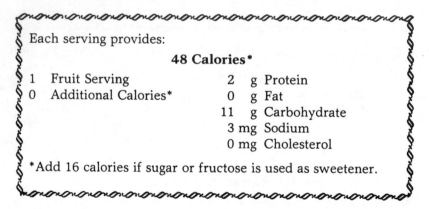

Each serving provides:

48 Calories*

1	Fruit Serving	2 g	Protein
0	Additional Calories*	0 g	Fat
		11 g	Carbohydrate
		3 mg	Sodium
		0 mg	Cholesterol

*Add 16 calories if sugar or fructose is used as sweetener.

Baked Pineapple Tapioca

Makes 4 servings

2   cups canned crushed pineapple (unsweetened), with 1/2 cup
       juice (Add water, if necessary, to equal 1/2 cup)
2   tablespoons plus 2 teaspoons quick-cooking tapioca
1/4   teaspoon lemon extract
       Dash ground cinnamon
3/4   cup hot water
       Sweetener equivalent to 8 teaspoons sugar

Preheat oven to 325°.
In a 1-quart casserole, combine all ingredients. Mix well. Let
stand 10 minutes.
Bake, uncovered, 40 minutes, or until tapioca granules are clear.
Serve hot or cold.

Each serving provides:

98 Calories*

1   Fruit Serving   0   g Protein
20 Additional Calories*   0   g Fat
                                25   g Carbohydrate
                                 2 mg Sodium
                                 0 mg Cholesterol

*Add 32 calories if sugar or fructose is used as sweetener.

Sautéed Pineapple

Makes 2 servings

1/4   of a fresh, ripe, medium pineapple, skin removed
2   teaspoons margarine
1/4   teaspoon ground cinnamon
      Sweetener equivalent to 2 teaspoons sugar

Slice pineapple into 1-inch slices.

Melt margarine in a small nonstick skillet over medium-high heat.

Sauté pineapple in margarine, turning frequently, until lightly browned on both sides. Remove from pan.

Combine sweetener and cinnamon and sprinkle evenly over pineapple.

Serve hot.

Each serving provides:

74 Calories*

1 Fat Serving	1	g Protein
1 Fruit Serving	4	g Fat
0 Additional Calories*	10	g Carbohydrate
	45	mg Sodium
	0	mg Cholesterol

*Add 16 calories if sugar or fructose is used as sweetener.

Pineapple-Grapefruit Salad

Tart and tangy, and so refreshing . . .

Makes 4 servings

1/4 of a fresh, ripe, medium pineapple, skin removed (or 1 cup canned, unsweetened, pineapple tidbits)
1 medium grapefruit, peeled, sectioned
1 cup plain lowfat yogurt
1 teaspoon vanilla extract
Sweetener equivalent to 8 teaspoons sugar

Cut pineapple and grapefruit into small bite-size tidbits.
Combine yogurt, vanilla and sweetener; add to fruit, mixing well.
Chill.

Each serving provides:

100 Calories*

1	Fruit Serving	5	g	Protein
1/2	Milk Serving	1	g	Fat
0	Additional Calories*	19	g	Carbohydrate
		40	mg	Sodium
		3	mg	Cholesterol

*Add 32 calories if sugar or fructose is used as sweetener.

Broiled Grapefruit Delight

Makes 2 servings

1   pink grapefruit, cut in half
2   teaspoons margarine, melted
1/2   teaspoon rum extract
     Sweetener equivalent to 1 teaspoon firmly-packed brown
     sugar

Place grapefruit on a broiler pan, cut-side up.
Combine margarine and rum extract and spread evenly over grapefruit.
Sprinkle with sweetener.
Broil 6 inches from heat 5 to 10 minutes, until hot and bubbly.

Each serving provides:

77 Calories*

1	Fat Serving	1 g	Protein
1	Fruit Serving	4 g	Fat
0	Additional Calories*	10 g	Carbohydrate
		44 mg	Sodium
		0 mg	Cholesterol

*Add 8 calories if brown sugar is used as sweetener.

Raspberry Melba Sauce

A gourmet's delight . . .

Makes 2 servings

1 cup raspberries, fresh or frozen (unsweetened)
2 tablespoons water
1 teaspoon cornstarch
Sweetener equivalent to 6 teaspoons sugar

In a small saucepan, combine raspberries and 1 tablespoon of the water. Bring to boil over medium heat.

Reduce heat to low and simmer a few minutes, until berries begin to fall apart.

In a small bowl or custard cup, dissolve cornstarch in remaining 1 tablespoon water. Add to berries. Cook, stirring, until mixture thickens, about 1 minute. Remove from heat.

Pour mixture through a strainer, into a small bowl. Stir in sweetener.

Serve hot or cold over fruit or frozen dietary dessert.

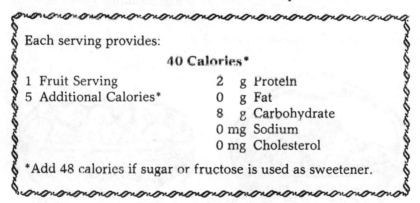

Each serving provides:

40 Calories*

1 Fruit Serving	2 g Protein
5 Additional Calories*	0 g Fat
	8 g Carbohydrate
	0 mg Sodium
	0 mg Cholesterol

*Add 48 calories if sugar or fructose is used as sweetener.

Cherry-Berry Sorbet

Unbelievably easy and delicious . . .

Makes 2 servings

20   frozen dark sweet cherries (unsweetened), still frozen
2   tablespoons water
1/4   teaspoon strawberry extract

In a blender container or food processor, combine all ingredients. Process just until smooth.
Serve immediately.

Each serving provides:

50 Calories

1 Fruit Serving

1   g   Protein
1   g   Fat
11   g   Carbohydrate
0   mg   Sodium
0   mg   Cholesterol

Bananas New Orleans

Fix it in minutes.

Makes 2 servings

2   teaspoons margarine
1/4   cup orange juice (unsweetened)
1   tablespoon honey
1/4   teaspoon rum extract
1/4   teaspoon vanilla butternut flavor
1   medium, ripe banana, sliced lengthwise, and then crosswise
       Dash ground cinnamon

In a small skillet, melt margarine over medium heat. Stir in orange juice, honey and extracts.

Add bananas. Sauté 5 minutes, turning bananas carefully several times.

Place 2 banana slices in each of 2 small serving bowls. Spoon sauce over bananas.

Sprinkle with cinnamon.

Serve hot.

Each serving provides:

137 Calories

1	Fat Serving	1	g Protein
1-1/4	Fruit Servings	4	g Fat
30	Additional Calories	26	g Carbohydrate
		46	mg Sodium
		0	mg Cholesterol

Baked Banana Crumble

Makes 4 servings

2   medium, ripe bananas, sliced lengthwise
1   teaspoon lemon juice
1/2   teaspoon ground cinnamon
       Sweetener equivalent to 4 teaspoons firmly-packed brown
       sugar
1   ounce graham cracker crumbs
1   tablespoon plus 1 teaspoon reduced-calorie margarine

Preheat oven to 375°.

Place bananas in a shallow baking dish that has been sprayed with a nonstick cooking spray. Sprinkle with lemon juice.

In a small bowl, combine cinnamon, sweetener and crumbs. Sprinkle over bananas. Dot with margarine.

Bake, uncovered, 20 minutes, until lightly browned.

Each serving provides:

99 Calories*

1/2	Bread Serving	1 g	Protein
1/2	Fat Serving	3 g	Fat
1	Fruit Serving	19 g	Carbohydrate
0	Additional Calories*	95 mg	Sodium
		0 mg	Cholesterol

*Add 16 calories if brown sugar is used as sweetener.

Banana Toast

An unbelievable eggless version of French toast!

Makes 2 servings

1   medium, ripe banana
1/4   cup skim milk
1/2   teaspoon vanilla extract
       Sweetener equivalent to 2 teaspoons sugar
2   slices white or whole wheat bread
2   teaspoons margarine
       Ground cinnamon

In a blender container, combine banana, milk, vanilla and sweetener. Blend until smooth.

Place bread in a shallow pan. Pour banana mixture over bread and turn bread several times, until it has absorbed the banana mixture.

Melt margarine in a nonstick skillet over medium-low heat.

Place bread carefully in skillet, using a spatula. Drizzle any remaining banana mixture over bread.

Brown toast carefully on both sides.

Sprinkle with cinnamon.

Each serving provides:

163 Calories*

1	Bread Serving	4	g Protein
1	Fat Serving	5	g Fat
1	Fruit Serving	27	g Carbohydrate
12	Additional Calories*	178	mg Sodium
		1	mg Cholesterol

*Add 16 calories if sugar or fructose is used as sweetener.

Banana Apricot Squares

An unusual and very effective blend of flavors . . .

Makes 2 servings

1	slice white or whole wheat bread, crumbled
1/3	cup nonfat dry milk
1	tablespoon plus 1 teaspoon reduced-calorie margarine
1/2	teaspoon double-acting baking powder
1	teaspoon vanilla butternut flavor
	Sweetener equivalent to 4 teaspoons sugar
1/2	medium, ripe banana, diced
1/2	cup canned apricots (unsweetened), chopped
2	tablespoons juice from apricots
1/4	teaspoon grated orange peel
1/4	teaspoon ground cinnamon
1/8	teaspoon ground nutmeg
	Dash ground cloves
	Dash ground ginger
2	2-1/2-inch graham cracker squares, crushed (1/2-ounce crumbs)

Preheat oven to 350°.

In a small bowl, combine bread, dry milk, margarine, baking powder, vanilla butternut flavor and sweetener. Mix well with a fork, pressing margarine into dry ingredients, until mixture forms a dough.

Press dough into the bottom of a 4 x 8-inch nonstick loaf pan.

Bake 5 minutes.

In a medium bowl, combine remaining ingredients, except graham cracker crumbs. Mix well. Spread mixture evenly over dough in pan. Sprinkle with reserved crumbs.

Bake 15 minutes.

Cool in pan. Chill. Cut into squares to serve.

Each serving provides:

183 Calories*

1	Bread Serving	7	g	Protein
1	Fat Serving	5	g	Fat
1	Fruit Serving	28	g	Carbohydrate
1/2	Milk Serving	373	mg	Sodium
0	Additional Calories*	2	mg	Cholesterol

*Add 32 calories if sugar or fructose is used as sweetener.

Banana Raisin Pudding

Makes 4 servings

1   medium, ripe banana
1-1/2 teaspoons lemon juice
2   eggs
1/3   cup nonfat dry milk
1/2   cup plain lowfat yogurt
2   slices white or whole wheat bread, crumbled
       Sweetener equivalent to 6 teaspoons sugar
1/2   teaspoon ground cinnamon
1/8   teaspoon ground nutmeg
1   teaspoon vanilla extract
1/4   cup raisins

Preheat oven to 350°.

In a blender container or food processor, combine all ingredients, *except* raisins. Blend until smooth. Stir in raisins.

Pour mixture into a 1-quart casserole or baking pan that has been sprayed with a nonstick cooking spray.

Bake, uncovered, 40 minutes, until set.

Serve hot or cold.

Each serving provides:

169 Calories*

1/2 Protein Serving   8 g Protein
1/2 Bread Serving   4 g Fat
1   Fruit Serving   25 g Carbohydrate
1/2 Milk Serving   147 mg Sodium
0   Additional Calories* 140 mg Cholesterol

*Add 24 calories if sugar or fructose is used as sweetener.

Sautéed Maple Peaches

Makes 4 servings

1	tablespoon plus 1 teaspoon margarine
1/2	cup orange juice (unsweetened)
1/2	teaspoon maple extract
1/4	teaspoon ground cinnamon
	Sweetener equivalent to 4 teaspoons firmly-packed brown sugar
3	medium, fresh peaches, peeled, and sliced 1/4-inch thick

Melt margarine in a 12-inch skillet over medium heat. Add orange juice, maple extract, cinnamon and sweetener.

Add peaches. Sauté, turning frequently, until tender, about 5 minutes.

Serve hot.

Each serving provides:

92 Calories*

1 Fat Serving	1	g Protein
1 Fruit Serving	4	g Fat
0 Additional Calories*	15	g Carbohydrate
	45	mg Sodium
	0	mg Cholesterol

*Add 16 calories if brown sugar is used as sweetener.

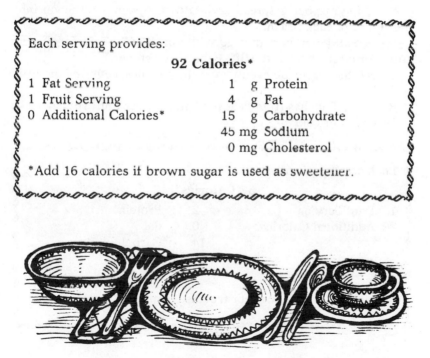

Snowcapped Peaches

A pretty dessert for a company dinner . . .

Makes 4 servings

8   canned peach halves (unsweetened)
2   tablespoons plus 2 teaspoons reduced-calorie raspberry *or* strawberry spread (16 calories per 2 teaspoons)
1/4   teaspoon raspberry *or* strawberry extract
1   egg white
1/4   teaspoon cream of tartar
       Sweetener equivalent to 5 teaspoons sugar

Preheat broiler.

Drain peaches well on paper towels. Place, cut-side up, in a shallow baking pan that has been sprayed with a nonstick cooking spray.

Combine raspberry spread and extract. Spoon 1 teaspoon into the center of each peach.

In a small bowl, beat the egg white until soft peaks form. Add cream of tartar; beat until stiff. Beat in sweetener.

Spread the meringue evenly over the peaches, covering the fruit spread.

Broil 5 to 6 inches from heat for 1 minute, or until golden.

Serve hot or cold.

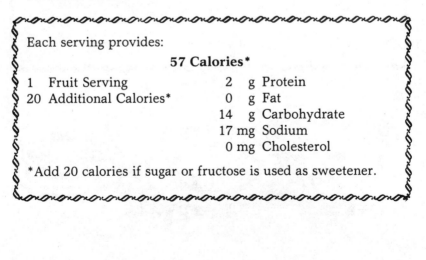

Each serving provides:

57 Calories*

1   Fruit Serving   2   g Protein
20 Additional Calories*   0   g Fat
                                   14   g Carbohydrate
                                   17 mg Sodium
                                    0 mg Cholesterol

*Add 20 calories if sugar or fructose is used as sweetener.

Baked Pears

Makes 2 servings

2   small pears (D'anjou, Bosc, or Bartlett are good choices for this dish.)
1/2 cup water
2   teaspoons lemon juice
2   teaspoons honey
1   ounce graham cracker crumbs (four 2-1/2 inch squares)
1/4 teaspoon ground cinnamon
2   teaspoons margarine

Preheat oven to 425°.

Peel pears and cut in half lengthwise. Scoop out core.

Place pears, core-side down, in a small shallow baking dish. Pour water around pears. Drizzle pears with lemon juice and honey.

Cover and bake 20 minutes, or until pears are tender. Uncover.

Sprinkle crumbs over pears. Sprinkle with cinnamon. Dot with margarine.

Bake, uncovered, an additional 10 minutes.

Each serving provides:

203 Calories

1	Bread Serving	2	g Protein
1	Fat Serving	6	g Fat
1	Fruit Serving	40	g Carbohydrate
20	Additional Calories	141	mg Sodium
		0	mg Cholesterol

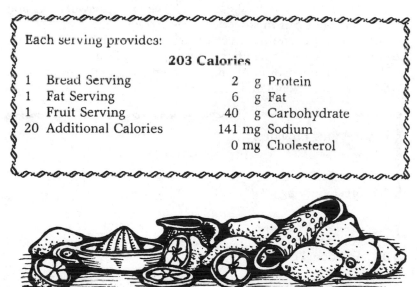

Apple Custard Squares

The tastiest of fruit puddings . . .

Makes 4 servings

1-1/2 ounces Grape-Nuts® cereal, crushed
1   tablespoon plus 1 teaspoon margarine, melted
4   eggs, slightly beaten
1-1/3 cups nonfat dry milk
1   teaspoon vanilla butternut flavor
1   teaspoon vanilla extract
       Sweetener equivalent to 8 teaspoons sugar
1/2   teaspoon ground cinnamon
1/8   teaspoon ground nutmeg
4   small, sweet apples, peeled and coarsely shredded (Golden
       Delicious or Rome Beauty are good choices.)

Preheat oven to 350°.

Combine crushed cereal and margarine in an 8-inch square baking pan. Mix until cereal is moistened. Press crumbs lightly in bottom of pan, forming a thin crust.

Bake 8 minutes.

In a large bowl, combine eggs, milk, flavorings, sweetener and spices. Mix well. Stir in shredded apples.

Spoon mixture over baked crust. Gently press apples down into custard. Sprinkle with additional cinnamon, if desired.

Bake 25 minutes, or until mixture is set and lightly browned.

Serve warm, or chill and serve cold.

Each serving provides:

301 Calories*

1	Protein Serving	16 g	Protein
1/2	Bread Serving	10 g	Fat
1	Fat Serving	37 g	Carbohydrate
1	Fruit Serving	319 mg	Sodium
1	Milk Serving	278 mg	Cholesterol
0	Additional Calories*		

*Add 32 calories if sugar or fructose is used as sweetener.

Baked Apple Alaska

Worth the effort!

Makes 4 servings

4   small, sweet apples, peeled, cored, cut in half lengthwise
      (McIntosh, Rome, or Jonathan would be good choices for
      this dish.)
      Sweetener equivalent to 2 tablespoons firmly-packed.brown
      sugar   ••
1/4   teaspoon ground cinnamon
Meringue
2   egg whites
1/4   teaspoon cream of tartar
      Sweetener equivalent to 6 teaspoons sugar

Preheat oven to 400°.

Place apples, cut-side down, in a shallow baking pan. Sprinkle
with sweetener and cinnamon. Pour water around apples to a
depth of 1/2-inch.

Cover and bake 30 minutes, or until apples are tender. Chill.

Just before serving:

Preheat oven to 450°.

Beat egg whites and cream of tartar on high speed of an electric
mixer until soft peaks form. Add sweetener and beat until stiff.

Place apples on a nonstick cookie sheet, cut side down. Frost
with meringue.

Bake 5 minutes, until just browned.

Serve immediately.

Each serving provides:

66 Calories*

1	Fruit Serving	2	g Protein
10	Additional Calories*	0	g Fat
		15	g Carbohydrate
		25	mg Sodium
		0	mg Cholesterol

*Add 24 calories if brown sugar is used as sweetener and 24
calories if sugar or fructose is used as sweetener in meringue.

Apple and Carrot Pudding

Makes 2 servings

1/2	cup grated carrot
1	small, sweet apple, peeled, grated
2	tablespoons raisins
2	eggs, separated
1	teaspoon lemon juice
3	tablespoons all-purpose flour
1/2	teaspoon ground cinnamon
	Sweetener equivalent to 2 teaspoons firmly-packed brown sugar
2	teaspoons margarine

Preheat oven to 350°.

In a medium bowl, combine carrot, apple, raisins, egg yolks, lemon juice, flour, cinnamon and sweetener. Mix well.

In a separate bowl, beat egg whites until stiff. Fold into carrot mixture.

Pour mixture into a small, shallow baking pan that has been sprayed with a nonstick cooking spray. Dot with margarine.

Bake, uncovered, 30 minutes, or until lightly browned.

Serve warm or cold.

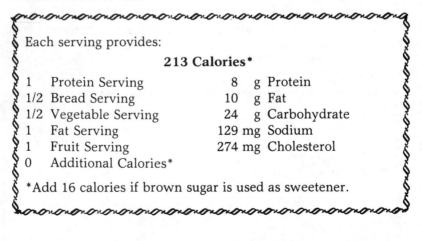

Each serving provides:

213 Calories*

1	Protein Serving	8	g Protein
1/2	Bread Serving	10	g Fat
1/2	Vegetable Serving	24	g Carbohydrate
1	Fat Serving	129	mg Sodium
1	Fruit Serving	274	mg Cholesterol
0	Additional Calories*		

*Add 16 calories if brown sugar is used as sweetener.

"Fried" Apples

Makes 4 servings

2   tablespoons margarine
4   small, sweet apples, cored, cut into rings 1/4-inch thick (McIntosh or Rome would be good in this dish.)
    Sweetener equivalent to 6 teaspoons sugar
1/2   teaspoon ground cinnamon
1/4   teaspoon ground nutmeg
1   teaspoon vanilla extract

In a large nonstick skillet, melt margarine over medium heat. Add apples. Cook, stirring frequently, until apples are tender, about 10 minutes.
Add sweetener, cinnamon, nutmeg, and vanilla.
Cook, stirring, 3 minutes.
Serve hot or cold.

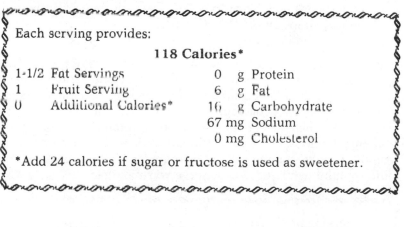

Each serving provides:

118 Calories*

1-1/2	Fat Servings	0 g	Protein
1	Fruit Serving	6 g	Fat
0	Additional Calories*	16 g	Carbohydrate
		67 mg	Sodium
		0 mg	Cholesterol

*Add 24 calories if sugar or fructose is used as sweetener.

Apple Crisp

Apples with a flair . . .

Makes 4 servings

4   small, sweet apples, peeled, cored and chopped (Golden Delicious, Rome, or McIntosh are good choices for this dish.)
1   cup water
1-1/2 teaspoons lemon juice
1   teaspoon ground cinnamon
1   teaspoon vanilla extract
       Sweetener equivalent to 6 teaspoons sugar
       Dash ground nutmeg

Topping

2/3   cup nonfat dry milk
1   teaspoon ground cinnamon
       Sweetener equivalent to 6 teaspoons sugar
2   tablespoons plus 2 teaspoons reduced-calorie margarine
3   ounces Grape-Nuts® cereal, crushed
       Dash ground nutmeg

Preheat oven to 375°. In a large saucepan, combine apples, water, lemon juice, cinnamon, vanilla, sweetener and nutmeg. Cook over medium heat until apples are tender, about 5 minutes, stirring frequently. Spread apple mixture in an 8-inch square baking pan or a 9-inch pie pan. In a small bowl, combine all topping ingredients. Blend with a fork until mixture is in the form of coarse crumbs. Sprinkle topping evenly over apples. Bake, uncovered, 20 minutes, until lightly browned. Serve warm or cold.

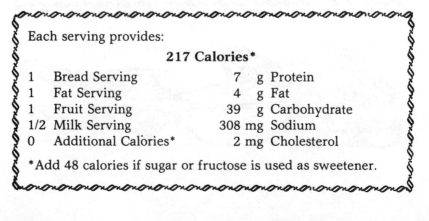

Each serving provides:

217 Calories*

1   Bread Serving   7   g Protein
1   Fat Serving   4   g Fat
1   Fruit Serving   39 g Carbohydrate
1/2 Milk Serving   308 mg Sodium
0   Additional Calories*   2   mg Cholesterol

*Add 48 calories if sugar or fructose is used as sweetener.

Applesauce Raisin Supreme

Makes 4 servings

1   cup applesauce (unsweetened)
1   teaspoon lemon juice
1/2 teaspoon grated orange peel
1/4 cup raisins, chopped
     Sweetener equivalent to 6 teaspoons sugar
1   egg white

In a large bowl, combine applesauce, lemon juice, orange peel, raisins and *half* of the sweetener. Mix well.

In another bowl, beat the egg white until stiff. Beat in remaining sweetener.

Fold egg white into applesauce mixture gently, but thoroughly. Chill. Serve within a few hours.

Each serving provides:

61 Calories*

1 Fruit Serving   2 g Protein
5 Additional Calories*   0 g Fat
                            14 g Carbohydrate
                            15 mg Sodium
                             0 mg Cholesterol

*Add 24 calories if sugar or fructose is used as sweetener.

Applesauce Cheese Mold

Makes 4 servings

1	envelope unflavored gelatin
1	cup orange juice (unsweetened)
2/3	cup lowfat cottage cheese
1	cup applesauce (unsweetened)
1/2	teaspoon ground cinnamon
1/8	teaspoon ground nutmeg
1	teaspoon vanilla extract
1/2	teaspoon maple extract (*or* rum extract)
	Sweetener equivalent to 6 teaspoons sugar

Sprinkle gelatin over 1/2 cup of the orange juice in a small saucepan. Let soften a few minutes. Heat over low heat, stirring frequently, until gelatin is completely dissolved.

Stir in remaining orange juice. Refrigerate mixture about 20 minutes, until gelatin is almost set.

In a blender container, combine gelatin mixture with remaining ingredients. Blend until smooth. Pour into a 3-cup mold.

Chill until firm. Unmold to serve.

Each serving provides

97 Calories*

1/2	Protein Serving	7	g	Protein
1	Fruit Serving	0	g	Fat
0	Additional Calories*	15	g	Carbohydrate
		156	mg	Sodium
		2	mg	Cholesterol

*Add 24 calories if sugar or fructose is used as sweetener.

Cakes, Pies, Cookies, and Candies

You've heard it said before, but now you can truly "have your cake and eat it, too." We've created a special grouping of scrumptious cakes, pies, cookies, and candies, where the taste has been heightened, while the calories have been lightened.

Many of our dessert offerings have the unique quality of containing enough protein per serving that you can actually eat a piece as part of your meal!

Forbidden foods are now within reach.

Enjoy! Enjoy! Enjoy!

Banana Cake

Everything goes into the blender for this easy and delicious cake.

Makes 8 servings

4   medium, ripe bananas, cut into chunks
4   eggs
2   tablespoons plus 2 teaspoons vegetable oil
1/2   teaspoon banana extract
1   teaspoon vanilla extract
      Sweetener equivalent to 12 teaspoons sugar
1-1/3 cups nonfat dry milk
1-1/2 teaspoons baking soda
4   slices whole wheat bread, crumbled

Preheat oven to 350°.

In a blender container, combine bananas, eggs, oil, extracts and sweetener. Blend until smooth.

Add remaining ingredients. Blend until all ingredients are moistened. Continue to blend for 1 minute.

Pour mixture into a nonstick Bundt pan that has also been sprayed with a nonstick cooking spray.

Bake 35 minutes, until lightly browned.

Cool 10 minutes in pan. Loosen with a knife and invert onto a rack to finish cooling.

Each serving provides:

205 Calories*

1/2	Protein Serving	9	g Protein
1/2	Bread Serving	8	g Fat
1	Fat Serving	25	g Carbohydrate
1	Fruit Serving	203 mg	Sodium
1/2	Milk Serving	140 mg	Cholesterol
0	Additional Calories*		

*Add 24 calories if sugar or fructose is used as sweetener.

Chocolate Peanut Butter Brownies

Mike's favorite!

Makes 8 servings

3/4	cup all-purpose flour
1	tablespoon plus 1 teaspoon cocoa (unsweetened)
1	teaspoon double-acting baking powder
1/8	teaspoon salt
3	eggs
1/4	cup plus 1 tablespoon peanut butter
1	teaspoon vanilla extract
1	teaspoon chocolate extract
1	tablespoon vegetable oil
1/4	cup plain lowfat yogurt
	Sweetener equivalent to 12 teaspoons sugar

Preheat oven to 350°.

In a small bowl, combine flour, cocoa, baking powder and salt.

In another bowl, combine remaining ingredients. Beat on low speed of an electric mixer until well blended.

Stir in dry ingredients. Mix by hand until all ingredients are moistened.

Place mixture in an 8-inch square baking pan that has been sprayed with a nonstick cooking spray.

Bake 15 minutes.

Cool in pan. Cut into squares to serve.

Each serving provides:

158 Calories*

1	Protein Serving	7	g Protein
1/2	Bread Serving	9	g Fat
1	Fat Serving	12	g Carbohydrate
9	Additional Calories*	178	mg Sodium
		103	mg Cholesterol

*Add 24 calories if sugar or fructose is used as sweetener.

Heavenly Chocolate Cake

Truly a heavenly dessert!

Makes 8 servings

1-1/2 cups all-purpose flour
3   tablespoons cocoa (unsweetened)
1   teaspoon double-acting baking powder
2/3   cup nonfat dry milk
2/3   cup water
1   tablespoon vinegar
1/4   cup margarine, softened
       Sweetener equivalent to 1/4 cup plus 4 teaspoons firmly-
       packed brown sugar
1/4   teaspoon salt
1   egg
1   teaspoon vanilla butternut flavor
1-1/2 teaspoons chocolate extract
1-1/2 teaspoons baking soda

Preheat oven to 350°. In a small bowl, sift flour, cocoa, and baking powder. In another bowl, combine milk and water. Add vinegar. In a large bowl, cream margarine, sweetener, salt and egg on low speed of an electric mixer. Add extracts. Beat until smooth. Add baking soda to milk. Alternately add milk and dry ingredients to margarine mixture, beating on low speed until all ingredients are moistened. Beat 1 minute on medium speed.

Spread batter in a 9-inch round cake pan that has been sprayed well with a nonstick cooking spray. Bake 15 to 20 minutes, until top of cake is dry. Cool in pan 15 minutes. Then loosen cake with a knife and invert onto a rack to finish cooling.

Each serving provides:

183 Calories*

1	Bread Serving	6	g Protein
1-1/2	Fat Servings	7	g Fat
1/4	Milk Serving	23	g Carbohydrate
12	Additional Calories*	269 mg	Sodium
		35 mg	Cholesterol

*Add 32 calories if brown sugar is used as sweetener.

Chocolate Zucchini Spice Cake

Very moist! You'll never know it's squash!

Makes 8 servings

3/4	cup all-purpose flour
1/4	teaspoon salt
1/2	teaspoon baking soda
1	teaspoon double-acting baking powder
1/2	teaspoon ground cinnamon
1/4	teaspoon ground nutmeg
1/4	teaspoon grated orange peel
1	tablespoon plus 1 teaspoon cocoa (unsweetened)
1	egg, beaten
	Sweetener equivalent to 9 teaspoons sugar
1/2	teaspoon chocolate extract
1/2	teaspoon vanilla extract
1	cup finely shredded, unpeeled zucchini

Preheat oven to 350°.

In a large bowl, combine flour, salt, baking soda, baking powder, cinnamon, nutmeg, orange peel and cocoa. Mix with a fork until blended. In another bowl, combine egg, sweetener and extracts. Mix well with a fork. Add wet mixture and zucchini to dry ingredients. Mix until just moistened.

Spoon mixture into an 8-inch round cake pan that has been sprayed with a nonstick cooking spray. Bake 20 minutes, until a toothpick inserted near the center of the cake comes out clean. Cool in pan.

Each serving provides:

62 Calories*

1/2	Bread Serving	2	g Protein
1/4	Vegetable Serving	1	g Fat
9	Additional Calories*	11	g Carbohydrate
		141	mg Sodium
		34	mg Cholesterol

*Add 18 calories if sugar or fructose is used as sweetener.

Pineapple Banana Cake

An interesting combination, very different and delicious!

Makes 8 servings

1-1/2	cups all-purpose flour
1/2	teaspoon baking soda
1/2	teaspoon ground cinnamon
1/4	teaspoon salt
	Sweetener equivalent to 12 teaspoons sugar
1/4	cup vegetable oil
1	egg
1	teaspoon vanilla extract
1/8	teaspoon banana extract
1/8	teaspoon lemon extract
1	cup canned crushed pineapple (unsweetened)
1/4	cup liquid from pineapple
1	medium, ripe banana, diced into 1/4-inch pieces

Preheat oven to 350°.

In a large bowl, sift flour, baking soda, cinnamon and salt.

In another bowl, combine sweetener, oil, egg, extracts and liquid from pineapple. Beat with a fork or wire whisk until well blended. Stir into dry ingredients. Add pineapple and banana. Stir until all ingredients are moistened.

Spoon mixture into a 9-inch round cake pan that has been sprayed with a nonstick cooking spray. Bake 50 minutes, until lightly browned. Cool in pan on a rack. Loosen cooled cake with a knife and remove carefully to a serving plate.

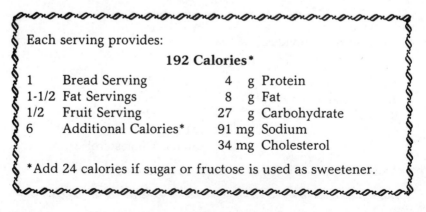

Each serving provides:

192 Calories*

1	Bread Serving	4	g	Protein
1-1/2	Fat Servings	8	g	Fat
1/2	Fruit Serving	27	g	Carbohydrate
6	Additional Calories*	91	mg	Sodium
		34	mg	Cholesterol

*Add 24 calories if sugar or fructose is used as sweetener.

Old World Apple Cake

You won't believe the New World ease!

Makes 8 servings

4   small, sweet apples, peeled and diced
4   eggs
2/3   cup nonfat dry milk
4   slices white or whole wheat bread, crumbled
1   cup part-skim ricotta cheese
1/2   teaspoon baking soda
1   teaspoon double-acting baking powder
2   teaspoons vanilla butternut flavor
1   teaspoon ground cinnamon
      Sweetener equivalent to 9 teaspoons sugar
Topping
1   tablespoon plus 1 teaspoon margarine, melted
1/4   teaspoon ground cinnamon
      Sweetener equivalent to 4 teaspoons sugar

Preheat oven to 350°. Place apples in an 8-inch square baking pan that has been sprayed with a nonstick cooking spray. In a blender container, combine remaining cake ingredients. Blend until smooth. Pour evenly over apples. Bake 40 minutes, until lightly browned.

Spread margarine over hot cake as soon as it comes from the oven. Combine remaining cinnamon and sweetener; sprinkle evenly over cake. Serve warm for best flavor.

Each serving provides:

185 Calories*

1	Protein Serving	10 g	Protein
1/2	Bread Serving	8 g	Fat
1/2	Fat Serving	19 g	Carbohydrate
1/2	Fruit Serving	252 mg	Sodium
1/4	Milk Serving	148 mg	Cholesterol
0	Additional Calories*		

*Add 26 calories if sugar or fructose is used as sweetener.

Carrot Cake with Vanilla Creme Frosting

Simply delicious!

Makes 8 servings

1-1/2 cups all-purpose flour
1 teaspoon *each* double-acting baking powder and baking soda
1-1/2 teaspoons ground cinnamon
1/2 teaspoon ground nutmeg
  Sweetener equivalent to 16 teaspoons sugar
2 tablespoons plus 2 teaspoons vegetable oil
4 eggs
1 teaspoon vanilla extract
1 cup canned crushed pineapple (unsweetened)
1/4 cup liquid from pineapple
1 cup finely shredded carrots
1/4 cup raisins
Frosting
1 cup part-skim ricotta cheese
1 teaspoon vanilla extract *or* vanilla butternut flavor
  Sweetener equivalent to 5 teaspoons sugar

Preheat oven to 350°. In a small bowl, combine dry ingredients. In a large bowl, combine sweetener, oil, eggs, vanilla and pineapple liquid. Beat on low speed of an electric mixer until smooth. Add dry ingredients; beat until just moistened. Stir in pineapple, carrots and raisins, mixing well. Spoon mixture into an 8-inch square baking pan that has been sprayed with a nonstick cooking spray. Bake 20 to 25 minutes. Cool in pan.
Combine frosting ingredients. Spread over cooled cake.

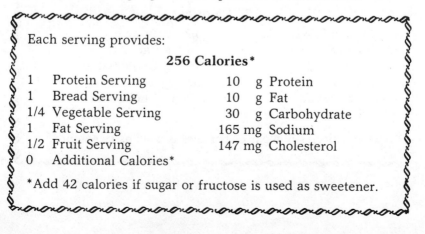

Each serving provides:

256 Calories*

1	Protein Serving	10	g Protein
1	Bread Serving	10	g Fat
1/4	Vegetable Serving	30	g Carbohydrate
1	Fat Serving	165	mg Sodium
1/2	Fruit Serving	147	mg Cholesterol
0	Additional Calories*		

*Add 42 calories if sugar or fructose is used as sweetener.

Rum Fruit Cake

*Instead of flour we've used graham cracker crumbs
for an interesting taste and texture.*

Makes 9 servings

4-1/2 ounces graham cracker crumbs (18 2-1/2-inch squares, crushed)
     Sweetener equivalent to 12 teaspoons sugar
1/8 teaspoon *each* ground cinnamon, cloves, allspice and nutmeg
3/4 teaspoon double-acting baking powder
1/2 teaspoon grated orange peel
1/8 teaspoon salt
1   egg, separated
1   teaspoon rum extract
1-1/2 cups canned fruit cocktail (unsweetened)
1/4 cup plus 2 tablespoons juice from fruit cocktail
3   tablespoons raisins

Preheat oven to 350°.

In a medium bowl, combine graham cracker crumbs, sweetener, spices, baking powder, orange peel and salt. Stir in egg yolk, rum extract and juice from fruit cocktail. Add fruit cocktail and raisins, mixing until well blended.

In a small, deep bowl, beat egg white on high speed of an electric mixer until stiff. Fold into fruit mixture gently, but thoroughly.

Spoon batter into a 4 x 8-inch loaf pan that has been sprayed with a nonstick cooking spray.

Bake 40 minutes, until top is dry. Cool in pan on a rack.

Each serving provides:

88 Calories*

1	Bread Serving	2	g	Protein
1/2	Fruit Serving	2	g	Fat
6	Additional Calories*	17	g	Carbohydrate
		170	mg	Sodium
		30	mg	Cholesterol

*Add 21 calories if sugar or fructose is used as sweetener.

Cinnamon Orange Coffee Cake

A very effective combination . . .

Makes 8 servings

Cake
3/4   cup all-purpose flour
2/3   cup nonfat dry milk
1/2   teaspoon grated orange peel
1/2   teaspoon baking soda
1/2   teaspoon double-acting baking powder
1/4   teaspoon salt
1/2   teaspoon ground cinnamon
1/4   cup plus 2 tablespoons frozen orange juice concentrate (un-
       sweetened), thawed
1/4   cup water
2   eggs
1/2   teaspoon orange extract
1   teaspoon vanilla extract
1   tablespoon plus 1 teaspoon margarine, melted
       Sweetener equivalent to 9 teaspoons sugar
Topping
2   tablespoons frozen orange juice concentrate (unsweetened),
       thawed
1/4   teaspoon ground cinnamon
       Sweetener equivalent to 1 teaspoon sugar

Preheat oven to 350°.

In a small bowl, combine and mix flour, dry milk, orange peel, baking soda, baking powder, salt and cinnamon.

In a larger bowl, combine remaining cake ingredients. Beat on low speed of an electric mixer until blended. Add dry ingredients. Beat on low speed until ingredients are just moistened. Beat on medium speed 1 minute.

Pour batter into an 8-inch round cake pan that has been sprayed with a nonstick cooking spray.

Bake 25 minutes, until a toothpick inserted in the center of the cake comes out clean.

Remove from oven and place pan on a rack to cool.

Spread remaining orange juice concentrate evenly over warm cake, using a pastry brush or the back of a spoon. Combine remaining cinnamon and sweetener and sprinkle evenly over cake.
Serve warm, for best flavor.

Each serving provides:

136 Calories*

1/4	Protein Serving	6	g Protein
1/2	Bread Serving	4	g Fat
1/2	Fat Serving	20	g Carbohydrate
1/2	Fruit Serving	180	mg Sodium
1/4	Milk Serving	70	mg Cholesterol
0	Additional Calories*		

*Add 20 calories if sugar or fructose is used as sweetener.

Pumpkin Log

What a treat!

Makes 8 servings

Cake

3/4	cup all-purpose flour
1	teaspoon double-acting baking powder
2	teaspoons ground cinnamon
1/2	teaspoon ground nutmeg
1/8	teaspoon ground allspice
1/8	teaspoon ground ginger
1/4	teaspoon salt
3	eggs
	Sweetener equivalent to 14 teaspoons sugar
1	teaspoon vanilla extract
1	tablespoon plus 1 teaspoon vegetable oil
1/4	cup water
1/2	cup canned pumpkin

Filling

1-1/4	cups part-skim ricotta cheese
1-1/2	teaspoons vanilla extract
1/2	teaspoon vanilla butternut flavor
	Sweetener equivalent to 6 teaspoons sugar

Preheat oven to 375°.

In a small bowl, sift flour, baking powder, spices and salt.

In another bowl, beat eggs on medium speed of an electric mixer for 5 minutes. Reduce mixer to low speed and beat in sweetener, vanilla, oil and water.

Add pumpkin and beat until blended. Add dry ingredients and beat on low speed until all ingredients are moistened.

Spread batter evenly in a 10 x 15-inch nonstick jelly roll pan that has also been sprayed with a nonstick cooking spray.

Bake 10 minutes. Let cake cool in pan 3 minutes, then loosen sides with a spatula. Run the spatula under the sides of the cake, loosening the entire cake. Turn cake out onto a towel. Roll into a log, with the towel, starting with the short side. Cool completely.

In a medium bowl, combine all filling ingredients, mixing well with a spoon.

Gently unroll cooled cake. Spread filling evenly over cake and roll up carefully.
Chill.

Each serving provides:

162 Calories*

1	Protein Serving	9 g	Protein
1/2	Bread Serving	8 g	Fat
1/8	Vegetable Serving	13 g	Carbohydrate
1/2	Fat Serving	230 mg	Sodium
0	Additional Calories*	115 mg	Cholesterol

*Add 40 calories if sugar or fructose is used as sweetener.

Honey Graham Spice Cake

An Old World favorite made easy and light . . .

Makes 4 servings

2   tablespoons *each* raisins and very hot water
2   ounces graham cracker crumbs (eight 2-1/2 inch squares, crushed)
2/3 cup nonfat dry milk
1   teaspoon double-acting baking powder
1/2 teaspoon baking soda
1   teaspoon ground cinnamon
1/2 teaspoon ground nutmeg
1/4 teaspoon ground allspice
2   eggs, slightly beaten
2   teaspoons *each* honey and vegetable oil
1/2 cup applesauce (unsweetened)
1   teaspoon vanilla extract
     Sweetener equivalent to 6 teaspoons sugar

Preheat oven to 375°. Combine raisins and water. Set aside. In a small bowl, combine graham cracker crumbs, dry milk, baking powder, baking soda and spices. In another bowl, combine raisins and water, eggs, honey, oil, applesauce, vanilla and sweetener. Mix with a fork until well blended. Stir dry ingredients into wet mixture. Mix well. Pour into a 4 x 8-inch nonstick loaf pan. Bake 25 minutes, until a toothpick inserted in the center of the cake comes out clean. Cool in pan 10 minutes. Invert onto a rack to finish cooling.

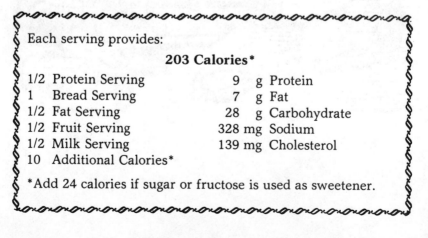

Each serving provides:

203 Calories*

1/2 Protein Serving   9   g Protein
1   Bread Serving   7   g Fat
1/2 Fat Serving   28 g Carbohydrate
1/2 Fruit Serving   328 mg Sodium
1/2 Milk Serving   139 mg Cholesterol
10   Additional Calories*

*Add 24 calories if sugar or fructose is used as sweetener.

Cinnamon Streusel Coffee Cake

So good with coffee!

Makes 8 servings

Streusel topping

1	tablespoon plus 1 teaspoon margarine, softened
3	tablespoons dry bread crumbs
1/2	teaspoon ground cinnamon
	Sweetener equivalent to 2 teaspoons sugar

Cake

1-1/4	cups plus 1 tablespoon all-purpose flour
1/4	teaspoon *each* salt and baking soda
2	teaspoons double-acting baking powder
	Sweetener equivalent to 10 teaspoons sugar
1	egg
2	tablespoons plus 2 teaspoons margarine, softened
1/2	cup plain lowfat yogurt
1-1/2	teaspoons vanilla extract

Preheat oven to 375°. In a small bowl, combine all topping ingredients. Mix well with a fork. Sift flour, salt, baking powder and baking soda into a small bowl. In a large bowl, combine sweetener, egg, margarine, yogurt and vanilla. Beat on low speed of an electric mixer until smooth. Stir dry mixture into wet ingredients. Mix until all ingredients are moistened. Spread batter in an 8-inch round nonstick cake pan. Sprinkle topping evenly over cake. Press topping lightly into cake. Bake 20 to 25 minutes, until a toothpick inserted in the center of the cake comes out clean. Cool in pan.

Each serving provides:

160 Calories*

1	Bread Serving	4	g Protein
1-1/2	Fat Servings	7	g Fat
19	Additional Calories*	19	g Carbohydrate
		280	mg Sodium
		35	mg Cholesterol

*Add 24 calories if sugar or fructose is used as sweetener.

Apricot Coffee Cake

Makes 8 servings

1-1/2   cups all-purpose flour
1/4   teaspoon salt
2   teaspoons double-acting baking powder
        Sweetener equivalent to 12 teaspoons sugar
1   egg
1/4   cup margarine, softened
1/3   cup nonfat dry milk
2/3   cup water
1   teaspoon vanilla extract
2   cups canned apricots (unsweetened), drained and chopped or
          sliced thin
        Ground cinnamon

Preheat oven to 375°.

In a small bowl, sift flour, salt and baking powder.

In another bowl, cream sweetener, egg and margarine on low speed of an electric mixer. Add dry milk, water and vanilla. Beat until blended.

Stir in dry ingredients. Stir until smooth.

Spread batter in an 8-inch square baking pan that has been sprayed with a nonstick cooking spray. Arrange apricots evenly over batter. Sprinkle liberally with cinnamon.

Bake 25 minutes, until a toothpick inserted in center of cake comes out clean.

Cool in pan.

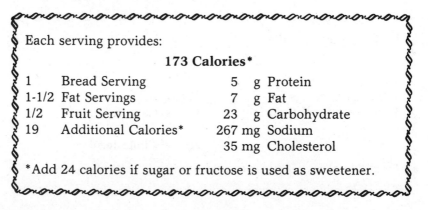

Each serving provides:

173 Calories*

1	Bread Serving	5	g Protein
1-1/2	Fat Servings	7	g Fat
1/2	Fruit Serving	23	g Carbohydrate
19	Additional Calories*	267	mg Sodium
		35	mg Cholesterol

*Add 24 calories if sugar or fructose is used as sweetener.

Cherry Kuchen

Makes 4 servings

4   slices white or whole wheat bread, crumbled
2/3   cup nonfat dry milk
2   tablespoons plus 2 teaspoons reduced-calorie margarine
1   teaspoon double-acting baking powder
1-1/2 teaspoons vanilla butternut flavor
       Sweetener equivalent to 4 teaspoons sugar
2   cups frozen dark sweet cherries (unsweetened), thawed
Topping
4   eggs
1   cup plain lowfat yogurt
1   teaspoon vanilla butternut flavor
1/2   teaspoon almond extract
       Sweetener equivalent to 9 teaspoons sugar

Preheat oven to 350°. In a medium bowl, combine bread, dry milk, margarine, baking powder, vanilla butternut flavor and sweetener. Mix with a fork until mixture resembles coarse crumbs. Pat crumbs in the bottom of an 8-inch square baking pan that has been sprayed with a nonstick cooking spray. Bake 10 minutes. Spread cherries evenly over crust. Beat eggs with a fork or a wire whisk. Beat in yogurt, remaining flavorings and remaining sweetener. Spread mixture evenly over cherries. Bake 30 to 40 minutes, until topping is set and lightly browned. Cool slightly. Cut into squares. Serve warm or cold.

Each serving provides:

316 Calories*

1 Protein Serving	16 g Protein
1 Bread Serving	12 g Fat
1 Fat Serving	35 g Carbohydrate
1 Fruit Serving	487 mg Sodium
1 Milk Serving	280 mg Cholesterol
0 Additional Calories*	

*Add 52 calories if sugar or fructose is used as sweetener.

Almond Oatmeal Bars

Quick and easy and makes a great breakfast on-the-go!

Makes 4 servings

3	ounces quick-cooking oats, uncooked
2/3	cup nonfat dry milk
1/2	teaspoon ground cinnamon
1/4	teaspoon ground nutmeg
	Dash ground allspice
1/2	teaspoon baking soda
1/2	teaspoon double-acting baking powder
1/4	cup raisins
1	cup applesauce (unsweetened)
1	teaspoon vanilla extract
3/4	teaspoon almond extract
	Sweetener equivalent to 6 teaspoons sugar

Preheat oven to 350°.

In a medium bowl, combine all dry ingredients and spices, mixing with a spoon.

Add remaining ingredients. Stir until mixture is completely moistened.

Spread mixture in an 8-inch square baking pan that has been sprayed with a nonstick cooking spray.

Bake 30 minutes, until lightly browned.

Cool slightly in pan. Cut into squares to serve.

Each serving provides:

187 Calories*

1	Bread Serving	8	g Protein
1	Fruit Serving	2	g Fat
1/2	Milk Serving	35	g Carbohydrate
0	Additional Calories*	149	mg Sodium
		2	mg Cholesterol

*Add 24 calories if sugar or fructose is used as sweetener.

Sticky Buns

So easy to do!

Makes 10 servings

3   tablespoons plus 1 teaspoon margarine, melted
2-1/2 teaspoons honey
       Sweetener equivalent to 2 tablespoons firmly-packed brown
       sugar
1/4 cup plus 1 tablespoon raisins
1   10-ounce package refrigerator biscuits (10 biscuits)

Preheat oven to 350°.

Combine margarine, honey and sweetener in the bottom of a 9-inch pie pan. Mix well and spread evenly in pan. Sprinkle raisins evenly over margarine mixture.

Arrange biscuits in pan.

Bake 20 minutes, until brown. Remove from oven and let sit 1 minute. Invert onto a serving plate.

Serve warm.

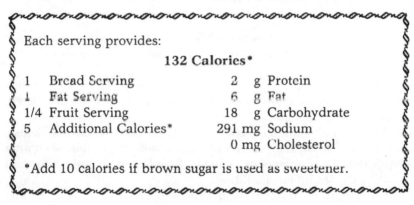

Each serving provides:

132 Calories*

1	Bread Serving	2	g Protein
1	Fat Serving	6	g Fat
1/4	Fruit Serving	18	g Carbohydrate
5	Additional Calories*	291 mg	Sodium
		0 mg	Cholesterol

*Add 10 calories if brown sugar is used as sweetener.

Marbled Cheese Pie

Lovely to look at, delightful to eat . . .

Makes 4 or 8 servings

Crust
8   2-1/2-inch graham cracker squares, crushed (2 ounces graham cracker crumbs)
2   teaspoons cocoa (unsweetened)
2   tablespoons margarine, melted
Filling
1-1/2 envelopes unflavored gelatin
1/2   cup water
2   cups part-skim ricotta cheese
1   cup evaporated skim milk
1-1/2 teaspoons vanilla extract
1-1/2 teaspoons vanilla butternut flavor
       Sweetener equivalent to 12 teaspoons sugar
1   tablespoon cocoa (unsweetened)
1   teaspoon chocolate extract

Preheat oven to 350°.

Combine crust ingredients in a 9-inch pie pan. Press crumbs onto sides and bottom of pan to form crust. Bake 8 minutes. Cool completely.

Sprinkle gelatin over water in a small saucepan. Let soften a few minutes. Heat over low heat until gelatin is completely dissolved, stirring frequently.

In a blender container, combine gelatin mixture, ricotta cheese, milk, vanilla, vanilla butternut and a *portion* of the sweetener equivalent to 10 teaspoons of sugar. Blend until smooth. Pour half of the mixture into a small bowl.

To remaining mixture, add remaining sweetener, cocoa, and chocolate extract. Blend until combined. Pour into a second bowl.

Chill both mixtures 10 minutes, or until slightly thickened.

Using 2 large spoons, drop mixtures alternately into cooled crust. Marble the top with a knife in a crisscross pattern.

Chill until firm.

For 4 servings

Each serving provides:

363 Calories*

2	Protein Servings	24	g Protein
1	Bread Serving	17	g Fat
1-1/2	Fat Servings	25	g Carbohydrate
1/2	Milk Serving	393	mg Sodium
6	Additional Calories*	41	g Cholesterol

*Add 48 calories if sugar or fructose is used as sweetener.

For 8 servings

Each serving provides:

182 Calories*

1	Protein Serving	12	g Protein
1/2	Bread Serving	9	g Fat
3/4	Fat Serving	13	g Carbohydrate
1/4	Milk Serving	197	mg Sodium
3	Additional Calories*	21	mg Cholesterol

*Add 24 calories if sugar or fructose is used as sweetener.

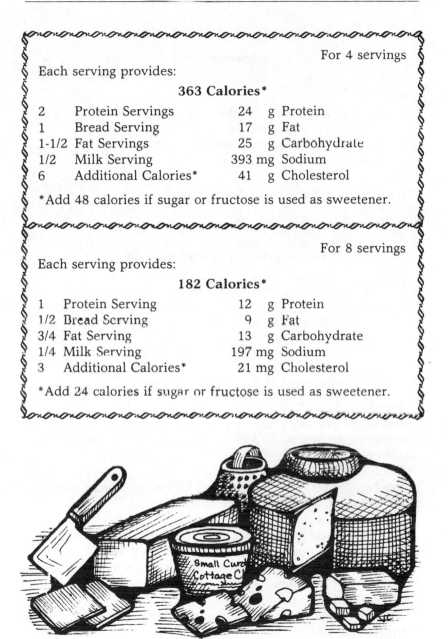

Strawberry-Topped Cheese Pie

(shown on cover)

Makes 6 servings

Crust

12   2-1/2-inch graham cracker squares, crushed (3 ounces graham cracker crumbs)
3   tablespoons margarine, melted
1/4   teaspoon ground cinnamon

Filling

2-1/4 cups part-skim ricotta cheese
3   eggs
1   tablespoon all-purpose flour
2   teaspoons vanilla extract
      Sweetener equivalent to 12 teaspoons sugar

Topping

1/2   cup orange juice (unsweetened)
1/2   cup water
1   tablespoon cornstarch
1   teaspoon strawberry extract
      Sweetener equivalent to 3 teaspoons sugar
      Few drops red food color
2   cups fresh strawberries, cut in half lengthwise

Preheat oven to 375°.

In a 9-inch pie pan, combine graham cracker crumbs, margarine and cinnamon. Mix well. Press crumbs onto bottom and sides of pan, forming a crust.

Bake 8 minutes.

In a blender container, combine all filling ingredients. Blend until smooth. Pour into crust.

Bake 30 minutes, until lightly browned. Cool slightly.

In a small saucepan, combine orange juice, water and cornstarch. Mix until cornstarch is completely dissolved.

Cook over medium heat, stirring constantly, until mixture comes to a full boil. Remove from heat. Stir in extract, remaining sweetener and red food color.

Arrange strawberries over top of pie. Spoon glaze evenly over berries.

Chill.

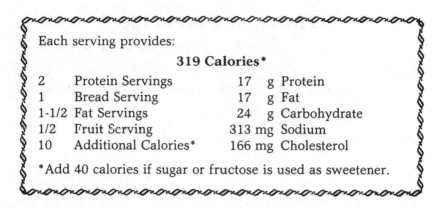

Each serving provides:

319 Calories*

2	Protein Servings	17	g Protein
1	Bread Serving	17	g Fat
1-1/2	Fat Servings	24	g Carbohydrate
1/2	Fruit Serving	313	mg Sodium
10	Additional Calories*	166	mg Cholesterol

*Add 40 calories if sugar or fructose is used as sweetener.

Pineapple Cheese Pie

Makes 4 or 8 servings

Crust
8   2-1/2-inch graham cracker squares, crushed (2 ounces graham cracker crumbs)
2   tablespoons margarine, melted
1/4   teaspoon grated lemon peel
Filling
1-1/2 envelopes unflavored gelatin
1/2   cup water
1-1/3 cups lowfat cottage cheese
1   cup orange juice (unsweetened)
1/4   teaspoon lemon extract
2   teaspoons vanilla extract
2/3   cup nonfat dry milk
      Sweetener equivalent to 9 teaspoons sugar
Topping
1   cup canned crushed pineapple (unsweetened)
1/4   cup juice from pineapple
      Sweetener equivalent to 3 teaspoons sugar
2   teaspoons cornstarch
2   tablespoons water

Preheat oven to 350°.

In a 9-inch pie pan, combine graham cracker crumbs, margarine and lemon peel. Mix well. Press onto bottom and sides of pan to form a crust. Bake 8 to 10 minutes, until browned. Cool completely.

Sprinkle gelatin over water in a small saucepan and let soften a few minutes. Heat over low heat until gelatin is completely dissolved, stirring frequently.

In a blender container, combine gelatin mixture with remaining filling ingredients. Blend until smooth. Pour into cooled crust. Chill until firm.

In a small saucepan, combine pineapple, juice and sweetener. Stir cornstarch into water in a small bowl and add to pineapple mixture. Cook over medium heat, stirring, until mixture comes to a boil. Boil 1 minute, stirring constantly. Spread evenly over pie. Chill.

For 4 servings
Each serving provides:

297 Calories*

1	Protein Serving	19	g	Protein
1	Bread Serving	8	g	Fat
1-1/2	Fat Servings	36	g	Carbohydrate
1	Fruit Serving	534	mg	Sodium
1/2	Milk Serving	5	mg	Cholesterol
5	Additional Calories*			

*Add 48 calories if sugar or fructose is used as sweetener.

For 8 servings
Each serving provides:

149 Calories*

1/2	Protein Serving	10	g	Protein
1/2	Bread Serving	4	g	Fat
3/4	Fat Serving	18	g	Carbohydrate
1/2	Fruit Serving	267	mg	Sodium
1/4	Milk Serving	3	mg	Cholesterol
3	Additional Calories*			

*Add 24 calories if sugar or fructose is used as sweetener.

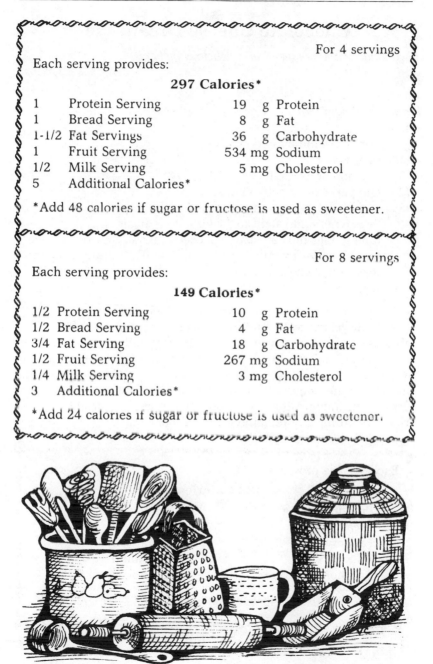

Chocolate Cheese Dream Pie

Two kinds of cheeses blend in a delicious pie!

Makes 8 servings

Crust
Prepare Graham Cracker Crust, page 409
Filling
2   envelopes unflavored gelatin
1-1/2 cups water
2/3   cup nonfat dry milk
1/2   cup part-skim ricotta cheese
2/3   cup lowfat cottage cheese
       Sweetener equivalent to 14 teaspoons sugar
2   tablespoons plus 2 teaspoons cocoa (unsweetened)
2   teaspoons *each* vanilla extract and vanilla butternut flavor
1   teaspoon chocolate extract
12   ice cubes

Preheat oven to 350°. Prepare crust. Cool completely.

Sprinkle gelatin over water in a small saucepan. Let soften a few minutes. Heat over low heat, stirring frequently, until gelatin is completely dissolved. In a blender container, combine gelatin mixture with remaining ingredients, *except* ice cubes. Blend until smooth. While continuing to blend, add ice cubes, 2 at a time. Blend until mixture thickens, about 1 minute. Spoon into cooled crust, discarding any remaining bits of ice. Chill.

Each serving provides:

133 Calories*

1/2	Protein Serving	10	g Protein
1/2	Bread Serving	5	g Fat
3/4	Fat Serving	11	g Carbohydrate
1/4	Milk Serving	211	mg Sodium
5	Additional Calories*	7	mg Cholesterol

*Add 28 calories if sugar or fructose is used as sweetener.

Fresh Orange Pie

A thick crunchy crust with refreshing fresh oranges!

Makes 8 servings

Crust

12   2-1/2 inch graham cracker squares, crushed (3 ounces graham
        cracker crumbs)
1/4   cup margarine, melted
1/4   teaspoon ground cinnamon
1/4   teaspoon grated orange peel

Filling

2   tablespoons plus 2 teaspoons cornstarch
1-1/2   cups orange juice (unsweetened)
1   tablespoon lemon juice
1/4   teaspoon orange extract
        Sweetener equivalent to 12 teaspoons sugar
2-1/2   cups fresh orange sections, drained (Navel oranges make the
        best choice.)

Preheat oven to 375°. Combine graham cracker crumbs with remaining crust ingredients in a 9-inch pie pan. Mix well. Press
crumbs onto bottom and sides of pan to form a crust. Bake 8
minutes. Cool completely. Dissolve cornstarch in a small amount of
the orange juice in a small saucepan. Add remaining orange juice,
lemon juice and orange extract. Bring mixture to a boil over
medium heat, stirring constantly. Boil 1 minute, stirring. Remove
from heat. Stir in sweetener and orange sections. Pour into cooled
crust. Chill.

Each serving provides:

153 Calories*

3/4	Bread Serving	3	g Protein
1-1/2	Fat Servings	7	g Fat
1	Fruit Serving	22	g Carbohydrate
10	Additional Calories*	138	mg Sodium
		0	mg Cholesterol

*Add 24 calories if sugar or fructose is used as sweetener.

Orange Sponge Pie

Our version of a Pennsylvania Dutch treat . . .

Makes 8 servings

Crust
Prepare Graham Cracker Crust, page 409, adding 1/4 teaspoon
  each grated orange peel and ground cinnamon
Filling

4	eggs, separated
	Sweetener equivalent to 12 teaspoons sugar
2	tablespoons all-purpose flour
1	teaspoon grated orange peel
1	teaspoon *each* orange extract and vanilla extract
1/2	cup frozen orange juice concentrate (unsweetened), thawed
2/3	cup nonfat dry milk
1/3	cup water
1	tablespoon plus 1 teaspoon reduced-calorie margarine

Preheat oven to 350°. Prepare crust. Cool completely.

In a medium bowl, combine egg yolks, *half* of the sweetener,
flour, orange peel, extracts, orange juice concentrate, dry milk,
water and margarine. Beat on low speed of an electric mixer until
combined. Beat on medium speed 1 minute. In a large bowl, beat
egg whites on medium speed until stiff. **Beat in remaining
sweetener.** Fold egg yolk mixture into egg whites gently, but
thoroughly. Pour mixture into cooled crust. Bake 25 minutes, until
golden. Cool on a wire rack 10 minutes. Chill.

Each serving provides:

164 Calories*

1/2	Protein Serving	7	g Protein
1/2	Bread Serving	8	g Fat
1	Fat Serving	17	g Carbohydrate
1/2	Fruit Serving	173 mg	Sodium
1/4	Milk Serving	138 mg	Cholesterol
7	Additional Calories*		

*Add 24 calories if sugar or fructose is used as sweetener.

Strawberry Cream Pie

Simply scrumptious!

Makes 6 servings

Crust
12   2-1/2 inch graham cracker squares, crushed (3 ounces graham
        cracker crumbs)
3   tablespoons margarine, melted
Filling
1-1/2   envelopes unflavored gelatin
3/4   cup water
1-1/2   cups part-skim ricotta cheese
1-1/2   teaspoons vanilla extract
3/4   teaspoon strawberry extract
        Sweetener equivalent to 12 teaspoons sugar
3   cups frozen strawberries (unsweetened) (*Do not thaw.*)

Preheat oven to 350°.

In a 9-inch pie pan, combine graham cracker crumbs and margarine. Mix well. Press crumbs onto bottom and sides of pan, forming a crust. Bake 8 minutes. Cool completely.

Sprinkle gelatin over water in a small saucepan. Let soften a few minutes. Heat, stirring frequently, over low heat until gelatin is completely dissolved. In a blender container, combine gelatin mixture, ricotta cheese, extracts and sweetener. Blend until smooth. Add frozen strawberries. Blend, stopping blender to stir frequently, until berries are puréed and mixture is smooth.

Spoon into cooled crust. Chill.

Each serving provides:

232 Calories*

1	Protein Serving	11	g Protein
1	Bread Serving	12	g Fat
1-1/2	Fat Servings	21	g Carbohydrate
1/2	Fruit Serving	242	mg Sodium
0	Additional Calories*	19	mg Cholesterol

*Add 32 calories if sugar or fructose is used as sweetener.

Pumpkin Cream Pie

Makes 8 servings

Crust

6	ounces Grape-Nuts® cereal, crushed
1/4	cup margarine, melted
1/8	teaspoon ground cinnamon

Filling

1	envelope unflavored gelatin
1/2	cup water
1	cup canned pumpkin
1-1/3	cups lowfat cottage cheese
1-1/2	teaspoons pumpkin pie spice
1	teaspoon vanilla extract
	Sweetener equivalent to 14 teaspoons sugar
2	egg whites
1/4	teaspoon cream of tartar

Preheat oven to 375°. In a 9-inch pie pan, combine all crust ingredients. Mix until crumbs are moistened. Press crumbs into the pan, forming a crust. Bake 8 minutes. Cool. Sprinkle gelatin over water in a small saucepan. Let soften a few minutes. Heat over low heat, stirring, until gelatin is dissolved. In a blender container, combine gelatin mixture, pumpkin, cottage cheese, pumpkin pie spice, vanilla, and a *portion* of the sweetener equivalent to 12 teaspoons of sugar. Blend until smooth. Pour into a bowl. In another bowl, beat egg whites and cream of tartar on high speed of an electric mixer until stiff. Beat in remaining sweetener. Fold egg whites into pumpkin mixture gently, but thoroughly. Spoon into cooled crust. Chill.

Each serving provides:

177 Calories*

1/2	Protein Serving	10	g	Protein
1	Bread Serving	6	g	Fat
1/4	Vegetable Serving	21	g	Carbohydrate
1-1/2	Fat Servings	452	mg	Sodium
5	Additional Calories*	1	mg	Cholesterol

*Add 28 calories if sugar or fructose is used as sweetener.

Almond Buttermilk Pie

A quick no-crust pie with a tangy surprise . . .

Makes 4 servings

1-1/2 cups buttermilk
4   eggs
1/4   cup reduced-calorie margarine
2   teaspoons vanilla extract
1   teaspoon almond extract
1/4   cup plus 2 tablespoons all-purpose flour
2   teaspoons double-acting baking powder
       Sweetener equivalent to 12 teaspoons sugar

Preheat oven to 350°.

In a blender container, combine all ingredients. Blend on low speed until all ingredients are moistened. Blend on high speed 1 minute.

Pour mixture into a 9-inch pie pan that has been sprayed with a nonstick cooking spray. Let stand for 5 minutes at room temperature.

Bake 35 minutes, until golden.

Cool 10 minutes, and then chill.

Each serving provides:

224 Calories*

1	Protein Serving	10	g Protein
1/2	Bread Serving	12	g Fat
1-1/2	Fat Servings	15	g Carbohydrate
1/2	Milk Serving	511	mg Sodium
0	Additional Calories*	278	mg Cholesterol

*Add 48 calories if sugar or fructose is used as sweetener.

Coconut Custard Cheese Pie

Rich and delicious!

Makes 6 servings

Crust

8	2-1/2-inch graham crackers, crushed (2 ounces graham cracker crumbs)
2	tablespoons margarine, melted
1/4	teaspoon coconut extract

Filling

2	cups part-skim ricotta cheese
4	eggs
1	tablespoon all-purpose flour
1-1/2	teaspoons vanilla extract
1/2	teaspoon vanilla butternut flavor
1	teaspoon coconut extract
1/3	cup nonfat dry milk
1/4	cup water
2	tablespoons shredded coconut (unsweetened)
	Sweetener equivalent to 12 teaspoons sugar

Preheat oven to 350°. In a 9-inch pie pan, combine all crust ingredients. Mix well until crumbs are moistened. Press crumbs onto bottom and sides of pan, forming a crust. Bake 8 minutes. Increase oven temperature to 375°. In a blender container, combine all filling ingredients. Blend until smooth. Pour into crust. Bake 25 minutes, until set and lightly browned. Cool slightly. Chill.

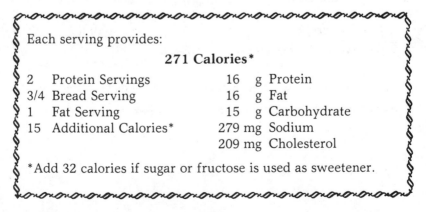

Each serving provides:

271 Calories*

2	Protein Servings	16 g	Protein
3/4	Bread Serving	16 g	Fat
1	Fat Serving	15 g	Carbohydrate
15	Additional Calories*	279 mg	Sodium
		209 mg	Cholesterol

*Add 32 calories if sugar or fructose is used as sweetener.

Graham Cracker Crust

8   2-1/2 inch graham cracker squares, crushed (2 ounces graham cracker crumbs)
2   tablespoons margarine, melted

Optional additions: (use any *one* of the following, if desired)
1/4   teaspoon grated orange *or* lemon peel
1/4   teaspoon ground cinnamon

Preheat oven to 350°.

In a 9-inch pie pan, combine graham cracker crumbs, margarine, and any one of the optional ingredients, if desired. Mix well, until crumbs are moistened.

Press crumbs onto bottom and sides of pan, forming a crust.

Bake 8 to 10 minutes, until browned.

This crust is delicious with cream, custard, cheese, and fruit fillings.

Each serving provides:

If used to serve:

4		6		8	
1	Bread Serving	3/4	Bread Serving	1/2	Bread Serving
1-1/2	Fat Servings	1	Fat Serving	3/4	Fat Serving
106	Calories	71	Calories	53	Calories
2	g Protein	1	g Protein	1	g Protein
8	g Fat	6	g Fat	4	g Fat
10	g Carbohydrate	7	g Carbohydrate	5	g Carbohydrate
160	mg Sodium	107	mg Sodium	80	mg Sodium
0	mg Cholesterol	0	mg Cholesterol	0	mg Cholesterol

Extra-Thick Graham Crust

For those who prefer a thicker crust . . .

12   2-1/2 inch graham cracker squares, crushed (3 ounces graham cracker crumbs)
3   tablespoons margarine, melted
1/4   teaspoon ground cinnamon, if desired

Preheat oven to 350°.
In a 9-inch pie pan, combine all ingredients. Mix well, until crumbs are moistened.
Press crumbs onto bottom and sides of pan, forming a crust.
Bake 8 to 10 minutes.

This crust is delicious with almost any cheese, cream, or fruit filling.

Each serving provides:
If used to serve:

4		6		8	
1-1/2	Bread Servings	1	Bread Serving	3/4	Bread Serving
2-1/4	Fat Servings	1-1/2	Fat Servings	1	Fat Serving
160	Calories	107	Calories	80	Calories
2	g Protein	1	g Protein	1	g Protein
10	g Fat	7	g Fat	5	g Fat
16	g Carbohydrate	11	g Carbohydrate	8	g Carbohydrate
240	mg Sodium	160	mg Sodium	120	mg Sodium
0	mg Cholesterol	0	mg Cholesterol	0	mg Cholesterol

Grape-Nuts® Crust

4-1/2 ounces Grape-Nuts® cereal, crushed
3   tablespoons margarine, melted
1/4   teaspoon cinnamon

Preheat oven to 350°.
In a 9-inch pie pan, combine all ingredients. Mix well until crumbs are moistened. Press crumbs onto bottom and sides of pan, forming a crust.
Bake 8 minutes.

This crust is especially good with pies that have apples, pears or peaches in the filling or in the topping.

Each serving provides:

If used to serve:

4			6			8		
1-1/2	Bread Servings		1	Bread Serving		3/4	Bread Serving	
2-1/4	Fat Servings		1-1/2	Fat Servings		1	Fat Serving	
190	Calories		127	Calories		95	Calories	
4	g Protein		3	g Protein		2	g Protein	
8	g Fat		6	g Fat		4	g Fat	
26	g Carbohydrate		17	g Carbohydrate		13	g Carbohydrate	
322	mg Sodium		215	mg Sodium		161	mg Sodium	
0	mg Cholesterol		0	mg Cholesterol		0	mg Cholesterol	

Shredded Wheat Crust

2-1/4 ounces shredded wheat cereal, crushed
2   tablespoons margarine, melted
1/4   teaspoon grated orange *or* lemon peel
1/4   teaspoon ground cinnamon
       Sweetener if desired

Preheat oven to 350°.

In a 9-inch pie pan, combine all ingredients. Mix well, until crumbs are moistened. Press crumbs onto bottom and sides of pan, forming a crust.

Bake 8 minutes.

This crust is a great alternative to a graham cracker crust.

Each serving provides:

If used to serve:

4		6		8	
3/4	Bread Serving	1/2	Bread Serving	1/4	Bread Serving
1-1/2	Fat Servings	1	Fat Serving	3/4	Fat Serving
108	Calories	72	Calories	54	Calories
2	g Protein	1	g Protein	1	g Protein
6	g Fat	4	g Fat	3	g Fat
12	g Carbohydrate	8	g Carbohydrate	6	g Carbohydrate
66 mg	Sodium	44 mg	Sodium	33 mg	Sodium
0 mg	Cholesterol	0 mg	Cholesterol	0 mg	Cholesterol

Bread Crumb Crust

An easy and inexpensive crust . . .

1/2   cup plus 1 tablespoon dry bread crumbs
3   tablespoons margarine, melted
1/4   teaspoon ground cinnamon
        Sweetener equivalent to 2 teaspoons sugar

Preheat oven to 350°.
In a 9-inch pie pan, combine all ingredients. Mix well, until crumbs are moistened.
Press crumbs onto bottom and sides of pan, forming a crust.
Bake 8 minutes.

This is an easy crust that can be used with many fillings. Try it without cinnamon and sweetener as an excellent crust for tuna, salmon, or vegetable pies.

Each serving provides:
If used to serve:

4		6		8	
3/4	Bread Serving	1/2	Bread Serving	1/4	Bread Serving
2-1/4	Fat Servings	1-1/2	Fat Serving	1	Fat Serving
134	Calories*	89	Calories*	67	Calories*
2	g Protein	1	g Protein	1	g Protein
10	g Fat	7	g Fat	5	g Fat
12	g Carbohydrate	8	g Carbohydrate	6	g Carbohydrate
208 mg Sodium		139 mg Sodium		104 mg Sodium	
0 mg Cholesterol		0 mg Cholesterol		0 mg Cholesterol	
*8 Additional calories if sugar or fructose is used as sweetener		*5 Additional calories if sugar or fructose is used as sweetener		*4 Additional calories if sugar or fructose is used as sweetener	

Pastry Crisps

Nice and crispy-crunchy . . .

Makes 8 servings
(about 5 crisps each serving)

1	cup plus 2 tablespoons all-purpose flour
	Pinch salt
1/4	teaspoon double-acting baking powder
1/4	teaspoon baking soda
1-1/2	ounces quick cooking oats, uncooked
	Sweetener equivalent to 9 teaspoons sugar
1/4	cup margarine, melted
1/4	cup plain lowfat yogurt

Topping

	Sweetener equivalent to 4 teaspoons sugar
1	teaspoon ground cinnamon

Preheat oven to 400°.

In a medium bowl, sift flour, salt, baking powder and baking soda. Stir in oats. Add sweetener, margarine and yogurt. Stir until well blended. Knead dough a few times until it holds together.

Roll dough between 2 sheets of wax paper into a rectangle 1/8-inch thick. Combine remaining sweetener and cinnamon and sprinkle evenly over dough.

Cut dough into 1 x 3-inch strips and place on a nonstick cookie sheet.

Bake 8 minutes, until golden.

Remove to a rack to cool. Divide evenly into 8 servings.

Each serving provides:

142 Calories*

1	Bread Serving	3	g	Protein
1-1/2	Fat Servings	6	g	Fat
6	Additional Calories*	18	g	Carbohydrate
		107	mg	Sodium
		0	mg	Cholesterol

*Add 26 calories if sugar or fructose is used as sweetener.

Crunchy Granola Bars

The kids will love this and so will the adults!

Makes 6 servings

4-1/2 ounces quick-cooking oats, uncooked
2   tablespoons honey
3/4   teaspoon almond extract
3/4   teaspoon coconut extract
       Sweetener equivalent to 3 teaspoons sugar
2   tablespoons vegetable oil
2   tablespoons hot water
       Ground cinnamon

Preheat oven to 250°.

In a medium bowl, combine all ingredients, *except* cinnamon, in the order given. Mix well with a spoon.

Place mixture on a nonstick cookie sheet. Shape into a rectangle 1/4-inch thick, slightly moistening your fingertips with water as you work.

Sprinkle with cinnamon.

Bake 1 hour.

Cut into squares immediately. Cool in pan. Divide into 6 even portions.

Each serving provides:

146 Calories*

1	Bread Serving	3	g Protein
1	Fat Serving	6	g Fat
20	Additional Calories*	20	g Carbohydrate
		1	mg Sodium
		0	mg Cholesterol

*Add 8 calories if sugar or fructose is used as sweetener.

Shortbread

A delicious lo-cal version of a traditional butter cookie . . .

Makes 4 servings
(6 cookies each serving)

3/4   cup all-purpose flour
1/2   teaspoon double-acting baking powder
1/4   cup reduced-calorie margarine
2   teaspoons butter flavor
       Sweetener equivalent to 6 teaspoons sugar

Preheat oven to 375°.

In a small bowl, combine flour and baking powder. Add remaining ingredients and blend well with a fork to form a dough.

Work dough into a ball with your hands. Divide into 24 pieces and roll each into a ball. Place on a nonstick cookie sheet. Flatten each cookie, using the bottom of a glass.

Bake 10 minutes, until bottoms are lightly browned. Remove to a rack to cool.

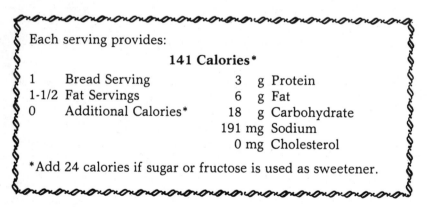

Each serving provides:

141 Calories*

1	Bread Serving	3	g Protein
1-1/2	Fat Servings	6	g Fat
0	Additional Calories*	18	g Carbohydrate
		191	mg Sodium
		0	mg Cholesterol

*Add 24 calories if sugar or fructose is used as sweetener.

Orange Cookies

Makes 4 servings
(6 cookies each serving)

3/4   cup all-purpose flour
1/2   teaspoon double-acting baking powder
1/4   cup reduced-calorie margarine
1   teaspoon orange extract
1/2   teaspoon grated orange peel
      Sweetener equivalent to 6 teaspoons sugar

Preheat oven to 375°.

In a small bowl, stir baking powder into flour. Add remaining ingredients and blend well with a fork to form a dough.

Work dough into a ball with your hands. Divide into 24 pieces and roll each into a ball. Place on a nonstick cookie sheet. Flatten each ball to 1/4-inch thick with a fork, in a crisscross pattern.

Bake 10 minutes, until bottoms are lightly browned. Remove to a rack to cool.

Each serving provides:

144 Calories*

1	Bread Serving	3	g	Protein
1-1/2	Fat Servings	6	g	Fat
0	Additional Calories*	18	g	Carbohydrate
		191	mg	Sodium
		0	mg	Cholesterol

*Add 24 calories if sugar or fructose is used as sweetener.

Pineapple Oatmeal Drops

An easy cookie with an unusual flavor . . .

Makes 2 servings
(8 cookies each serving)

3/4   ounces quick-cooking oats, uncooked
3   tablespoons all-purpose flour
1/2   teaspoon double-acting baking powder
1/3   cup nonfat dry milk
1/2   teaspoon ground cinnamon
       Sweetener equivalent to 4 teaspoons sugar
1/2   cup canned crushed pineapple (unsweetened), drained
2   tablespoons juice from pineapple
1/2   teaspoon vanilla extract

Preheat oven to 350°.
In a medium bowl, combine all dry ingredients. Stir to combine.
Stir in remaining ingredients, stirring until mixture is well blended.
Drop mixture by teaspoonfuls onto a nonstick cookie sheet. (Makes 16 cookies.)
Bake 15 minutes, until lightly browned.
Let cool in pan 5 minutes. Remove to a rack to finish cooling.

Each serving provides:

171 Calories*

1   Bread Serving   7 g Protein
1/2 Fruit Serving   1 g Fat
1/2 Milk Serving   33 g Carbohydrate
0   Additional Calories*   169 mg Sodium
                                2 mg Cholesterol

*Add 32 calories if sugar or fructose is used as sweetener.

Oatmeal Raisin Drops

Makes 8 servings
(4   cookies each serving)

1/2   cup plus 1 tablespoon all-purpose flour
3-3/4 ounces quick-cooking oats, uncooked
1/2   teaspoon double-acting baking powder
1/2   teaspoon baking soda
1/4   teaspoon ground cinnamon
       Sweetener equivalent to 1/4-cup firmly-packed brown sugar
1/4   cup plus 1 tablespoon plus 1 teaspoon reduced-calorie margarine
1   egg
1   teaspoon vanilla extract
2   tablespoons water
1/2   cup raisins

Preheat oven to 375°.

In a medium bowl, combine flour, oats, baking powder, baking soda, cinnamon and sweetener. Add margarine. Mix well with a fork until mixture resembles coarse crumbs.

Beat egg with vanilla and water. Stir into dry ingredients. Add raisins and stir until all ingredients are moistened.

Drop mixture by teaspoonfuls onto a nonstick cookie sheet, making 32 cookies.

Bake 10 to 12 minutes, until lightly browned.

Remove to a rack to cool.

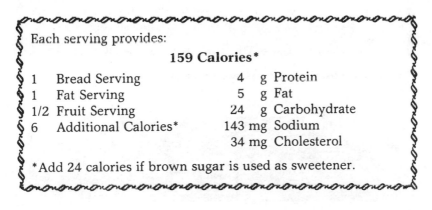

Each serving provides:

159 Calories*

1	Bread Serving	4	g	Protein
1	Fat Serving	5	g	Fat
1/2	Fruit Serving	24	g	Carbohydrate
6	Additional Calories*	143	mg	Sodium
		34	mg	Cholesterol

*Add 24 calories if brown sugar is used as sweetener.

Banana Drop Cookies

Makes 2 servings
(6 cookies each serving)

3/4   ounce quick-cooking oats, uncooked
3   tablespoons all-purpose flour
1/4   teaspoon double-acting baking powder
1/4   teaspoon baking soda
1/4   teaspoon banana extract
1/2   teaspoon vanilla butternut flavor
1/2   medium, ripe banana, mashed
       Sweetener equivalent to 3 teaspoons sugar

Preheat oven to 375°.

In a small bowl, combine oats, flour, baking powder and baking soda. Add remaining ingredients and stir until blended.

Drop mixture by teaspoonfuls onto a nonstick cookie sheet, making 12 cookies.

Bake 10 minutes, until lightly browned.

Remove to a rack to cool.

Each serving provides:

116 Calories*

1   Bread Serving   3   g Protein
1/2 Fruit Serving   1   g Fat
0   Additional Calories*   23   g Carbohydrate
                              80 mg Sodium
                              0 mg Cholesterol

*Add 24 calories if sugar or fructose is used as sweetener.

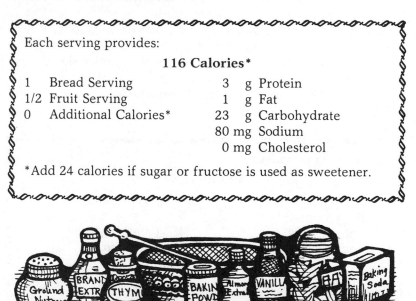

Apple Chews

A real quickie . . .

*Makes 2 servings
(8 cookies each serving)*

1   small, sweet apple, unpeeled, coarsely grated
2/3   cup nonfat dry milk
1/2   teaspoon double-acting baking powder
1/4   teaspoon ground cinnamon
1   teaspoon vanilla extract
1   egg white
1   ounce graham cracker crumbs (four 2-1/2 inch squares, crushed)
       Sweetener equivalent to 4 teaspoons sugar

Preheat oven to 350°.
In a small bowl, combine all ingredients. Mix well with a fork until well blended.
Drop mixture by teaspoonfuls onto a nonstick cookie sheet, making 16 cookies.
Bake 15 minutes, until lightly browned.
Remove to a rack to cool.

Each serving provides:

190 Calories*

1   Bread Serving
1/2 Fruit Serving
1   Milk Serving
10   Additional Calories*

11   g Protein
2   g Fat
32   g Carbohydrate
355 mg Sodium
4   mg Cholesterol

*Add 32 calories if sugar or fructose is used as sweetener.

Frozen Butter Mints

They melt in your mouth.

Makes 2 servings

1/3	cup nonfat dry milk
1/8	teaspoon peppermint extract
1/4	teaspoon vanilla butternut flavor
2	tablespoons water
	Sweetener equivalent to 2 teaspoons sugar

In a small bowl, combine all ingredients. Mix thoroughly.

Line a flat pan with wax paper.

Drop mixture by teaspoonfuls onto wax paper. Place in freezer for at least 20 minutes.

Eat candies right from the freezer.

Each serving provides:

48 Calories*

1/2	Milk Serving	5 g	Protein
0	Additional Calories*	0 g	Fat
		6 g	Carbohydrate
		65 mg	Sodium
		2 mg	Cholesterol

*Add 16 calories if sugar or fructose is used as sweetener.

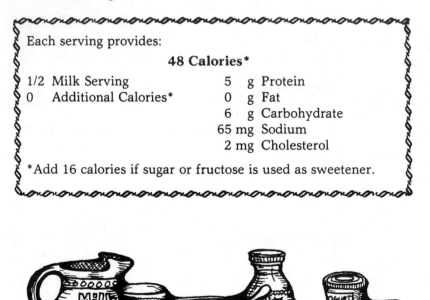

Chocolate Raisin Crunch

Makes 4 servings

2/3	cup nonfat dry milk
1	tablespoon plus 1 teaspoon cocoa (unsweetened)
	Sweetener equivalent to 8 teaspoons sugar
1	teaspoon vanilla extract
2	tablespoons plus 2 teaspoons water†
2	tablespoons raisins
1-1/2	ounces corn flakes cereal

In a small bowl, combine dry milk and cocoa.

Add remaining ingredients in order given, mixing well.

Press mixture into the bottom of a 4 x 8-inch nonstick loaf pan. Cover and refrigerate until firm.

To serve, cut into squares.

†If you use sugar or fructose as sweetener, use only 1 tablespoon plus 2 teaspoons water.

Each serving provides:

111 Calories*

1/2	Bread Serving	7	g Protein
1/4	Fruit Serving	0	g Fat
1/2	Milk Serving	20	g Carbohydrate
5	Additional Calories*	199	mg Sodium
		2	mg Cholesterol

*Add 32 calories if sugar or fructose is used as sweetener.

A note about adding water to the following candy recipes:

Different sweeteners react in different ways when combined with dry milk and water. When making the following candies, add the water a little at a time. If mixture is too soft to roll into balls, chill until firm, and then roll. If mixture is too dry, add water, a few drops at a time.

Marzipan

Makes 1 serving
(4 candies each serving)

1/3   cup nonfat dry milk
        Sweetener equivalent to 4 teaspoons sugar
1/4   teaspoon almond extract
1/4   teaspoon vanilla extract
2   drops food color, any color
2-1/2 teaspoons water†

In a small bowl, combine all ingredients, adding water last. Mix well.

Divide mixture evenly and roll into 4 balls. Place on wax paper, cover with plastic wrap, and chill.

†If you are using sugar or fructose as sweetener, use only 1-1/2-teaspoons of water. (See note on adding water to candies, at top of page.)

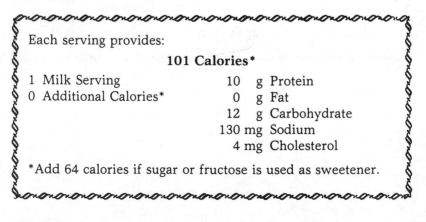

Each serving provides:

101 Calories*

1 Milk Serving   10   g Protein
0 Additional Calories*   0   g Fat
                            12   g Carbohydrate
                           130 mg Sodium
                             4 mg Cholesterol

*Add 64 calories if sugar or fructose is used as sweetener.

Rum Balls

These delightful morsels will be a favorite.

Makes 2 servings
(3 candies each serving)

1/3 cup nonfat dry milk
2   teaspoons cocoa (unsweetened)
1/2 ounce graham cracker crumbs (two 2-1/2 inch squares, crushed)
     Sweetener equivalent to 6 teaspoons sugar
1/2 teaspoon vanilla extract
1/4 teaspoon rum extract
1   tablespoon plus 1 teaspoon water†

In a small bowl, combine dry milk and cocoa. Mix together, pressing out lumps with the back of a spoon.

Set aside 2 teaspoons of the graham cracker crumbs. Add remaining crumbs and all remaining ingredients to cocoa mixture, adding water last.

Divide mixture evenly and roll into 6 balls. Roll balls in reserved crumbs. Cover and chill.

(Variation: In place of rum extract, try 1/4 teaspoon almond extract *or* 1/8 teaspoon peppermint extract.)

†If you are using sugar or fructose as sweetener, use only 2-3/4 teaspoons of water. (See note on adding water to candies, page 424.)

Each serving provides:

87 Calories*

1/2 Bread Serving	7	g Protein
1/2 Milk Serving	1	g Fat
5 Additional Calories*	12	g Carbohydrate
	113	mg Sodium
	2	mg Cholesterol

*Add 48 calories if sugar or fructose is used as sweetener.

Coconut Bon Bons

Sure to satisfy your sweet tooth . . .

Makes 1 serving
(4 candies each serving)

2 teaspoons finely shredded coconut (unsweetened)
1/3 cup nonfat dry milk
Sweetener equivalent to 4 teaspoons sugar
1/2 teaspoon coconut extract
1/4 teaspoon vanilla extract *or* vanilla butternut flavor
2-1/2 teaspoons water†

Set aside 1/2 teaspoon of the coconut.

In a small bowl, combine remaining coconut with all of the remaining ingredients, adding water last. Mix well.

Divide mixture evenly and roll into 4 balls. Roll balls in reserved coconut.

Cover and chill.

†If you are using sugar or fructose as sweetener, use only 1-1/2-teaspoons of water. (See note on adding water to candies, page 424.)

Each serving provides:

118 Calories*

1 Milk Serving
20 Additional Calories*

11 g Protein
2 g Fat
13 g Carbohydrate
131 mg Sodium
4 mg Cholesterol

*Add 64 calories if sugar or fructose is used as sweetener.

Sauces and Toppings

Sauces can enhance even the simplest of meals. From our Cinnamon Yogurt Sauce for fruit to our Apricot Brandy Sauce for chicken, we offer you some uniquely different combinations that will allow you to create many exciting finished items.

Honey Mustard Sauce

Serve with sliced meat, chicken or cheese.

Makes 6 servings
(2 tablespoons each serving)

1/2   cup prepared mustard
1/4   cup honey
2   teaspoons soy sauce

Combine all ingredients in a small bowl. Mix until well blended.

Each serving provides:

40 Calories

40 Additional Calories

1   g Protein
1   g Fat
13 g Carbohydrate
407 mg Sodium
0   mg Cholesterol

Chili Orange Barbecue Sauce

Brush on chicken or meat while broiling or grilling.

Makes 4 servings
(2 tablespoons each serving)

1/4   cup plus 2 tablespoons chili sauce
1   tablespoon plus 1 teaspoon vegetable oil
2   tablespoons frozen orange juice concentrate (unsweetened), thawed

Combine all ingredients. Baste chicken or meat.

Each serving provides:

81 Calories

1   Fat Serving
1/4 Fruit Serving
25   Additional Calories

1   g Protein
5   g Fat
10 g Carbohydrate
344 mg Sodium
0   mg Cholesterol

Apricot Brandy Sauce

Delicious on leftover chicken or turkey . . .

Makes 4 servings
(3 tablespoons each serving)

2   teaspoons cornstarch
1/2   cup water
1/4   cup reduced-calorie apricot spread (16 calories per 2 tea-
       spoons)
1-1/2 teaspoons brandy extract
1   packet instant chicken flavored broth mix

In a small saucepan, dissolve cornstarch in water. Add remaining ingredients. Bring to a boil over medium-low heat, stirring frequently. Boil 3 minutes, stirring.

Serve hot or cold.

Each serving provides:

32 Calories

32 Additional Calories

    0 g Protein
    0 g Fat
    8 g Carbohydrate
208 mg Sodium
    0 mg Cholesterol

Orange "Butter"

Serve on cooked carrots or sweet potatoes or on French toast or bread.
Makes 2 servings
(2 teaspoons each serving)

1   tablespoon plus 1 teaspoon reduced-calorie margarine
1/2 teaspoon grated orange peel
1/4 teaspoon orange extract

Combine all ingredients in a small bowl. Mix well. Serve, or chill for later servings.

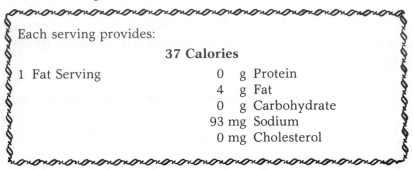

Each serving provides:

37 Calories

1 Fat Serving

0 g Protein
4 g Fat
0 g Carbohydrate
93 mg Sodium
0 mg Cholesterol

Baked Potato Topper

Doubles as a salad dressing . . .

Makes 8 servings
(2 tablespoons each serving)

1   cup plain lowfat yogurt
1/2   teaspoon dill weed
1-1/2 teaspoons dried chives
1/4   teaspoon salt
1/8   teaspoon pepper
2   teaspoons imitation bacon bits

Combine all ingredients and mix well. Chill.

Each serving provides:

20 Calories

1/4 Milk Serving	2 g Protein
3 Additional Calories	1 g Fat
	2 g Carbohydrate
	111 mg Sodium
	2 mg Cholesterol

Strawberry Yogurt Sauce

Great with fresh fruit salad or over cottage cheese . . .

Makes 4 servings
(1/2 cup each serving)

1   cup plain lowfat yogurt
1   cup strawberries, fresh or frozen (unsweetened)
1   teaspoon vanilla extract
      Sweetener equivalent to 4 teaspoons sugar

In a blender container, combine all ingredients. Blend until smooth.

Chill.

Each serving provides:

53 Calories*

1/4	Fruit Serving	4 g	Protein
1/2	Milk Serving	1 g	Fat
0	Additional Calories*	7 g	Carbohydrate
		40 mg	Sodium
		3 mg	Cholesterol

*Add 16 calories if sugar or fructose is used as sweetener.

Cinnamon Yogurt Sauce

Delicious over baked apples or over cooked winter squash . . .

Makes 4 servings
(1/4 cup each serving)

1   cup plain lowfat yogurt
1   teaspoon ground cinnamon
1   teaspoon vanilla extract
    Sweetener equivalent to 4 teaspoons sugar

In a small bowl, combine all ingredients, mixing well. Chill.

Each serving provides:

43 Calories*

1/2 Milk Serving	3 g Protein
0 Additional Calories*	1 g Fat
	4 g Carbohydrate
	39 mg Sodium
	3 mg Cholesterol

*Add 16 calories if sugar or fructose is used as sweetener.

Strawberry Sauce

Be creative. This sauce will enhance lots of foods.

Makes 2 servings
(1/2-cup each serving)

1   cup frozen strawberries, thawed and drained (Measure while
     frozen.)
1   tablespoon reduced-calorie strawberry spread (16 calories
     per 2 teaspoons)

Combine and use as desired.
Variation: Use reduced-calorie orange marmalade in place of
     strawberry spread.

Each serving provides:

39 Calories

1/2 Fruit Serving   0   g Protein
12   Additional Calories   0   g Fat
                                10   g Carbohydrate
                                 2 mg Sodium
                                 0 mg Cholesterol

Hot Fudge Sauce

Makes a great fondue for fresh fruit!

Makes 2 servings
(1/4 cup each serving)

1   tablespoon cocoa (unsweetened)
1-1/2 teaspoons cornstarch
1/2   cup evaporated skim milk
          Sweetener equivalent to 4 teaspoons sugar
1/2   teaspoon vanilla extract
1/4   teaspoon chocolate extract

In a small saucepan, combine cocoa and cornstarch. Mix well, pressing out all lumps with the back of a spoon.

Stir in evaporated milk. Stir until cornstarch and cocoa are dissolved.

Cook, stirring constantly, over medium-low heat, until mixture boils. Remove from heat. Stir in sweetener and extracts.

Serve hot.

Each serving provides:

71 Calories*

1/2 Milk Serving   5 g Protein
15 Additional Calories* 1 g Fat
                          10 g Carbohydrate
                          74 mg Sodium
                          3 mg Cholesterol

*Add 32 calories if sugar or fructose is used as sweetener.

Chocolate Pineapple Sauce

Delicious on frozen dietary dessert or on ricotta cheese . . .

Makes 2 servings
(1/2 cup each serving)

1	tablespoon plus 1 teaspoon cocoa (unsweetened)
2/3	cup nonfat dry milk
1	teaspoon vanilla extract
1/2	cup canned crushed pineapple (unsweetened)
2	tablespoons juice from pineapple
	Sweetener equivalent to 4 teaspoons sugar

In a small bowl, combine cocoa and dry milk. Mix, pressing out any lumps with the back of a spoon.

Add remaining ingredients and mix well.

Serve, or refrigerate for later servings.

Each serving provides:

146 Calories*

1/2	Fruit Serving	10 g	Protein
1	Milk Serving	1 g	Fat
10	Additional Calories*	24 g	Carbohydrate
		133 mg	Sodium
		4 mg	Cholesterol

*Add 32 calories if sugar or fructose is used as sweetener.

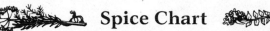

Spice Chart

A guide to flavorful combinations

	Soups	Salads/ Dressings	Fish/ Seafood	Meat	Poultry	Fruit	Vegetables	Eggs/ Cheese	Desserts
Allspice						✔	✔		
Anise									✔
Basil	✔	✔	✔	✔	✔		✔	✔	
Bay leaf	✔		✔	✔	✔		✔		
Cardamom				✔					✔
Celery seed		✔	✔				✔		
Chili powder		✔		✔	✔				
Chives	✔	✔			✔		✔	✔	
Cinnamon						✔		✔	✔
Cloves	✔			✔		✔			✔
Coriander	✔		✔	✔					✔
Cumin				✔	✔				
Curry			✔	✔	✔				
Dill	✔	✔	✔		✔		✔	✔	
Fennel	✔		✔	✔					
Ginger			✔	✔		✔	✔		✔
Mace	✔								✔
Marjoram	✔	✔		✔	✔		✔	✔	
Nutmeg				✔		✔	✔	✔	✔
Oregano	✔	✔	✔	✔	✔		✔	✔	
Paprika		✔	✔		✔				
Rosemary			✔	✔	✔		✔		
Saffron	✔		✔		✔				
Sage	✔			✔					
Savory	✔			✔			✔		
Tarragon		✔	✔		✔		✔	✔	
Thyme	✔	✔		✔	✔		✔		

Index

Almond
  Almond Bread Puff, 91
  Almond Buttermilk Pie, 407
  Almond Oatmeal Bars, 394
Almost a Quiche, 115
Almost French-Fried Onion Rings, 232
Appetizers
  Chili-Cheddar Cheese Ball, 97
  Crab and Cheese Ball, 70
  Spinach Cheese Puffs, 120
  Yogurt Cheese and Cheddar Log, 71
Apples
  Apple and Carrot Pudding, 372
  Apple-Cheddar Custard, 124
  Apple Chews, 421
  Apple Crisp, 374
  Apple Custard Squares, 370
  Apple Kugel, 278
  Baked Apple Alaska, 371
  Cottage Apple Bake, 129
  Dutch Apple Pancake, 84
  "Fried" Apples, 373
  Multi-Grain Apple Muffins, 285
  Old World Apple Cake, 383
  Our Waldorf Salad, 18
  Pumpkin Apple Muffins, 288
  Surprise Apple Bean Cake, 319
  Sweet Potatoes and Apples, 264
Applesauce
  Applesauce Cheese Mold, 376
  Applesauce Pancakes, 85
  Applesauce Raisin Supreme, 375
  Quick and Creamy Applesauce
    Dessert, 72
Apricots
  Apricot Brandy Sauce, 429
  Apricot Coffee Cake, 392
  Apricot-Glazed Carrots, 235
  Apricot-Glazed Chicken, 175
  Banana Apricot Squares, 364
Artichoke Hearts, Marinated, 24
Asparagus
  Asparagus Cheese Tart, 111
  Asparagus Vinaigrette, 40

Bacon and Egg Salad, 79
Baked Apple Alaska, 371
Baked Banana Crumble, 362
Baked Cracked Wheat, 275
Baked Custard, 89
Baked Lentils and Tomatoes, 315
Baked Orange Squash, 255
Baked Pears, 369
Baked Pineapple Tapioca, 355
Baked Potato Topper, 431
Baked Squash Southern Style, 252
Bananas
  Baked Banana Crumble, 362
  Banana Apricot Squares, 364
  Banana Bavarian, 62
  Banana Bran Muffins, 284
  Banana Cake, 378
  Banana Drop Cookies, 420
  Banana Fritters, 88
  Banana Puff, 86
  Banana Raisin Pudding, 366
  Banana Toast, 363
  Banana New Orleans, 361
  Pineapple Banana Cake, 382
  Tofu Banana Cream Pie, 330
  Tofu Banana Fritters, 327
  Tofu, Peanut Butter and Banana
    Spread, 328
Barbecued Beef Liver, 200
Barbecued Beef Loaf, 214
Barbecued Black-Eyed Peas, 314
Barbecued Franks, 216
Barley
  Barley-Cheddar Sauté, 273
  Barley-Mushroom Soup, 13
Basic Cooking Directions for Legumes,
  303
Basic Cooking Directions for
  Vegetables, 227
Beans, Green
  Dilly Beans, 41
  Easiest Bean Salad, 311
  Italian Green Bean Salad, 26
  Green Beans and Tomatoes, 233

Beans, Kidney
  Bean-Stuffed Eggplant, 305
  Cheesy Beans and Rice, 306
  Easiest Bean Salad, 311
  Garlic and Bean Soup, 12
  Kidney Beans Provençal, 317
  Prairie Bean Tortillas, 304
  Roman Tuna Salad, 312
  Tangy Baked Kidney Beans, 316
Beans, Lima
  Pepper-Bean Casserole, 313
Beans, Pink
  Pink Bean "Pumpkin" Pie, 318
  Prairie Bean Tortillas, 304
Beans, Pinto
  Surprise Apple Bean Cake, 319
Beans, Soybeans
  Bean Stroganoff, 309
  Mushroom Soy Loaf Supreme, 310
  Soybean Soufflé, 308
Beef
  Barbecued Beef Loaf, 214
  Chili Meatloaf, 213
  Hungarian Meatballs and
    Sauerkraut, 218
  Meatloaf Florentine, 212
  Meat Sauce and Spaghetti Squash,
    219
  Pepper Steak, 215
  Steak Diane, 210
  Terijaki Steak, 211
Beer Bread, 294
Beets á l'Orange, 236
Bengal Seafood Salad, 157
Best Cole Slaw, 29
Best Stewed Tomatoes, 241
Bleu Cheese Dressing, 50
Blueberries
  Blueberry Bread 'n Butter Pudding,
    351
  Blueberry Cheese Pudding, 107
  Blueberry Clafouti, 352
  Elegant Floating Islands, 55
  Red, White and Blueberry Parfaits,
    102
Biscuits (Also see Rolls, Muffins)
  Cheese Pinwheels, 301
  Quick Onion Biscuits, 296
  Yogurt Biscuits, 300
Bouillabaise, 159
Bread Crumb Crust, 413

Bread Pudding
  Blueberry Bread 'n Butter Pudding,
    351
  Pineapple Cheese Bread Pudding,
    283
Breaded Fillet of Fish, 134
Breaded Turkey Cutlets, 183
Breads (Also see Biscuits, Muffins,
    Rolls)
  Beer Bread, 294
  Onion Bread, 298
  Orange Raisin Bread, 292
  Peanut Butter Bread, 337
  Pumpkin Bread, 291
  Skillet Cheese Corn Bread, 293
Broccoli
  Broccoli Cheese Puff, 113
  Broccoli Pancakes, 121
  Chicken and Broccoli Bake, 179
  Cream of Broccoli Soup, 9
  Lemon Broccoli, 245
Broiled Grapefruit Delight, 358
Brown Rice and Vegetable Salad, 31
Brussels Sprouts, Savory, 242
Buckwheat-Cheese Bake, 274
Buttermilk Potatoes, 261

Cabbage
  Best Cole Slaw, 29
  Cabbage Soup, 3
  Cabbage with Mustard Sauce, 246
  No Noodle Fruit Kugel, 126
  Pineapple Slaw, 42
  Red Cabbage Salad, 37
Caesar Salad, 32
Cakes
  Almond Oatmeal Bars, 394
  Apricot Coffee Cake, 392
  Banana Apricot Squares, 364
  Banana Cake, 378
  Carrot Cake with Vanilla Creme
    Frosting, 384
  Cherry Kuchen, 393
  Chocolate Peanut Butter Brownies,
    379
  Chocolate Zucchini Spice Cake, 381
  Cinnamon Orange Coffee Cake, 386
  Cinnamon Streusel Coffee Cake, 391
  Heavenly Chocolate Cake, 380
  Honey Graham Spice Cake, 390
  Old World Apple Cake, 383

Peanut Butter-Banana Squares, 345
Peanut Butter-Scotch Bars, 342
Pineapple Banana Cake, 382
Pumpkin Log, 388
Rum Fruit Cake, 385
Surprise Apple Bean Cake, 319
Calves Liver Stroganoff, 202
Candies
  A Note About Adding Water to
    Candy Recipes, 424
  Chocolate Peanut Butter Bars, 336
  Chocolate Raisin Crunch, 423
  Coconut Bon Bons, 426
  Frozen Butter Mints, 422
  Marzipan, 424
  Peanut Butter Fruit Candy, 341
  Peanut Butter Fudge, 344
  Rum Balls, 425
Carribean Fish, 135
Carrots
  Apple and Carrot Pudding, 372
  Apricot-Glazed Carrots, 235
  Carrot and Raisin Salad, 20
  Carrot Cake with Vanilla Creme
    Frosting, 384
  Carrot Loaf, 234
  Carrot Slaw, 36
  Cream of Carrot Soup, 10
Cauliflower
  Cauliflower Cheese Bake, 116
  Cauliflower Tofu Bake, 323
  Mock Mashed Potatoes, 244
  Italian Cauliflower Salad, 39
Cheese, Bleu
  Bleu Cheese Dressing, 50
Cheese, Cheddar
  Apple-Cheddar Custard, 124
  Barley-Cheddar Sauté, 273
  Broccoli Cheese Puff, 113
  Cheese Pinwheels, 301
  Cheesy Beans and Rice, 306
  Cheddar 'n Onion Muffins, 286
  Chili-Cheddar Cheese Ball, 97
  Easy Cheesy, 112
  Noodles and Cheese Casserole, 96
  Potato Cheese Casserole, 114
  Spinach Cheese Puffs, 120
  Spinach 'n Herb Bake, 117
  Tofu Cheddar Squares, 322
  Tomato Cheddar Bake, 123
  Yogurt Cheese and Cheddar Log, 71
  Zucchini Cheese Bake, 95

Cheese, Cottage (Also see Pies)
  Applesauce Cheese Mold, 376
  Asparagus Cheese Tart, 111
  Blueberry Cheese Pudding, 107
  Broccoli Pancakes, 121
  Buckwheat-Cheese Bake, 274
  Cheese Herbed Onions, 93
  Cheesy Thousand Island Dressing,
    49
  Cinnamon Raisin Cheese Squares,
    130
  Cottage Apple Bake, 129
  Cottage Cheese Cinnamon Toast,
    109
  Cottage Cheese Latkes, 128
  Dessert Zucchini Fritters, 249
  Easy Cheesy, 112
  Eggplant Pastitsio, 122
  Mealtime Zucchini Fritters, 248
  No Noodle Fruit Kugel, 126
  Noodles and Cheese Casserole, 96
  Pineapple Bavarian Cream, 100
  Potato Cheese Casserole, 114
  South Sea Salad, 21
  Spaghetti Squash Kugel, 127
  Strawberry Cheese Mold, 104
  Sweet Cheese Puff, 125
  Tropical Cheese Pudding, 103
  Zucchini Cheese Bake, 95
Cheese, Mozzarella
  Italian Veggie Bake, 94
  Zucchini-Mozzarella Casserole, 247
Cheese, Parmesan
  Cheesy Herb Dressing, 46
  Macaroni Parmesan, 281
  Parmesan Noodles, 280
Cheese Pies (See Pies)
Cheese, Ricotta (Also see Pies)
  Cauliflower-Cheese Bake, 116
  Cheese-Stuffed Pita, 98
  Chocolate Ricotta, 99
  Creamy Egg Salad, 119
  Italian Baked Spinach, 230
  Italian Eggplant and Cheese
    Casserole, 92
  Pears Belle Helene, 108
  Pineapple Cheese Bread Pudding,
    283
  Pineapple-Orange Danish Toast, 110
  Plum Cheese Cobbler, 105
  Quick Peach Melba, 101

Cheese, Ricotta (*Continued*)
  Red, White and Blueberry Parfaits, 102
  Rum Raisin Pudding, 106
Cheese, Swiss
  Almost a Quiche, 115
  Quiche For One, 118
  Seafood Quiche, 158
Cherries
  Cherry-Berry Sorbet, 360
  Cherry Kuchen, 393
Cheesy Beans and Rice, 306
Chesapeake Bay Crab Puffs, 147
Chewy Fruit Squares, 350
Chicken (*Also see* Cornish Hens)
  Apricot-Glazed Chicken, 175
  Chicken and Broccoli Bake, 179
  Chicken and Peppers, 162
  Chicken Cacciatore, 170
  Chicken Delicious, 176
  Chicken Dijon, 177
  Chicken in Wine Sauce, 164
  Chicken Rice Soup, 6
  Chicken Scampi, 161
  Cream of Chicken Soup, 5
  Golden Crowned Chicken, 166
  Honey Crunch Chicken, 172
  Lazy Day Chicken, 173
  Orange Barbecue Chicken, 167
  Oriental Chicken and Mushrooms, 163
  Peachy Spiced Chicken, 171
  Pineapple Mandarin Chicken, 165
  Polynesian Chicken Salad, 174
  Savory Roast Chicken, 178
  Spice-Glazed Chicken, 169
  Wine Barbecued Chicken, 168
Chicken Liver (*See* Liver)
Chick Peas, Herbed Patties, 307
Chili-Cheddar Cheese Ball, 97
Chili Meatloaf, 213
Chili Orange Barbecue Sauce, 428
Chocolate
  Chocolate Cheese Dream Pie, 402
  Chocolate Fluff, 59
  Chocolate Peanut Butter Bars, 336
  Chocolate Peanut Butter Brownies, 379
  Chocolate Peanut Butter Log, 332
  Chocolate Peanut Butter Pudding, 339
  Chocolate Pineapple Sauce, 436

  Chocolate Raisin Crunch, 423
  Chocolate Ricotta, 99
  Chocolate Tofu Cheese Pie, 329
  Chocolate Upside-Down Pudding, 66
  Chocolate Zucchini Spice Cake, 381
  Creamy Chocolate Pudding, 60
  Heavenly Chocolate Cake, 380
  Hot Fudge Sauce, 435
  Tofu Chocolate Pudding, 326
Cinnamon
  Cinnamon Orange Coffee Cake, 386
  Cinnamon Raisin Cheese Squares, 130
  Cinnamon Streusel Coffee Cake, 391
  Cinnamon Yogurt Muffins, 289
  Cinnamon Yogurt Sauce, 433
Clams
  Clam Dip, 68
  Clams Casino, 146
  Manhattan Clam Chowder, 4
Coconut Bon Bons, 426
Coconut Custard Cheese Pie, 408
Coffee Cakes (*See* Cakes)
Company Egg Cups, 81
Company Fruit Compote, 349
Cookies
  Apple Chews, 421
  Banana Drop Cookies, 420
  Crunchy Granola Bars, 415
  Oatmeal Raisin Drops, 419
  Orange Cookies, 417
  Pastry Crisps, 414
  Peanut Butter Cookies, 338
  Pineapple Oatmeal Drops, 418
  Shortbread, 416
Cooking Chart For Grains, 269
Cooking Chart For Vegetables, 226
Corn
  Corn Soufflé, 266
  Mexi-Corn, 267
  Peanut Butter Corn Muffins, 335
  Skillet Cheese Corn Bread, 293
Cornish Hens
  Cranberry Stuffed Cornish Hens, 180
  Deviled Cornish Hens, 181
Cottage Apple Bake, 129
Cottage Cheese (*See* Cheese, Cottage)
Country Veal Loaf, 189
Crab
  Chesapeake Bay Crab Puffs, 147

Crab and Cheddar Casserole, 148
Crab and Cheese Ball, 70
Cracked Wheat, Baked, 275
Cranberries
Cranberry Salad Mold, 22
Cranberry Stuffed Cornish Hens, 180
Cream of Broccoli Soup, 9
Cream of Carrot Soup, 10
Cream of Chicken Soup, 5
Creamy Chocolate Pudding, 60
Creamy Egg Salad, 119
Creamy Italian Dressing, 47
Creamy Orange Dressing, 51
Creamy Rice and Raisin Pudding, 65
Creole Seafood Chowder, 7
Crunchy Granola Bars, 415
Cucumbers
Cucumber and Onion Salad, 30
Cucumber-Dill Dressing, 44
Tangy Cucumber Salad, 33
Custard
Apple-Cheddar Custard, 124
Apple Custard Squares, 370
Baked Custard, 89

Dessert Zucchini Fritters, 249
Deviled Chicken Livers, 199
Deviled Cornish Hens, 181
Deviled Veal Chops, 192
Dijon Dressing, 45
Dilled Squash, 251
Dilly Beans, 41
Dips
Clam Dip, 68
Onion Dip, 67
Dutch Apple Pancake, 84

Easiest Bean Salad, 311
Easy Cheesy, 112
Eggplant
Bean-Stuffed Eggplant, 305
Eggplant Pastitsio, 122
Eggplant Supreme, 228
Italian Eggplant and Cheese
Casserole, 92
Middle East Eggplant Salad, 38
Eggs
Almond Bread Puff, 91
Apple Custard Squares, 370
Applesauce Pancakes, 85
Bacon and Egg Salad, 79
Baked Custard, 89
Banana Fritters, 88

Banana Puff, 86
Carrot Loaf, 234
Company Egg Cups, 81
Creamy Egg Salad, 119
Dutch Apple Pancake, 84
Fruittata, 83
Lemon Soufflé, 87
Orange Upside-Down French Toast,
90
Peanut Butter French Toast, 343
Spanish Omelet, 80
Spinach Frittata, 82
Spinach Pancakes, 78
Elegant Floating Islands, 55
Extra-Thick Graham Crust, 410

Favorite Rice Casserole, 272
Fish (Also see Salmon, Tuna, and Sea-
food)
Breaded Fillet of Fish, 134
Carribean Fish, 135
Fish Cakes, 139
Fish Parmigiana, 133
French Fish, 137
Italian Baked Fish, 138
Lemony Stuffed Fish, 142
Oriental Tofu Fish Cakes, 320
Potato-Fish Patties, 143
"Pretend" Salmon Salad, 141
Snapper Creole, 136
Sole and Peppers, 132
Springtime Broiled Fish, 140
Frankfurters
Barbecued Franks, 216
Franks and Kraut, 217
French Fish, 137
French Herbed Shrimp, 149
French Herbed Veal Roast, 190
French Onion Soup, 2
French Toast
Almond Bread Puff, 91
Banana Toast, 363
Orange Upside-Down French Toast,
90
Peanut Butter French Toast, 343
French Tomato Dressing, 48
French Veal Cutlets, 194
Fresh Orange Pie, 403
"Fried" Apples, 373
Frittatas (See Eggs)
Fritters (See Pancakes)
Frozen Butter Mints, 422

Frozen Desserts
  Cherry-Berry Sorbet, 360
  Orange Freeze, 61
  Three Fruit Sherbert, 74
  Tortoni, 57
Fruit (*Also see* individual names)
  Company Fruit Compote, 349
  Fruit Soup, 8
  Fruit Yogurt, 75
  Fruittata, 83
  No Noodle Fruit Kugel, 126
  Peanut Butter-Dressed Fruit Salad,
    346

Garlic and Bean Soup, 12
Golden Crowned Chicken, 166
Gourmet Zucchini Salad, 27
Graham Cracker Crust, 409
Grains (*See* individual names)
Grape
  Chewy Fruit Squares, 350
  Grape Gelatin Dessert, 354
Grapefruit
  Broiled Grapefruit Delight, 358
  Pineapple-Grapefruit Salad, 357
Grape-Nuts® Raisin Pudding, 277
Grape-Nuts® Crust, 411
Green Beans (*See* Beans, Green)
Green Beans and Tomatoes, 233
Green Peppers (*See* Peppers, Green)
Grilled Ham Steak, 220

Ham
  Ham Barbecue, 221
  Grilled Ham Steak, 220
Heavenly Chocolate Cake, 380
Herbed Chick Pea Patties, 307
Herbed Chicken Livers, 198
Herbed Potato Salad, 28
Herbed Yogurt Dressing, 43
Honey Crunch Chicken, 172
Honey Crunch Peanut Spread, 333
Honey Graham Spice Cake, 390
Honey Mustard Sauce, 428
Hot Fudge Sauce, 435
Hot German Potato Salad, 35
Hungarian Meatballs and Sauerkraut,
  218

Island Sweet Potato Pudding, 265
Italian
  Italian Baked Fish, 138

Italian Baked Spaghetti Squash, 250
Italian Baked Spinach, 230
Italian Cauliflower Salad, 39
Italian Eggplant and Cheese
  Casserole, 92
Italian Green Bean Salad, 26
Italian Grilled Veal, 193
Italian Stuffed Squash, 253
Italian Tofu "Meatballs", 321
Italian Turkey Burgers, 184
Italian Veggie Bake, 94

Jelly Muffins, 290

Kidney Beans Provençal, 317
Kugel (*See* Pudding)

Lamb
  Lemony Lamb Chops, 223
  Roast Leg of Lamb, 222
Latkes (*See* Pancakes)
Lazy Day Chicken, 173
Legumes (*See* individual names)
  Basic Cooking Directions For
    Legumes, 303
Lemon
  Lemon Broccoli, 245
  Lemon-Broiled Scallops, 144
  Lemon Soufflé, 87
  Lemony Lamb Chops, 223
  Lemony Stuffed Fish, 142
Lentils, Baked and Tomatoes, 315
Light-as-Air Peaches, 63
Liver
  Barbecued Beef Liver, 200
  Calves Liver Stroganoff, 202
  Chicken Livers and Pasta, 204
  Chicken Livers Provencal, 205
  Deviled Chicken Livers, 199
  Herbed Chicken Livers, 198
  Liver and Bacon Spread, 207
  Liver-Ka-Bobs, 203
  Paté en Aspic, 206
  Piquant Livers and Noodles, 201
  Sherried Liver Spread, 208

Macaroni
  Eggplant Pastitsio, 122
  Macaroni Parmesan, 281
  Pasta á Pesto, 282
  Tuna Seashell Salad, 153
Manhattan Clam Chowder, 4

Marbled Cheese Pie, 396
Marinated Artichoke Hearts, 24
Marinated Green and Gold Salad, 25
Marinated Pork Roast, 224
Marinated Vegetable Salad, 34
Marzipan, 424
Mealtime Zucchini Fritters, 248
Meat (See individual names)
Meatballs, Hungarian and Sauerkraut,
  218
Meatloaf
  Chili Meatloaf, 213
  Country Veal Loaf, 189
  Meatloaf Florentine, 212
Meat Sauce and Spaghetti Squash, 219
Mexi-Corn, 267
Middle East Eggplant Salad, 38
Miracle Italian Tuna Pie, 152
Mock Mashed Potatoes, 244
Mock-Sausage and Peppers, 185
Molds
  Applesauce Cheese Mold, 376
  Cranberry Salad Mold, 22
  Peaches 'n Creme Mold, 73
  Strawberry Cheese Mold, 104
  Tangy Tomato Aspic, 23
  Yogurt Fruit Mold, 76
Muffins
  Banana Bran Muffins, 284
  Cheddar 'n Onion Muffins, 286
  Cinnamon Yogurt Muffins, 289
  Jelly Muffins, 290
  Multi-Grain Apple Muffins, 285
  Peanut Butter Corn Muffins, 335
  Peanut Butter and Raisin Muffins,
    340
  Pumpkin Apple Muffins, 288
  Zucchini Muffins, 287
Mushrooms
  Barley-Mushroom Soup, 13
  Mushrooms, Onions and Peppers,
    237
  Mushroom Soup, 11
  Mushroom Soy Loaf Supreme, 310
  Oriental Chicken and Mushrooms,
    163
  Peas and Mushrooms, 259
  Quick Mushroom Salad, 33

No Noodle Fruit Kugel, 126
Noodles
  Apple Kugel, 278

Noodles and Cheese Casserole, 96
Parmesan Noodles, 280
Pineapple Kugel For One, 279
Piquant Livers and Noodles, 201
Tuna Noodle Casserole, 151

Oats and Oatmeal
  Almond Oatmeal Bars, 394
  Crunchy Granola Bars, 416
  Oatmeal Raisin Drops, 419
  Multi-Grain Apple Muffins, 285
  Pineapple Oatmeal Drops, 418
Old World Apple Cake, 383
Omelets (See Eggs)
Onions
  Almost French-Fried Onion Rings,
    232
  Cheese Herbed Onions, 93
  Cucumber and Onion Salad, 30
  French Onion Soup, 2
  Mushrooms, Onions and Peppers,
    237
  Onion Bread, 298
  Onion Dip, 67
  Onion Rolls, 297
  Quick Onion Biscuits, 296
  Sweet and Sour Braised Onions,
    231
Orange
  Baked Orange Squash, 255
  Chewy Fruit Squares, 350
  Creamy Orange Dressing, 51
  Fresh Orange Pie, 403
  Orange Barbecue Chicken, 167
  Orange "Butter", 430
  Orange Cookies, 417
  Orange Freeze, 61
  Orange Raisin Bread, 292
  Orange Sponge Pie, 404
  Orange Tapioca, 353
  Orange Upside-Down French Toast,
    90
Oriental
  Oriental Chicken and Mushrooms,
    163
  Oriental Fried Rice, 271
  Oriental Tofu Fish Cakes, 320
Our Own Potatoes, 262
Our Waldorf Salad, 18

Pancakes
  Applesauce Pancakes, 85

Pancakes (*Continued*)
Banana Fritters, 88
Broccoli Pancakes, 121
Cottage Cheese Latkes, 128
Dessert Zucchini Fritters, 249
Dutch Apple Pancake, 84
Herbed Chick Pea Patties, 307
Mealtime Zucchini Fritters, 248
Potato Latkes, 263
Raisin Rice Patties, 270
Spinach Pancakes, 78
Tofu Banana Fritters, 327
Parmesan Noodles, 280
Parsnips, Whipped Spiced, 257
Pasta á Pesto, 282
Pastry Crisps, 414
Paté
Paté en Aspic, 206
Salmon Paté, 155
Peaches
Light-as-Air Peaches, 63
Peaches 'n Creme Mold, 73
Peachy Spiced Chicken, 171
Quick Peach Melba, 101
Sautéed Maple Peaches, 367
Snowcapped Peaches, 368
Peanut Butter
Chocolate Peanut Butter Bars, 336
Chocolate Peanut Butter Brownies, 379
Chocolate Peanut Butter Log, 332
Chocolate Peanut Butter Pudding, 339
Honey Crunch Peanut Spread, 333
Peanut Butter and Raisin Muffins, 340
Peanut Butter-Banana Squares, 345
Peanut Butter Bread, 337
Peanut Butter Cookies, 338
Peanut Butter Corn Muffins, 335
Peanut Butter Date Spread, 347
Peanut Butter-Dressed Fruit Salad, 346
Peanut Butter French Toast, 343
Peanut Butter Fruit Candy, 341
Peanut Butter Fudge, 344
Peanut Butter Pineapple Spread, 334
Peanut Butter-Scotch Bars, 342
Tofu, Peanut Butter and Banana Spread, 328
Pears
Baked Pears, 369

Pears Belle Helene, 108
Peas
Barbecued Black-Eyed Peas, 314
Peas and Mushrooms, 259
Peas New Orleans, 258
Snow Peas Surprise, 238
Peppers, Green
Chicken and Peppers, 162
Mock-Sausage and Peppers, 185
Mushrooms, Onions and Peppers, 237
Pepper-Bean Casserole, 313
Pepper Steak, 215
Sole and Peppers, 132
Persian Cream Pudding, 54
Pie Crusts
Bread Crumb Crust, 413
Extra-Thick Graham Crust, 410
Graham Cracker Crust, 409
Grape-Nuts® Crust, 411
Shredded Wheat Crust, 412
Pies
Almond Buttermilk Pie, 407
Chocolate Cheese Dream Pie, 402
Chocolate Tofu Cheese Pie, 329
Coconut Custard Cheese Pie, 408
Fresh Orange Pie, 403
Marbled Cheese Pie, 396
Orange Sponge Pie, 404
Pineapple Cheese Pie, 400
Pink Bean "Pumpkin" Pie, 318
Pumpkin Cream Pie, 406
Strawberry Cream Pie, 405
Strawberry-Topped Cheese Pie, 398
Tofu Banana Cream Pie, 330
Piña Colada Fluff, 58
Pineapple
Baked Pineapple Tapioca, 355
Chocolate Pineapple Sauce, 436
Piña Colada Fluff, 58
Pineapple Acorn Squash, 256
Pineapple Banana Cake, 382
Pineapple Bavarian Cream, 100
Pineapple Cheese Bread Pudding, 283
Pineapple Cheese Pie, 400
Pineapple-Grapefruit Salad, 357
Pineapple Kugel For One, 279
Pineapple Mandarin Chicken, 165
Pineapple Oatmeal Drops, 418
Pineapple-Orange Danish Toast, 110

Pineapple Slaw, 42
Sautéed Pineapple, 356
Pink Bean "Pumpkin" Pie, 318
Piquant Livers and Noodles, 201
Plum Cheese Cobbler, 105
Polynesian Chicken Salad, 174
Pork, Marinated Roast, 224
Potatoes, Sweet
Island Sweet Potato Pudding, 265
Sweet Potatoes and Apples, 264
Sweet Potato Rolls, 299
Potatoes, White
Baked Potato Topper, 431
Buttermilk Potatoes, 261
Herbed Potato Salad, 28
Hot German Potato Salad, 35
Our Own Potatoes, 262
Potato Cheese Casserole, 114
Potato-Fish Patties, 143
Potato Kugel, 260
Potato Latkes, 263
Potato Soup, 14
Poultry (See individual names)
Prairie Bean Tortillas, 304
"Pretend" Salmon Salad, 141
Puddings (Also see Bread Pudding)
Apple and Carrot Pudding, 372
Apple Kugel, 278
Baked Pineapple Tapioca, 355
Banana Bavarian, 62
Banana Raisin Pudding, 366
Chocolate Fluff, 59
Chocolate Upside-Down Pudding, 66
Creamy Chocolate Pudding, 66
Creamy Rice and Raisin Pudding, 65
Elegant Floating Islands, 55
Grape-Nuts® Raisin Pudding, 277
Island Sweet Potato Pudding, 265
No Noodle Fruit Kugel, 126
Orange Tapioca, 353
Persian Cream Pudding, 54
Piña Colada Fluff, 58
Pineapple Kugel For One, 279
Potato Kugel, 260
Rum Raisin Pudding, 106
Spaghetti Squash Kugel, 127
Tofu Chocolate Pudding, 326
Tofu Rice Pudding, 325
Tropical Cheese Pudding, 103
Vanilla Tapioca Pudding, 64
Pumpkin
Pumpkin Apple Muffins, 288

Pumpkin Bread, 291
Pumpkin Cream Pie, 406
Pumpkin Log, 388

Quiche
Almost a Quiche, 115
Quiche For One, 118
Seafood Quiche, 158
Quick and Creamy Applesauce Dessert, 72
Quick Mushroom Salad, 33
Quick Onion Biscuits, 296
Quick Peach Melba, 101

Raisins
Applesauce Raisin Supreme, 375
Banana Raisin Pudding, 366
Carrot and Raisin Salad, 20
Chocolate Raisin Crunch, 423
Cinnamon Raisin Cheese Squares, 130
Creamy Rice and Raisin Pudding, 65
Grape-Nuts® Raisin Pudding, 277
Raisin Rice Patties, 270
Rum Raisin Pudding, 106
Raspberry Melba Sauce, 359
Ratatouille, 229
Red Cabbage Salad, 37
Red, White and Blueberry Parfaits, 102
Rice
Brown Rice and Vegetable Salad, 31
Cheesy Beans and Rice, 306
Chicken Rice Soup, 6
Creamy Rice and Raisin Pudding, 65
Favorite Rice Casserole, 272
Oriental Fried Rice, 271
Raisin Rice Patties, 270
Tofu Rice Pudding, 325
Roast Leg of Lamb, 222
Roast Turkey Breast with Peach Sauce, 186
Rolls and Buns (Also see Muffins)
Onion Rolls, 297
Scones, 295
Sticky Buns, 395
Sweet Potato Rolls, 299
Roman Tuna Salad, 312
Rum Balls, 425
Rum Fruit Cake, 385
Rum Raisin Pudding, 106

Salad Dressings
  Baked Potato Topper, 431
  Bleu Cheese Dressing, 50
  Cheesy Herb Dressing, 46
  Cheesy Thousand Island Dressing, 49
  Creamy Italian Dressing, 47
  Creamy Orange Dressing, 51
  Cucumber-Dill Dressing, 44
  Dijon Dressing, 45
  French Tomato Dressing, 48
  Herbed Yogurt Dressing, 43
Salads
  Asparagus Vinaigrette, 40
  Bacon and Egg Salad, 79
  Bengal Seafood Salad, 157
  Best Cole Slaw, 29
  Brown Rice and Vegetable Salad, 31
  Caesar Salad, 32
  Carrot and Raisin Salad, 20
  Carrot Slaw, 36
  Cucumber and Onion Salad, 30
  Creamy Egg Salad, 119
  Dilly Beans, 41
  Easiest Bean Salad, 311
  Eggplant Supreme, 228
  Gourmet Zucchini Salad, 27
  Herbed Potato Salad, 28
  Hot German Potato Salad, 35
  Italian Cauliflower Salad, 39
  Italian Green Bean Salad, 26
  Marinated Artichoke Hearts, 24
  Marinated Green and Gold Salad, 25
  Marinated Vegetable Salad, 34
  Middle East Eggplant Salad, 38
  Our Waldorf Salad, 18
  Pineapple-Grapefruit Salad, 357
  Pineapple Slaw, 42
  Polynesian Chicken Salad, 174
  "Pretend" Salmon Salad, 141
  Quick Mushroom Salad, 33
  Red Cabbage Salad, 37
  Roman Tuna Salad, 312
  South Sea Salad, 21
  Tangy Cucumber Salad, 33
  Tangy Tomato Aspic, 23
  Tropical Ambrosia Salad, 19
  Tuna Seashell Salad, 153
Salmon
  Salmon Paté, 155
  Superb Salmon Loaf, 156

Sandwiches
  Cheese-Stuffed Pita, 98
  Cottage Cheese Cinnamon Toast, 109
  Pineapple-Orange Danish Toast, 110
Sauces and Toppings
  Apricot Brandy Sauce, 429
  Baked Potato Topper, 431
  Chili Orange Barbecue Sauce, 428
  Chocolate Pineapple Sauce, 436
  Cinnamon Yogurt Sauce, 433
  Honey Mustard Sauce, 428
  Hot Fudge Sauce, 435
  Orange "Butter", 430
  Raspberry Melba Sauce, 359
  Strawberry Sauce, 434
  Strawberry Yogurt Sauce, 432
  Whipped Topping, 56
Sauerkraut
  Franks and Kraut, 217
  Hungarian Meatballs and Sauerkraut, 218
  Simmered Sauerkraut, 243
Sautéed Maple Peaches, 367
Sautéed Pineapple, 356
Savory Roast Chicken, 178
Savory Sprouts, 242
Scallops
  Lemon-Broiled Scallops, 144
  Terijaki Scallops, 145
Scones, 295
Seafood (Also see individual names)
  Bengal Seafood Salad, 157
  Bouillabaise, 159
  Creole Seafood Chowder, 7
  Seafood Quiche, 158
Sherried Liver Spread, 208
Shortbread, 416
Shredded Wheat Crust, 412
Shrimp (Also see Seafood)
  French Herbed Shrimp, 149
  Shrimp Scampi, 150
Simmered Sauerkraut, 243
Skillet Cheese Corn Bread, 293
Snapper Creole, 136
Snow Peas Suprise, 238
Snowcapped Peaches, 368
Sole and Peppers, 132
Soufflés
  Corn Soufflé, 266
  Lemon Soufflé, 87
  Soybean Soufflé, 308

Soup
  Barley-Mushroom Soup, 13
  Bouillabaise, 159
  Cabbage Soup, 3
  Chicken Rice Soup, 6
  Cream of Broccoli Soup, 9
  Cream of Carrot Soup, 10
  Cream of Chicken Soup, 5
  Creole Seafood Chowder, 7
  French Onion Soup, 2
  Fruit Soup, 8
  Garlic and Bean Soup, 12
  Manhattan Clam Chowder, 4
  Mushroom Soup, 11
  Potato Soup, 14
  Tomato Squash Soup, 15
  Vegetable Soup for a Crowd, 16
South Sea Salad, 21
Soybeans (See Beans, Soybeans)
Spaghetti Squash Kugel, 127
Spanish Omelet, 80
Spice Chart, 437
Spice-Glazed Chicken, 169
Spinach
  Italian Baked Spinach, 230
  Spinach Cheese Puffs, 120
  Spinach Frittata, 82
  Spinach 'n Herb Bake, 117
  Spinach Pancakes, 78
Spreads
  Chili-Cheddar Cheese Ball, 97
  Crab and Cheese Ball, 70
  Honey Crunch Peanut Spread, 333
  Liver and Bacon Spread, 207
  Paté en Aspic, 206
  Peanut Butter Date Spread, 347
  Peanut Butter Pineapple Spread, 334
  Sherried Liver Spread, 208
  Tofu, Peanut Butter and Banana
    Spread, 328
  Yogurt Cheese and Cheddar Log, 71
Springtime Broiled Fish, 140
Squash, Acorn and Butternut
  Baked Orange Squash, 255
  Pineapple Acorn Squash, 256
  Tomato Squash Soup, 15
Squash, Yellow and Zucchini
  Baked Squash — Southern Style, 252
  Chocolate Zucchini Spice Cake, 381
  Dessert Zucchini Fritters, 249
  Dilled Squash, 251
  Gourmet Zucchini Salad, 27

  Italian Stuffed Squash, 253
  Marinated Green and Gold Salad, 25
  Mealtime Zucchini Fritters, 248
  Zucchini Cheese Bake, 95
  Zucchini-Mozzarella Casserole, 247
  Zucchini Muffins, 287
Squash, Spaghetti
  Italian Baked Spaghetti Squash, 250
  Meat Sauce and Spaghetti Squash,
    219
  Spaghetti Squash Kugel, 127
Steak Diane, 210
Sticky Buns, 395
Strawberries
  Fruit Soup, 8
  Red, White and Blueberry Parfaits,
    102
  Strawberries 'n Creme Breakfast
    Cereal, 276
  Strawberry Cheese Mold, 104
  Strawberry Cream Pie, 405
  Strawberry Ice Cream in a Flash, 53
  Strawberry Sauce, 434
  Strawberry-Topped Cheese Pie, 398
  Strawberry Yogurt Sauce, 432
Superb Salmon Loaf, 156
Surprise Apple Bean Cake, 319
Sweet and Sour Braised Onions, 231
Sweet Cheese Puff, 125
Sweet Potatoes (See Potatoes, Sweet)

Tangy Baked Kidney Beans, 316
Tangy Cucumber Salad, 33
Tangy Tomato Aspic, 23
Tapioca
  Orange Tapioca, 353
  Vanilla Tapioca Pudding, 64
Terijaki Scallops, 145
Terijaki Steak, 211
Three Fruit Sherbert, 74
Tofu
  Cauliflower Tofu Bake, 323
  Chocolate Tofu Cheese Pie, 329
  Italian Tofu "Meatballs", 321
  Oriental Tofu Fish Cakes, 320
  Tofu Banana Cream Pie, 330
  Tofu Banana Fritters, 327
  Tofu Cheddar Squares, 322
  Tofu Chocolate Pudding, 326
  Tofu Parmigiana, 324
  Tofu, Peanut Butter and Banana
    Spread, 328

Tofu (Continued)
Tofu Rice Pudding, 325
Tomatoes
Baked Lentils and Tomatoes, 315
Best Stewed Tomatoes, 241
French Tomato Dressing, 48
Green Beans and Tomatoes, 233
Tangy Tomato Aspic, 23
Tomato Cheddar Bake, 123
Tomato Pie, 239
Tomato Squash Soup, 15
Tomatoes Provencal, 240
Tortoni, 57
Tropical Ambrosia Salad, 19
Tropical Cheese Pudding, 103
Tuna
Miracle Italian Tuna Pie, 152
Roman Tuna Salad, 312
Tuna Mousse, 154
Tuna Noodle Casserole, 151
Tuna Seashell Salad, 153
Turkey
Breaded Turkey Cutlets, 183
Italian Turkey Burgers, 184
Mock-Sausage and Peppers, 185
Roast Turkey Breast with Peach
Sauce, 186
Turkey Divan, 182

Vanilla Tapioca Pudding, 64
Veal
Country Veal Loaf, 189
Deviled Veal Chops, 192
French Herbed Veal Roast, 190
French Veal Cutlets, 194
Italian Grilled Veal, 193
Veal and Rosemary, 188
Veal Chops Italiano, 191
Veal in Dilled Cream Sauce, 195
Veal Oriental, 196

Vegetables (Also see individual names)
Basic Cooking Directions for
Vegetables, 227
Cooking Chart for Vegetables, 226
Italian Veggie Bake, 94
Marinated Vegetable Salad, 34
Ratatouille, 229
Vegetable Soup for a Crowd, 16

Whipped Spiced Parsnips, 257
Whipped Topping, 56
Wine Barbecued Chicken, 168

Yogurt
Baked Potato Topper, 431
Cinnamon Yogurt Muffins, 289
Cinnamon Yogurt Sauce, 433
Clam Dip, 68
Crab and Cheese Ball, 70
Creamy Orange Dressing, 51
Cucumber-Dill Dressing, 44
Elegant Floating Islands, 55
Fruit Yogurt, 75
Herbed Yogurt Dressing, 43
Onion Dip, 67
Peaches 'n Creme Mold, 73
Quick and Creamy Applesauce
Dessert, 72
Three Fruit Sherbert, 74
Strawberry Yogurt Sauce, 432
Yogurt Biscuits, 300
Yogurt Cheese, 69
Yogurt Cheese and Cheddar Log, 71
Yogurt Fruit Mold, 76

Zucchini (See Squash, Yellow and
Zucchini)